Short-term Counselling in Higher Education

CU00806502

As the demand for counselling from students across higher education (HE) increases year on year, counselling services are continually seeking to explore creative ways of working under the pressure that results from this rise in client numbers. One of the most frequent responses to increased demand is limiting the number of sessions that individual students may have. Until *Short-term Counselling in Higher Education*, there has been no text that provides a contextual, theoretical and practical input to this evolving way of working.

This book explores constructive ways of providing very short-term counselling within a higher education context. Using case studies and employing up-to-date statistics from the sector, the book gives readers a clear understanding of the nature of professional challenges and offers ways of addressing these, including managing waiting lists, developing policies to facilitate timely intervention and understanding the limitations of what short-term therapy can offer.

Short-term Counselling in Higher Education explores the implications of working in higher education counselling services in this very short-term way, and as such it will be an essential resource for counsellors, heads of counselling services and student services managers in higher education, helping to find ways of delivering effective short-term interventions within existing counselling services.

Dr David Mair is Head of Counselling and Wellbeing at the University of Birmingham, and a BACP Senior Accredited Counsellor/Psychotherapist. He has worked in higher education for over 20 years and has a particular interest in encouraging and supporting diversity and equality as well as exploring how counselling can help to meet the needs of the current generation of emerging adults.

"This is an extremely timely book as it comes out when over 100,000 students are accessing counselling services per year throughout the UK HE sector, with demand both in terms of student numbers and expectations increasing on university counselling services. This book addresses the major issues and challenges faced by student service managers and counselling services in the HE sector. The chapters in this book are written by some of the leading therapeutic experts and Heads of University Counselling Services and give extremely thoughtful as well as practical insights into each of the topics covered. It is an essential book for anyone who works or is interested in the world of student counselling and student mental health today."

−Alan Percy, Head of Counselling, University of Oxford

"Universities in the UK, and across the world, continue to report increases in the numbers and complexity of students of all ages whose mental health and wellbeing are compromised during their studies. Whilst we remain committed to working with our students to achieve the best possible experience and outcomes from their higher education we are doing this in an environment where resources have probably never been more challenged. Mair and associates have given us a critical and timely exploration of the ways we can manage these complex new demands. This work provides a vital new perspective on counselling in higher education and the ways we can work together to ensure our students succeed."

−Ben Lewis, Director, Student Support & Wellbeing,
Cardiff University; Chairman, AMOSSHE,
The Student Services Organisation

"*Short-term Counselling in Higher Education* offers an insight into the background and pertinent issues in the HE psychotherapy sector today.

With therapists in this field seeing approaching 10% of the HE student population per year, this timely book discusses the increasing use of student counselling services, clarifying the nature of the ultra short-term therapy offered, its effectiveness and the integration of approaches from lower- to higher-intensity interventions.

With a leaning towards the pragmatic and utilitarian, Mair brings together leading clinicians and researchers in the field. This excellent book describes the landscape of the HE counselling sector, clarifies the variety of approaches to the work and ultimately will develop skills of both experienced and new clinicians alike, who will be there to help our next generation transit through this important time in their development, should they need it."

−Jeremy Christey, Chair, University and Colleges Division of
the BACP; Director, Students Against Depression;
Practising Counselling Psychologist

Short-term Counselling in Higher Education

Context, Theory and Practice

Edited by David Mair

Routledge
Taylor & Francis Group

LONDON AND NEW YORK

First published 2016
by Routledge
2 Park Square, Milton Park, Abingdon, Oxon OX14 4RN

and by Routledge
711 Third Avenue, New York, NY 10017

Routledge is an imprint of the Taylor & Francis Group, an informa business

© 2016 David Mair

British Library Cataloguing in Publication Data
A catalogue record for this book is available from the British Library

Library of Congress Cataloging-in-Publication Data
Short-term counselling in higher education : context, theory and practice /
   edited by David Mair.
      pages cm
   1. Counseling in higher education.   2. Short-term counseling.   I. Mair,
David Clare, 1949–
   LB2343.S526 2016
   378.1'94—dc23
   2015019618

ISBN: 978-1-138-79412-2 (hbk)
ISBN: 978-1-138-79413-9 (pbk)
ISBN: 978-1-315-75107-8 (ebk)

Typeset in Times New Roman
by Apex CoVantage, LLC
Printed by Ashford Colour Press Ltd.

Contents

Figures

Tables

Notes on contributors

Jo Ames is an Accredited member of BACP and over the last 16 years has worked in the youth voluntary sector, Child & Adolescent Mental Health Service (CAMHS), privately and within two West Midlands universities. After completing training to Advanced Diploma level in online counselling, she now has over 12 years' experience of working online. She has developed and provided online services for adults, young people and students, which reflects her passion for increasing accessibility to professional counselling services. Jo is the current chair of the Association for Counselling & Therapy Online (ACTO). Employed by the University of Birmingham as Online Counsellor Lead, she has transitioned online counselling service to a new platform that includes one-to-one web conferencing functions. Describing herself as "tech-challenged", she has gained additional knowledge and experience through online gaming, which has led to a greater appreciation and understanding of inhabiting virtual worlds and relating to people online from across the globe.

Sue Anderson works as a counsellor at the University of Birmingham Counselling and Wellbeing Service where she is also Deputy Head of Service. She qualified in counselling in 1999 having previously worked for 20 years as a local authority social worker specialising in child protection, mental health and HIV and AIDS. She has worked as a counsellor and clinical supervisor in several settings – a local authority and NHS mental health service, the Brook Advisory Service, Barnardos and in private practice. She has worked as a counsellor and supervisor over the past 15 years at Birmingham City University and the University of Birmingham. Sue is a BACP Senior Accredited counsellor, an EMDR Europe Accredited Practitioner and holds a post-graduate qualification in supervision. Sue has previously published social work texts on child sexual abuse and services for carers of people living with HIV/AIDS.

Alex Coren initially trained as a psychiatric social worker working both in adult mental health and in child and family guidance. After training as a psychoanalytic psychotherapist he worked as a psychotherapist in both secondary and tertiary education predominantly at Kings College London and Oxford University. He was Director of the Psychodynamic Studies Programme at Oxford

University and has written extensively in the fields of education and short-term therapy. His books include *A Psychodynamic Approach to Education* (Sheldon Press) and *Short Term Psychotherapy* (Palgrave).

John Cowley has worked as a counsellor/psychotherapist for over 30 years in both primary care and the education sector. During his extensive counselling career he has been Deputy Chair of BACP, Chair of AUCC, a special interest group of BACP and Chair of BACP's Equality and Diversity Forum. A passionate believer in Social Justice, he initiated and chaired BACP's Criminal Justice forum. He is currently Head of Counselling Health and Wellbeing at Cardiff University, regarded as a successful and innovative provision for students. In this role his service developed the Cardiff Model, recognised in 2010 as BACP's Innovation Award winner. John has carried out development and consultancy work both in the UK and Sri Lanka. In 2006 he was awarded a fellowship of BACP.

Géraldine Dufour is Head of Counselling at the University of Cambridge, where she oversees the provision of psychological support for the collegiate university, leading a large team of counsellors, CBT therapists, mindfulness teachers and mental health advisors. She previously managed the counselling service at Birmingham City University, where she started her career as a university counsellor over 10 years ago. Current Chair of HUCS, a special interest group of BACP Universities and Colleges where she sits on the executive committee, she is also a member of a number of national committees relating to student mental health and wellbeing. She has a special interest in developing the skills of counsellors having lectured on MA in Counselling at Leicester and Birmingham University. Géraldine started her career working in social care, moving on to counselling drug and alcohol users, sexual abuse survivors and young people. One counselling experience that was particularly helpful in developing her assessment skills was that of working in a community alcohol team. There she conducted in-depth assessments of clients with very complex needs and severe co-morbidity of mental illnesses and addictions.

Vicky Groves has worked in student counselling at Cardiff University for over 17 years and during this time her role has changed and developed frequently and considerably. Having always been actively curious about what helps students stay at university and gain the most out of their experience, and troubled by seeing long waiting lists for counselling support, Vicky was delighted to research new ways of working, and proud to be one of the "architects" of the Cardiff Model. Her particular interests lie in change management, anxiety and eating disorders. Vicky's Masters (CBT) dissertation explored post-traumatic stress disorder (PTSD) in patients complaining of chest pain following apparently successful cardiac surgery. This research was motivated by her time as a coronary care nurse. Vicky has also trained in Eye Movement Desensitisation and Reprocessing (EMDR) and is excited about future developments in this area, being hopeful that they will lead to EMDR helping with many types of difficulties, not just PTSD. Vicky is a BACP Senior Accredited counsellor and supervisor.

Pat Hunt was Head of the University Counselling Service at the University of Nottingham for 11 years before retiring from this post in 2014. Between 2009 and 2014 Pat played a leading role in establishing a new counselling service at the University of Nottingham's international campus in Ningbo, China. She served on the executive committee of the Heads of University Counselling Services national body (HUCS) for six years and was chair of HUCS from 2009 to 2010. Pat is a Psychotherapist accredited through the UK Council for Psychotherapy (UKCP), a trustee on the UKCP board and was elected Vice-Chair of UKCP in 2015.

Peter Jenkins is a Senior Lecturer in Counselling at the University of Manchester, where he is programme director for the MA Counselling, which is based on an integrative model. He has been a member of both the Professional Conduct Committee of the BACP and the Ethics Committee of the UKCP. He has published widely on legal aspects of therapy, and has run numerous training workshops on this topic. His books include *Counselling, Psychotherapy and the Law* (Sage, second edition, 2007) and, as co-author with Dr Debbie Daniels, *Therapy with Children* (Sage, second edition, 2010). Additionally, he has produced a number of DVDs and training packs on children's rights. Peter originally trained and worked as a social worker, before moving to teaching in a college of further education and then training as a counsellor. He worked as a part-time student counsellor in FE for 15 years, and then at several universities, where he continued to work part-time, as a student and staff counsellor for a further 15 years, in addition to lecturing and running counselling courses. He has been actively involved as an Honorary Counsellor in the University of Manchester Staff and Student Counselling Service since 2002.

Dorothy Louden has been involved in counselling for over 25 years, as a counsellor, supervisor, trainer and facilitator. She is a Senior Accredited BACP therapist and an EMDR accredited practitioner. She first developed an interest in the effects of trauma as a result of her own experiences while growing up. She went on to train in several trauma specific models of counselling. She has worked in education for over 20 years and managed a counselling service in a FE college for over 12 years. She sat on the AUCC FE sub-committee (as it was then) for several years and worked as a volunteer safeguarding trainer for Dudley safeguarding board. She currently works as a counsellor at the University of Birmingham. Dorothy originally trained as a nurse and has worked as a volunteer youth leader for many years.

David Mair, MBACP (Senior Accredited), is Head of Counselling and Wellbeing at the University of Birmingham. He has worked in HE for over 20 years, first with international students, and then in a variety of counselling roles. His particular interests include the needs of LGBTQ students in HE – an area he explored in his doctoral research – issues affecting international students' mental health, and mindful approaches to wellbeing. He has been a member of the BACP-UC Advisory Committee, and also of the HUCS (Heads of University Counselling Services) executive.

Kitty McCrea qualified as a psychotherapist in 1995 following a career in teaching and education management. She has 20 years' experience as a UKCP registered psychotherapist and BACP Senior Accredited counsellor. Her involvement with the higher education counselling sector began in 1994 as a student counsellor at Bedfordshire College of Higher Education (later part of De Montfort University, Leicester). Kitty was appointed Head of Counselling at De Montfort University in 2001, a post she held until 2007. For the last 10 years she has worked collaboratively with colleagues across the sector towards establishing an HE Practice Research Network involving a common data set. Kitty has worked for CORE IMS since 2007 and in this role provides pre- and post-sales support, training and management consultancy to counselling services in a range of sectors, but with specific responsibility for the HE sector. She is particularly interested in helping services identify and manage problems around data quality and in using outcome measurement data to help improve service quality.

Denise Meyer, C.Psychol and MBACP (Senior Accredited), has worked in the HE counselling sector since 1995, with experience in four different universities. She is currently the lead Senior Counsellor in the University of Portsmouth Student Wellbeing Services. Her doctoral research project, the student-focused depression self-help website Students Against Depression, won the BACP Innovation in Counselling & Psychotherapy Award in 2006. Denise recently stepped away from active management of the site but still offers consultation and advice to its owners, the Charlie Waller Memorial Trust.

Samantha Tarren initially worked as a counsellor in a range of GP surgeries then moved to set up a counselling service at the Art and Design College in Cleveland. She has an MA (distinction) in counselling from Ripon and York, St John. In 2000 she moved to take up the post of University Counsellor at Warwick University and then became Deputy Head of Counselling and subsequently Head of Counselling of the University Counselling Service.

Introduction

David Mair

"I'll need at least a term to finish working with this client."

I well remember hearing a colleague, many years ago, talking in these terms about a client she was working with in a university counselling service. In those days, long-term, open-ended work was much more the norm. Counsellors not uncommonly worked with clients for an entire academic year, or even throughout their degree programme. Issues such as clients cancelling or not arriving for sessions were typically reckoned as "part of the work", expressions of insecure attachment or ambivalence to therapy that needed to be allowed, thought about and worked through. Nowadays, many services have clear policies, based on providing equitable access to services, about DNAs and cancellations, which potentially override therapeutic concerns. My colleague was voicing "private practice mentality" applied directly to an institutional context, but even then I felt concern about the possibility that a young person had become so dependent on a relationship with a therapist that they would need a minimum of 11 weeks to say goodbye and bring the work to a close.

The environment in most university counselling services today is very different. Long-term, open-ended work has all but disappeared and with it the associated therapist passivity, and encouragement of transference as a chief way of working. Instead, counsellors are much more aware of the educationally-driven nature of the setting in which they are located, and of the need to keep academic work clearly in the forefront of any therapeutic work undertaken. They have accepted the reality expressed in a recent report into student mental wellbeing in higher education that "institutions are academic, not therapeutic, communities" (Universities UK, 2015, p. 4). Many therapists have undergone training in models of work with a much more clearly articulated short-term focus, such as CBT, ACT or DIT,[1] leading to a more active therapist stance, where transference moves off centre-stage in the work and there is greater awareness of the risk of encouraging unhealthy dependency in clients at a life-stage where independence needs to be fostered and supported.

But while counsellors may have accepted that they do not work in therapeutic institutions, universities cannot so easily declare themselves to be independent territories, separate from the rest of society where therapeutic concepts have burgeoned and where therapists of all kinds are now mainstream. Universities may indeed place academic achievement at the heart of their mission statements, but those who enrol at universities do not only have academic achievement in mind as they embark on a three-year undergraduate course, a Masters degree or a doctoral research programme. Developmental issues are unavoidable for young adults, or indeed for anyone engaging in a course of study. Academic study is not undertaken merely to achieve a certificate, but in pursuit of an imagined and hoped-for future about which there may be anxiety and uncertainty. Therapeutic work is not, therefore, incompatible with academic achievement. In light of institutions' and governments' "widening participation" agenda, it is an essential component of institutional support that underpins that achievement. Yet counselling is seen by some as a kind of soft option for the feeble; I once heard at a conference, a senior manager express surprise that "intelligent" students were accessing counselling. The impression was that it provided a space for a "cosy chat", but was hardly key to the serious academic work of the institution. Indeed, there is no legal requirement for universities to provide counselling services for their students: a telephone helpline might suffice at a purely legal level. Ethically, however, it is not so easy for institutions to side-step the provision of robust support services. The Universities UK report mentioned earlier acknowledges this:

> The task for institutions is to help students capitalise on the positive mental health benefits of higher education while identifying and providing appropriate support to those who are more vulnerable to its pressures. Providing them with the support they need to fulfil their potential is not only in the interest of the institution, but also in the interest of society as a whole.
>
> (Universities UK, 2015, p. 9)

Nevertheless, while counsellors have adapted their understanding of what it means to offer therapy in an educational environment, and the nature of the interventions provided has evolved significantly over the last 20 years to a point where short-term work is now the norm, there may still be academics or managers who look askance at the provision of therapy by the institution, or who believe that a kind of one-size-fits-all advice-giving service could easily replace the work of well-trained and experienced therapists. This book, therefore, while intended for therapists who are undertaking the demanding work required of them in an HE setting,[2] also speaks to those who commission and support such services. Counselling work can be hard to articulate – it can sound vague and insubstantial. The reality is quite the opposite: university counsellors are required to think hard, fast and carefully about the needs of a wide range of individuals who are struggling to cope with the demands of academic work and of life itself. They need to understand the demands of academic work and the insecurities it can provoke – not just from an intellectual standpoint, but from first-hand experience. They also need to be able to work with individuals who may be intellectually extremely bright, but who may struggle to express vulnerability or deal with distress.

Such work is exhausting, and care is needed to avoid burn-out. Counsellors cannot have a "quiet day" where they attend to filing. They are constantly required to engage in depth with individuals or groups who express high levels of distress, which it is their task to understand and contain, rather than "solve" or "explain". So while universities are definitely not per se therapeutic communities, they cannot ignore the therapeutic needs of a significant proportion of their population, or the need to support counsellors in the demanding work they undertake.

Short-term work in HE counselling services is now the norm, and I, for one, am glad that the days when counsellors took a term to say good-bye to a client are over. Such extended exchanges could lead one to wonder whose needs were actually being addressed – the client's or the therapist's. But it is not easy to work in a consistently short-term way with its relentless round of beginnings and endings, high throughput of clients and rapidly rising demand for counselling support in young adults. This book addresses the context in which we work, how that context shapes our task and also explores theory and practice, which equip the therapeutic enterprise. The intention is that it may offer insights to strengthen competence and awareness in therapists, and elicit understanding and support in managers in the sector.

Dr David Mair, February 2015.

Notes

1 Cognitive Behaviour Therapy, Acceptance and Commitment Therapy, Dynamic Interpersonal Therapy
2 As Tarren states in Chapter 11 of this book, short-term counselling can be exhausting, physically and emotionally. Sitting with distressed individuals for up to five hours a day is work that requires emotional robustness in practitioners, and a supportive institutional environment.

References

Universities UK (2015) Student mental wellbeing in higher education, London. Available from: www.universitiesuk.ac.uk/highereducation/Pages/StudentMentalWellbeing-Guide.aspx#.VOsk-haoHXc– (accessed 23rd February 2015).

Context

Chapter 1

The rise and rise of higher education and therapeutic culture

David Mair

there is . . . a growing need for more *effective* . . . counselling to be made available to more clients within a climate of limited resources in time and funding. The usual response is to presume that *short-term* or brief psychological therapy is indicated. This suggestion is seen by many practitioners as a meagre and cheese-paring solution which puts cost-effective solution above considerations of quality. Even among those who extol the qualities of the brief psychotherapies there can be discerned an uneasy defensiveness, especially with regard to the appropriateness of short-term interventions for many client groups. The implication is that in the best of all possible worlds, longer-term psychotherapy would be the response of choice.

(Elton-Wilson, 1996, p. 6)

This book explores the work of counsellors across institutions of higher education (HE). Many services within this setting are "overstretched and under-resourced" (Royal College of Psychiatrists, 2011, p. 44), largely due to the huge increase in students seeking support for psychological and emotional distress. At its inception, the Association for Student Counselling (ASC) envisaged an ideal counsellor-student ratio of one counsellor for every 750 students (Bell, 1996). No modern institution comes close to that ideal, which now seems almost utopian. Demand has, therefore, stimulated development of new ways of providing support, often characterised by a limit to the number of sessions offered. In many university services, a ceiling of three to six sessions is now typical,[1] constituting, effectively, a new form of intervention. "Short-term" therapy in established therapy models such as CBT, CAT or DIT[2] is, typically, 16 sessions. A way of working that sets a predetermined limit to the number of sessions to be provided at such a low level could therefore be called "very short-term" therapy. Throughout this book, written by contributors with many years' experience in this field, one key question hovers: is it really possible to work effectively and meaningfully in a very short-term way with clients who seek counselling, sometimes with severe and entrenched issues?

In order to answer this question, we need a clear understanding of the nature of the work of counselling services within HE. Applying assumptions relevant in other settings is unhelpful. University students' presenting issues are nearly always affected by academic work and other institutional dynamics. Structural considerations as simple as term dates, the timing of exams, the number of teaching or supervision contact hours within a department, all directly affect therapeutic work, the needs that clients bring to us and the possibility of what can be offered. Working within such institutions without a clear appraisal of these practicalities, and a broader understanding of what coming to university represents for students, leaves a counsellor impoverished in her ability to provide timely and appropriate interventions.

McCaffery (2010) argues that in order to manage well in HE there are "four knows" that must be mastered:

1   knowing your environment
2   knowing your university
3   knowing your department, and
4   knowing yourself (p. 5)

Axiomatic in McCaffery's proposition is the notion that it is impossible to function well, or intelligently, within an environment one does not adequately understand. Although university counselling services may sometimes feel distanced from the funding, teaching, research and administration of the rest of the institution, it is dangerous for services and staff to operate as though the financial, political and sociological context in which we exist is unimportant. I contend that it is only when we understand the purpose of our institutions – current and future aspirations, constraints under which they operate – that we can meaningfully and intelligently engage with senior managers and stakeholders and be considered an integral part of those institutions. "Knowledge" takes many forms: factual knowledge is an obvious starting point, but counsellors are clear that hidden (unconscious) knowledge is often most powerful in determining outcomes.

Knowing your environment – knowing your university

In 1939, there were 50,000 students studying at 21 universities in Britain. Most were in Arts faculties (at Oxford and Cambridge the proportion was 80 per cent and 70 per cent respectively). By 1980, numbers of students had increased to around 300,000, and there were 46 institutions of higher education. Recent figures suggest that there are currently around 2.5 million students studying at 130 British universities. On the eve of the Second World War, 2 per cent of the late adolescent population went to university; by the mid-1960s, the figure had risen to 6 per cent. The figure is now 45 per cent. Whereas in previous generations the norm was for students to be physically present on campus, there is now a growing trend for online courses, distance learners and part-time students.

Table 1.1 Number of UK HE institutions and students, 1939–2012

Year	Number of British universities	Number of students
1939	21	50,000
1980	46	300,000
2012	130	2,500,000

Source: Collini, 2012

These figures, highlighting the dramatic increase in student numbers over the last century, mask particular increases in postgraduate students to over 530,000, and also obscure the fact that whereas the Arts once dominated, students now study mainly vocational or professional subjects, often on a part-time basis. The figures also conceal the fact that women now slightly outnumber men whereas in the early twentieth century these institutions were almost exclusively male (Collini, 2012). International students are also concealed within these figures, yet their significance continues to grow as numbers (and fees) increase year on year.

As the student population has grown, so the purpose and function of universities has evolved. Universities have been seen across different historical periods as "seminaries, finishing schools, government staff colleges, depositories of culture, nurseries of citizenship, and centres of scientific research . . . (and) now . . . plcs" (Collini, 2012, p. 34). That author identifies at least three different "types" of university: the "Oxbridge model" – residential, tutorial and character-forming; the "Scottish/London model" – metropolitan, professional, meritocratic; and the "civic or Redbrick model" – local, practical, aspirational. This is without even considering the impact since 1992 of the re-classification of former polytechnics (38 of which gained university status): some of these institutions are now the largest universities in the UK (in terms of student numbers) and are not "research-intensive" institutions. Many UK universities are members of different groupings (e.g. "The Russell Group", "U21") reflecting their particular origins and aspirations, and promoting members' interests in areas of research, teaching and funding. Over a century, British higher education has been transformed, and it is a matter of opinion as to whether "standards are falling, philistinism is rampant . . . even the barbarians are going to the dogs . . . (or) . . . challenges and opportunities abound, partnerships with industry beckon . . . and we're all investing in the future like billy-oh" (Collini, 2012, p. 20).

There is, perhaps, no more potent way in which recent political changes have impacted on universities than in the area of funding. Billig (1996) comments that whereas until the Thatcher era universities were funded to carry out research, post-Thatcher they now carry out research in order to attract funding – a fundamental shift. Funding is awarded primarily in support of science, medicine and technology, and this bias constitutes a control mechanism, determining what comes to be valued as "proper" research. Now, knowledge is not valued simply for its own sake, but must be justified in terms of economic impact. The result is an increasing emphasis on "efficiency" and "impact" as validators of academic effort, and this culture of "UK HE plc" impinges upon staff and students alike in these institutions.[3]

Funding, and charging fees to the majority of students in England and Wales, exemplifies the way in which HE is an evolving sector. While a notion of "the student as customer" is sometimes seen as driving emphasis on quality student support, there appears to be little evidence that universities treat students as customers in any conventional sense, or that students perceive themselves to have real consumer powers: "Look around any university campus as students flow between classes . . . and it will be observed that they exhibit none of the characteristics of the penny-wise consumer in a retail outlet." (Shattock, 2010, p. 104). While there has never been a time when universities were not reinventing themselves, adapting to and reflecting developments in government policy, financial forces are undoubtedly major drivers behind institutional change and restructuring.[4]

At a broader level, social changes impact upon our institutions, the people who run them and those who study within them, and are factors that represent another key aspect of "knowing your environment".

Identity and narratives-of-self in Western culture

Questions of identity may be a particular feature of modern, Western society. Our current way of life creates the need to ask and answer questions that simply did not exist for earlier generations, and may still not be relevant (or possible) for contemporary members of other, non-Western cultures (McAdams, 1993).

Since the end of the Second World War, traditional ways of living in the West have been eroded with increasing rapidity: class divisions have become blurred or eradicated; traditional religion has declined in influence; established family patterns – chiefly marriage – have begun to give way to other, more varied forms of relationship; self-identities based on sexual attraction or behaviour (lesbian, gay, bisexual, transgender, queer) are now no longer marginal in society; careers and education have become ever more varied, with technology spawning myriad new occupations (alongside the demise of traditional heavy industry jobs); the media, and especially the internet, have brought people into contact with images of ways of living that simply did not exist until very recently or were beyond the reach of all but a few. The range of options, the need to choose and the pressure that this can create are new to contemporary society. British sociologist Anthony Giddens suggests that we are living in a period of post-traditional late modernity, which contrasts with pre-modern (traditional) culture (Giddens, 1991). In late-modern societies, Giddens suggests, identity becomes an inescapable concern for everyone. At the heart of this endeavour, he argues, is the individual's attempt to construct a story about him or herself, which will provide a sense of coherence and stability:

> A person's identity is not to be found in behaviour, nor – important though this is – in the reactions of others, but in the capacity *to keep a particular narrative going*.
>
> (Giddens, 1991, p. 54)

To "keep a particular narrative going" requires considerable effort, given the range of possibilities available. Psychologist Kenneth Gergen (1991) argues that we have reached a point in Western society where the self has become "saturated" – that the world is so full of potential meanings and stories that individuals are becoming overwhelmed. For some, the choice of meanings and roles evokes playfulness and possibility; for others, a lack of fixed points of meaning becomes disturbing, threatening to flood the individual with despair. Gergen's view shifts us away from Giddens' late-modern society, towards a place of post-modernity. Gergen refers to the resultant personal saturation and fragmentation as "multiphrenia", defined by Holstein and Gubrium (2000) as "a life condition characterized by the consumption of myriad self signifiers, none of which is privileged over the other, but all of which are allegedly genuine, each competing for the self we can be" (p. 60)

While the few students who entered HE at the start of the twentieth century were chiefly from privileged backgrounds, with largely certain, pre-determined futures, this is no longer the case. "Knowing your environment" and "knowing your institution", therefore, is a far from simple process. For counsellors to offer genuinely insightful and discerning support to distressed individuals, it is incumbent upon us to achieve understanding and awareness of the social and political past and present: without such "knowledge" we are like swimmers swept along in currents of which we have no understanding or awareness. Sociological and political knowledge enables us, at least to some extent, to provide meaningful interventions for individuals and institutions.

Universities and narratives of self

> Before adolescence, we have no life story. We have no identity.
>
> (McAdams, 1993, p. 40)

Those who work therapeutically with late adolescents and young adults are engaging with them at a significant stage of life. This is when individuals begin to confront issues of identity and ideology, and start the process of crafting a sense of who they are, clarifying their values and deciding how they want to live their lives. Typical questions (though rarely formulated as succinctly) are: "Who am I?", "Who do I want to be?", "What values are important to me?" and "How can I create satisfying and enriching relationships?" Answers reached at this stage in life may resonate across an individual's life affecting not only an individual, but an entire generation. Cohler and Hostetler (2003) suggest that

> young adulthood, roughly between the ages of nineteen and twenty-five, represents a "reminiscence bump," which then becomes a kind of filter for a distinctive worldview unique to this *generation*, and which members of this generation carry across the course of their life and into old age.
>
> (p. 558)

Although by no means all students accessing university counselling services are late adolescents/young adults, the majority are and understanding the developmental tasks of this particular life-stage is essential when working to support students. Many theorists, e.g. Erikson (1959), Gould (1978), Levinson (1996) and Havighurst (1953), have attempted to tabulate common transitional stages of life. Although their theories differ in subtle ways, they all agree that "development occurs when individuals have to deal with different social demands" (Handry & Kloep, 2012, p. 17). Gould in particular emphasises loss as underpinning these developmental stages between the ages of 17 and 25 when two significant realisations typically emerge: "I have to leave my parents' world" and "I'm nobody's baby now" (ibid, p. 18). All agree that moving from one life-stage to another is frequently stressful and is distinguished by "periods of adjustment, balance and stability" (ibid, p. 18). Arnett (2004) argues that in Western culture, the achievement of adulthood has become a protracted process: key stages such as attaining financial independence, marriage and the birth of a first child all occur much later for today's "emerging adults" than past generations. Arnett argues that the ages of 17 to 29 now represent an "in-between" stage of life, between adolescence and adulthood, characterised by high levels of self-focus, a wide range of options where a young person is free to experiment with temporary jobs, long trips abroad, relationships and identities, and also, importantly, high levels of insecurity.[5]

Late adolescents and emerging adults, then, face a daunting task: the search for a personal life-story, a narrative, that will prove sufficiently robust as a foundation for their journey through life and provide a sense of meaning and identity. Counsellors and psychotherapists are part of highly individualistic Western culture, assisting individuals in the creation or repair of meaningful life-stories in ways previously provided by institutions such as the extended family or the church (McLeod, 1997, 2004). We are engaged in supporting individuals who are grappling with their "project of the self" (Benwell & Stokoe, 2006, p. 24). We recognise – to some degree at least – that the self is a *reflexive project* – "an endeavour that we continuously work and reflect on. We create, maintain and revise a set of biographical narratives – the story of who we are, and how we came to be where we are" (Gauntlett, 2008, p. 107).

How and where do adolescents find the space and time to engage in this crucial "project of the self"? In a society that provides endless inducements to consume other people's stories (particularly via the cult of celebrity), what opportunities exist for a new generation to create their own stories, their own life-narrative and to find a sense of meaning in them?

University as a developmental space

One space in which emerging adults may engage with the identity-building process is the transitional zone between home and full-time work, adolescence and adulthood, provided by universities. Besides offering educational opportunities, universities provide a "halfway house" between the freedom of childhood and the demands of adulthood, a context in which to experiment and learn about capabilities and limitations (Rana, 2000).

Universities thus provide a "psychosocial moratorium" (McAdams, 1993, p. 92) in the essential process of constructing a narrative of "who I am". Undergraduate, and indeed postgraduate years are, hopefully, about more than just getting a degree. Universities are also places where the work of identity-formation, of coming to a preliminary understanding about one's place in the world, can occur. However, the shift in culture within institutions of higher education to a more business-based model (Billig, 1996; Mann, 2008) has a trickle-down effect on the experience of students. It raises levels of performance anxiety, and inhibits the sense of undergraduate years being about more than just gaining a qualification. Yet, identity issues cannot easily be supressed, and they are uppermost in students' presenting issues at university counselling services. Many students approach these services with concerns about academic work but these issues are often underpinned by deeper anxieties about relationships, self-esteem and unresolved conflicts within families of origin (AUCC, 2002). Indeed, academic work – eliciting the need to prove oneself in competition against one's peers – may magnify existing insecurities about the self and bring them to the fore.

The impact of change

If discerning the sociological, political, economic, psychological and emotional currents that eddy around us, often unseen, is key to understanding our work as therapists within universities, so too is an awareness of how these currents manifest themselves in the clients we support. It is easy to "know" that the number seeking counselling support in HE has grown enormously in the last decade. Where stigma once prevented many from seeking the psychological help they needed, a new openness and willingness to reveal and talk about emotional problems has emerged within Western culture (Royal College of Psychiatrists, 2011). This willingness has led to a sharp rise in demand for university counselling services over the last decade, and in expectations of what therapists can offer – some of which reflect idealistic hopes rather than sober reality.

A recent survey of heads of UK university counselling services (Mair, 2014) revealed the following examples of increases in the numbers of students registering for counselling over a 10-year period.

Table 1.2 Students seen in 11 HE counselling services, 2002–12

Institution	Students seen 2002	Students seen 2012	% increase
1	238	458	93
2	556	1203	116
3	326	572	75
4	324	650	101
5	230	295	28
6	380	576	52
7	119	312	162
8	362	792	119
9	213	674	216
10	718	1186	65
11	362	798	120

These data reveal that over a decade, many services have experienced what can only be called an explosion in demand. Alongside the increase in numbers, there is a suggestion that the level of severity of reported distress has also risen: a 2008 survey of four HE institutions found that 29 per cent of respondents described clinical levels of psychological distress and in 8 per cent of cases this was moderate to severe or severe (Royal College of Psychiatrists, 2011, p. 23).[6]

Although some services have seen modest increases in staffing to help cope with this demand, others have not. Despite increasing pressure to meet the demands of students who are more willing to seek support and help for personal issues than previous generations, many services have not received additional resourcing and have had to introduce changes to the way such demand is absorbed. Some make more use of unpaid "associate" staff or "trainees" to help meet demand for individual counselling. Evening, and in some cases Saturday, opening is widespread throughout the sector as demand for fast access to support grows. In some instances, out-sourcing of counselling provision has seemed to be the only way to meet demand. One of the dangers of under-investing in support services is that they become weakened, and start to perform poorly, struggling to maintain quality and effectiveness thus hastening their demise. By contrast, "services that are well maintained can add value to an institution in often unmeasurable ways, [although] costs of . . . maintenance can seem high when the most obvious measures of institutional competition can be demonstrated elsewhere" (Shattock, 2010, p. 40).

"Knowing our environment" requires that we ask why it is that demand has increased so dramatically in recent years. What factors are at play here? In the spirit of "knowing", we need to consider why it is that the last decade has seen such a rise in numbers accessing university counselling services.

Higher education, students and help-seeking behaviour

> University students are a very steady group. The fact that large numbers come to a student health service for help with psychological problems is determined by the nature of their work. Whereas an engineer's apprentice or a farmer's boy can suffer the normal depression and anxieties of growing up without his employment being much affected, it is impossible for a student to suffer even transitory disturbance without his work suffering. He (sic) then begins to drop behind his colleagues; this produces a secondary anxiety which in turn also adversely affects his study and makes his problems worse in a vicious circle. It is because student life demands such a continuously high standard of intellectual efficiency, not because students are psychiatric weaklings, that the incidence of those attending for psychological help are high, and their treatment is important.
>
> (Malleson, 1963, p. 43)

These words, penned over half a century ago, ring as true today as when first written. Nick Malleson, "the driving force behind the founding of the Association for Student Counselling" (Bell, 1996, p. 12), clearly encapsulates the vulnerability to psychological and emotional distress of students who, paradoxically, need to be able to perform at the peak of their intellectual abilities at a time in life when they may be most prone to the stresses of late adolescence/ emerging adulthood.

Malleson understood why it is that students, especially, are vulnerable to stress, depression and other psychological, emotional and psychiatric disturbance. He described the spiralling impact of depression or anxiety on academic work, the falling behind that further compounds the depression, which in turn further affects work, and so on. He understood why numbers of students seeking support from then fledgling health centres and, eventually, counselling services should be so high: because of *the setting itself and the demands it imposes*.

As with any consideration of issues as complex as "reasons why people seek support", a categorical assertion is unwise. Theories abound as to why numbers seeking support have risen so dramatically, yet there is no conclusive evidence as to why this should be so. The likelihood is that there are several factors, which together drive this surge. I explore some of the most salient as follows.

Young people today are less resilient than they used to be

This view is based on a sense that contemporary youth have grown up in a risk-averse culture with over-protective parents and a consequent lack of exposure to settings and relationships that would, in previous generations, have strengthened self-reliance, an ability to accept set-backs and an early realisation and acceptance that life is not always fair. Typical headlines in the press encapsulate this impression:

'Spoon-fed' students lack resilience needed at Oxbridge

(Paton, 2010)

Children 'no longer allowed to fail', Tanya Byron warns. Growing numbers of middle-class children are suffering mental health problems after being "raised in captivity" by over-protective parents, a leading psychologist has warned.

(Paton, 2012)

Children and adolescents, it is argued, have become accustomed to having every need met, and met quickly, with smart-phones ("a masterclass in distraction", Chodron, 2013), computers and parents themselves providing on-demand, instantaneous responses. There is a widespread popular impression that education has been "dumbed down", with subjects taught and exams set so that no one ever fails. Some (e.g. Ecclestone & Hayes, 2008) assert that the rise of so-called "therapeutic education" has created a situation where "it is widely assumed that staff and students may need counselling to cope with all aspects of university life" (p. 86). The rise of a culture where any and every emotional disturbance must be soothed with adjustments to submission dates or exams does not promote the development of resilience in emerging adults.

Consequently, when students are thrown into a highly competitive environment such as a university course community, many find themselves unable to cope. Swedish psychologist David Eberhard (2013) describes the raising of children in a social environment that places their needs above those of adults, arguing that parents have unwittingly set their children up for high levels of depression and distress when they later discover that the world does not, in fact, revolve around their needs. If this argument is true, then the rise in numbers of students seeking counselling is, in part, due to young people being generally unable to tolerate demands in life with which their parents and grandparents would have stoically coped. Lack of resilience is seen as an acquired inability to withstand the inevitable losses, frustrations and disappointments of life.

Life is more pressurised nowadays for young people

This claim, which locates the source of increased distress in the external rather than internal world, posits that it is modern life itself, making demands on people unknown by previous generations, that explains why more students seek counselling support. Here, as discussed previously, the increasing competitiveness of life combines with growing insecurity and instability about identity and roles within society to create a potent mix within some individuals of anxiety, depression or apathy. Increased demand for counselling, then, represents a kind of existential crisis in the formation of meaningful life-narratives within Western culture. The competitiveness of modern life, often exacerbated by parental anxiety that off-spring should out-perform their peers, carries the risk that children internalise a message that the only thing that counts are results and success (Carey, 2014). Whereas in former generations one's place in society, along with a degree of cer-tainty about job/career, stability of family structure and personal identity meant that issues of individual choice and the resulting anxiety were more muted, and organised religion provided a background "meaning-of-life" narrative, nowadays almost every aspect of life is fraught with the concern that results from a plethora of options. A report by the Royal College of Psychiatrists in 2011 cited external sources of distress as key to understanding recent rises in the severity of the men-tal health issues with which students present at university counselling services:

> The prevalence of . . . causal factors for mental disorder in young people in general has also shown substantial changes in the past two decades. These include increased rates of family breakdown, consumption of alcohol and illegal drugs, and unemployment.
>
> (p. 21)

"Facebook envy" – the ability of youth to compare themselves (usually unfa-vourably) to literally millions of other young people around the world – was absent for previous generations. Now, young people are bombarded with adver-tising images and celebrity-obsessed journalism that invite them to strive con-stantly to acquire more, to *be* more, generating feelings of inadequacy (physical, emotional and financial) and yet at the same time instilling beliefs that we should all, somehow, achieve permanent happiness. This insidious form of perfectionism constantly undermines self-esteem. Children are tested at school from a young age; competition for access to "elite" institutions of education is immense; the need to secure well-paid, prestigious jobs acute. Whereas higher education was, during the "golden years" of the 1960s, '70s and '80s, free, coming to univer-sity now entails taking on a large debt to be repaid over many years. For some students, the experience of HE itself has been transformed from an enquiry-led process, to a results-driven one:

> the old fashioned 'Slow Food' feel of traditional British scholarship, where academics took their time to make and mature idiosyncratic ideas, has given way to a new 'Fast Food' American-style approach which focuses on serving up the latest fashionable ideas and meeting short-term goals. The demands on our time, as staff and students, are increasing each year, and there seems to be less time available to meet those demands.
>
> (Stanley, 2014)

Sometimes taught in industrial-sized lecture theatres, with little contact with key academic staff (themselves stretched to breaking point), HE can, for some, be a huge strain. Such pressures mean that it should be no surprise that young people need greater help, and seek it in increasing numbers from counsellors and others, in navigating a highly pressurised, competitive and demanding social environment. Where pressures to perform are not mitigated by strong emotional support networks, the resulting pressure can feel too much to bear.

> Getting into Oxbridge was traumatic for me because of my pushy mother who just enjoyed bragging about it. When I tried to take an overdose she accused me of embarrassing her. She treated me better when I did well in exams. The result was that I worked harder to win her love. When I had a mental break-down she accused me of trying to get my own way. I hate her guts now because I realise she didn't love me, she just loved my achievements.
>
> (Carey, 2014, p. 90)

Cultural enfeeblement and the Fundamental Attribution Error

A further reason cited for the rise in numbers of people willing to seek professional help for personal emotional and psychological issues is that of "cultural enfeeblement". As therapy services become embedded within institutions and wider culture, and thereby normalised, a powerful narrative is disseminated within society that emotional difficulties and issues should not be tolerated, and that everyone should expect to feel happy most, if not all, of the time. The "cultural enfeeblement" argument is articulated clearly by sociologist Kenneth Gergen.

> As we furnish the population with hammers of mental deficit, everyone needs pounding . . . the culture *learns how to be* mentally ill . . . depression has become such a cultural commonplace that it is virtually an invited reaction to failure, frustration or disappointment.
>
> (2006, p. 129)

This "cultural enfeeblement" narrative is strengthened by the proliferation of medical diagnoses for feelings that in previous generations would simply have been accepted as part of the normal ups and downs of life. The DSM,[7] the "Bible" of the psychiatric community, has come under sustained criticism from many quarters for proliferating the number of diagnosable syndromes. A recent NHS newsletter (2013) summarised this critique as twofold:

1   An unhealthy influence of the pharmaceutical industry on the revision from DSM-edition IV to V.
2   An increasing tendency to medicalise patterns of behaviour and mood that are not particularly extreme.

The prescription of antidepressants in rich, Western countries is now at a level unimaginable to previous generations, with GPs and mental health services unable to cope with levels of mental health distress with which patients present (Greenberg, 2011). With access to talking therapies and mental health services under enormous pressure, antidepressants, known to work with moderate-severe depression, may now be prescribed as a first intervention, even though evidence for their effectiveness at this level is scarce.

The "cultural enfeeblement" proposition suggests that the provision of therapy, and the creation of discourses of syndromes and other mental health deficiencies, in and of itself reduces resilience within individuals. Others critique different aspects of the therapy project. Principally, there is the idea that therapy *individualises* problems, and tends to ignore sociological or political causes of suffering (Morrall, 2008). In a university setting, for example, it might be possible for counsellors to be working with "depression" (possibly diagnosed by a GP working within a medical model), which, viewed from another perspective, could be redefined as "oppression" (from societal expectations that a university degree is essential for future careers, or from institutional issues such as poor housing or bad teaching). By individualising suffering, it is argued, therapy effectively disempowers people, encouraging self-blame and inculcating a sense of personal failure. Therapists unwittingly collude with oppressive practices in institutions by implying that the individual can/should be able to deal with distress within themselves. We thus become blocks to meaningful change in the environment that could, by itself, alleviate suffering.

The Fundamental Attribution Error (FAE) is the thesis that people typically, and erroneously "attribute another person's behaviour to their dispositional qualities, rather than situational factors" (Heider, 1958; Ross, 1977, cited in Langdridge and Butt, 2004, p. 359). So whereas therapists will typically engage with an individual's internal experience of depression or stress and explore developmental, cognitive or psychodynamic causes for distress, the FAE posits that a personal focus ignores other more significant external factors (e.g. high fees, living in expensive, cramped, noisy accommodation with incompatible strangers, poor teaching, vast lecture theatres), which, when attended to, significantly alleviate individual suffering and distress. Could it be that counsellors unconsciously collude with narratives of personal deficiency – if not always, at least at times – by emphasising the individual's responsibility for overcoming suffering that is entirely understandable when environmental considerations are taken into account? One important implication of this argument is that counsellors within HE must use their knowledge of common causes of distress, especially those that have their root in policies or practices of their institution, and develop mechanisms for feeding these back to relevant committees with the power to make appropriate changes. This is a clear argument for maintaining such services "in-house". External providers of counselling are unlikely to be in a position to develop the feedback mechanisms and relationships that could enable such positive environmental change to take place – especially if to do so meant that they were perceived as exceeding the bounds of their limited "helping" role.

Agency and structure: what drives help-seeking behaviour?

The theories outlined in this chapter, apparently contradictory when taken in isolation, in fact reinforce each other when considered together. Lack of individual resilience combined with greater external expectations and pressures is a potent source of personal distress, especially when experienced against a stronger cultural narrative of "mental health" that locates responsibility for personal distress within the individual. Essentially, these ideas are based on differing emphases on the centrality of *agency* (the ability of an individual to determine personal choices) and *structure* (the unavoidable constraints placed upon us by our social, political, economic and geographical environment) and the way these forces interact to influence and determine our internal and external emotions, behaviours and life-narratives. While both agency and structure are key considerations when understanding ("knowing") personal distress, it is perhaps true to say that counsellors may tend to lend more weight to the former rather than the latter. A key aspect of knowing ourselves, therefore, must be the development of awareness of the interplay of structure and agency, and an ability to appropriately engage with and influence our institutions and those who manage them.

Managing demand: very short-term work with students

With so many factors at play within the context of an HE institution, it is not easy to "know" with complete certainty what drives increasing demand for counselling services. Nevertheless, data confirms that this demand exists and shows no sign of abating. Given this context, this book is primarily concerned with theory and practice in working within a very short time frame with students who present with varying degrees of distress at university counselling services. While a few universities continue to offer open-ended therapy with no set limit to the number of sessions a student can have, a majority, due to demand, now impose limits. This can vary, but three to six sessions is becoming the norm in most student counselling services. Even in services with no formal limit to the number of sessions available, the average number of sessions attended by student-clients is between four and five (Wallace, 2014, p. 16).

Essential questions to consider in responding to this rise in demand include:

• What is the "real need" (Ecclestone, 2014) being expressed by this student? (Assessment is key here: see Dufour, Chapter 4.)
• Is this need best understood as a lack of internal resilience, or as an understandable struggle with a demanding external environment?

- Can this need be addressed via services that engage with outer world adjustments and changes, or through counselling with its greater emphasis on inner world awareness and development?

Indeed, one fact that university counsellors need to consider when meeting a client for the first time is that not every student who contacts us will actually want, need or be able to use counselling. This is a vital realisation, but one that is easily overlooked. Not recognising that this is so can create unhelpful complications for the client, the therapist and the service. Students who are in fact looking for support because of practical difficulties within the institution (e.g. wanting to change courses, study-skill problems or housing issues), or who approach us in the aftermath of a distressing event, can be left confused if a counsellor seeks to reframe such issues as instances of personal internalised (agency) lack, rather than recognising them as institutional/externalised (structural) issues. Clients who "dropout" of counselling may be expressing uncertainty or dissatisfaction with their encounter with a therapist due to a reattribution of issues from structure to agency[8]. For others, the intensity of a 50-minute individual session with a counsellor may simply be too much and therapists need to be able to tailor sessions to the needs of individual students. Crucially, we need to be able to distinguish between those who contact us because they are "in crisis", those who are "just visiting" and those who are "ready to engage" (Elton-Wilson, 1996). Many students contact counselling services as a result of a crisis – a relationship ending, a failed exam, parental separation. Such crises do not mean that clients are "motivated to engage fully in personal psychological change" (ibid, p. 15). Others are testing us out – perhaps in a few years they may be able to stand the intensity of introspection, and the challenge to self, entailed in therapy. Those who are genuinely "ready to engage" will be relatively few in number given the demands of such internal self-examination. Could it be that many of the students who have come forward in recent years for "counselling" may actually benefit more from referral to an ancillary service (Wellbeing, Mental Health, Welfare Tutor, Chaplaincy etc.) where structural issues can be addressed more effectively, and where psychoeducational input can normalise and "decontaminate" common emotional responses to typical life-events?

> The responsibility of the intake interviewer is to attempt as accurate an assessment of the immediate needs of the client, and to be prepared to empower an oppressed client with appropriate information as to their rights and the availability of other professional specialisations and sources of self-help. The subtle dividing line between the need for external support and internal change is the crucial dividing factor which underlies an honest offer of psychotherapeutic engagement.
>
> (Elton-Wilson, 1996, p. 16)

Having the confidence as therapists and as counselling services to gently say "no" to students who approach us is an indication of maturity and non-defensiveness about our role. Clarity about what counselling is, and is not, its strengths and limitations, must underpin our work; *readiness and willingness to commit to personal change* is one of the most important factors to discern in any intake/assessment interview. Developing relationships with other campus services, enabling smooth onward referrals that do not communicate rejection to a student, is essential to effectively meeting the real needs of "emerging adults".

This, of course, begs the question: do we actually need counsellors at all in universities? If relatively few students are ready to engage in psychological change, and those who may be are constrained by the practicalities of term-endings and other unavoidable interruptions to therapeutic work, and if many of the issues with which clients present are setting-driven, would we not be better simply employing generalist advisors who can provide practical information at much lower cost? If counselling services have become so stretched that some can only offer five sessions of "support", are they really offering anything that is qualitatively distinct from other helping services?

While the work of newly emerging professionals such as wellbeing advisors, mental health advisors and vulnerable student officers is appropriate and important, there remains a level of therapeutic engagement that can only be undertaken by clinicians with appropriate levels of training and experience. Counsellors need to be non-defensive in their interaction with other professionals: signposting students according to needs is key to embracing the BACP ethical framework (www. bacp.co.uk), which requires us to respect client autonomy. But while many students *may* be "in crisis" or "just visiting", the quality of response and intervention they receive is absolutely central to their experience of being helped. Time and again, research shows that it is the quality of relationship that emerges between a counsellor and her client that is crucial to psychological change and this relationship will be distinguished by a respectful and enabling stance (Asay & Lambert, 2004). Students in distress may feel that they need rescuing and approach counsellors with a hope that they will airlift them out of difficulty. The ability of counsellors to *contain* distress *without rescuing* can foster the ability to tolerate distress within our clients and is a key, essential difference in the work we do compared to other helping services.

A therapeutic alliance can be built, which strengthens clients' internal worlds and encourages them to draw on inner resources, to think more clearly and to move forwards, accessing their own adult coping skills. Whereas other services may be focused on facilitating changes to the external world to enable students to be as free from stress as possible, counsellors will always retain an important role in working with the inner world – helping clients to understand how *they* play a role in sustaining or exacerbating problems, clarifying the impact of the past in the present and providing a quality of hearing – along with an ability to challenge – that can only be the result of a deep "knowing" of psychological, philosophical and emotional processes. "Knowing" about issues such as developmental stages, and having the scaffolding of knowledge provided by therapeutic models, enables a depth and quality of response to students that transcends information giving. Three to six sessions may not be much quantitatively; qualitatively, much can be communicated by practitioners who have done the hard work within themselves of developing personal awareness, and who can engage compassionately yet challengingly with their clients.

Such "knowledge" and inner personal work informs our interactions and interventions, and fast-route training is no substitute for it. The ability to contain high levels of risk, to respond to the aftermath of a student death, or a sexual assault, to work with entrenched issues such as self-harm or eating issues is not something that can be undertaken by minimally-trained staff, or those without sufficient self-understanding not to impose their own views or solutions onto their clients. One of the most important aims of higher education, that of producing graduates who not only have knowledge of their field, but more importantly have acquired an ability to ask good questions about that field, is mirrored in the counselling encounter. Counsellors do not attempt to provide all the answers, but help clients to ask better questions about themselves, other people and the world around them.

The practical issues of how such support can be offered within a very short-term framework are the subjects of the rest of this book. We start with an overview of theory behind approaches to short-term work (Coren), and a consideration of legal issues underpinning the ever-vexing issue of managing risk and exercising "duty of care" (Jenkins). The fundamental importance of assessment as the starting point for all good therapy comes – appropriately – first in the "Practice" section of the book (Dufour) and issues of service evaluation and demonstrating impact are next (McCrea). This is followed by a description of an established model for guiding short-term work (Cowley and Groves) and then by exploration of short-term work with typical, but often problematic, issues that students bring to our services (Hunt, Meyer, Anderson and Louden). The challenges of engaging with entrenched, somatic issues are considerable but these authors contend that much can be done with a good model and an expectation of change. The use of technology for reaching out to the "digital generation" is explored (Ames) and the book ends with an exploration of the importance of self-care and institutional support for therapists who undertake this demanding work (Tarren) – how, in effect, we can survive the demands of clients, parents and managers while staying true to our theoretical foundations and ethical frameworks.

"Counselling students" is not a phrase that necessarily conveys the complexity, subtlety and challenge of the work undertaken in university counselling services across the country. "Knowing" – as McCaffery enjoins – is a demanding and at time stressful process. But the richness of the work, and the potential for significant, positive impact in a person's life, remains a powerful draw to engage in a profession that at times still struggles for acceptance, but provides institutions and individuals with the space and time in which emotional and psychological growth can occur within the context of academic achievement.

Notes

1 Though how rigidly these limits are applied varies from service to service.
2 Cognitive Behaviour Therapy, Cognitive Analytical Therapy, Dynamic Interpersonal Therapy.
3 Nevertheless, Billig may be overstating his argument that recent governments have wreaked havoc upon university funding, imposing fees on students that previous generations never had to pay. According to Collini, "taking another perspective it is the 1960s and 1970s that can be made to appear exceptional, the first and last decades in which Britain tried to sustain a substantial but still rigorously selective, wholly state-funded system of high-quality undergraduate-centred universities" (2012, p. 21).
4 Universities now receive only around 40 per cent of their funding from the state, compared to 80 per cent in the 1980s (Shattock, 2010, p. 32).
5 While such models of development may have some benefit in helping to understand broad patterns, they have all been criticised for being particularly ethnocentric, typically ignoring non-Western cultures where adolescence may not exist, and where the possibilities, freedoms and insecurities of "emerging adulthood" are unknown. Equally, they may more accurately encapsulate middle-class rather than working-class experience.
6 Others, however, question the notion that severity in morbidity has increased significantly (RCP, 2011, p. 31).
7 The *Diagnostic and Statistical Manual of Mental Disorders* (DSM), published by the American Psychiatric Association, offers a common language and standard criteria for the classification of mental disorders. The DSM is now in its fifth edition, DSM-5, published on May 18, 2013.
8 Of course, it may not always be possible to separate agency/structure issues, and even when a presenting issue appears to be chiefly in a matter of structure, there may be some agency issues that need to be addressed. However, remembering the Fundamental Attribution Error, counsellors would be well advised to exercise caution before embarking on significant, thorough-going personal exploration before a clear, immediate external problem has been addressed/resolved.

References

Arnett, J. J. (2004) *Emerging Adulthood: The Winding Road from the Late Teens through the Twenties*, Oxford, Oxford University Press.
Asay, T. P. & Lambert, M. J. (2004) The Empirical Case for the Common Factors in Therapy: Quantitative Findings, in Hubble, M. A., Duncan, B. L. and Miller, S. D. (Eds) *The Heart and Soul of Change: What Works in Therapy*, Washington D.C., American Psychological Association.
AUCC (2002) Annual Survey of Counselling in Further and Higher Education 2002/03.
BACP (n.d.) *Ethical principles of counselling and psychotherapy*. Available from: www.bacp.co.uk/ethical_framework/ethics.php (accessed 9th November 2013).
Bell, E. (1996) *Counselling in Further and Higher Education (Counselling in Context)*, London, Sage.
Benwell, B. & Stokoe, E. (2006) *Identity and Discourse*, Edinburgh, Edinburgh University Press.
Billig, M. (1996) *Thinking and Arguing: A Rhetorical Approach to Social Psychology*, Cambridge, Cambridge University Press.
Carey, T. (2014) *Taming the Tiger Parent: How to Put Your Child's Well-Being First in a Competitive world*, London, Robinson.

Chodron, P. (2013) *How To Meditate: A Practical Guide To Making Friends With Your Mind*, Boulder, CA, Sounds True.

Cohler, B J. & Hostetler, A. (2003) Linking Life Course and Life Story: Social Change and the Narrative Study of Lives over Time, in Mortimer, J. T. (Ed.) *Handbook of the Life Course*, Hingham, MA, Kluwer Academic Publishers.

Collini, S. (2012) *What Are Universities For?* London, Penguin.

Eberhard, D. (2013) *How Children Took Power (Hur Barnen Tok Makten)*, Sweden, Pocketförlaget.

Ecclestone, K. & Hayes, D. (2008) *The Dangerous Rise of Therapeutic Education*, Abingdon, Routledge.

Ecclestone, K (2014) "'Real Need' or 'Real Life'". Presentation to Heads of University Counselling Services, King's College, London, 14th November 2014.

Elton-Wilson, J (1996) *Time Conscious Psychological Therapy: A Life-Stage to Go Through*, Abingdon, Routledge.

Erikson, E. H. (1959) Identity and the life cycle. *Psychological Issues, Monograph 1*. New York, International University Press.

Gauntlett, D. (2008) *Media, Gender and Identity: An Introduction (2nd Edition)*, Abingdon, Routledge.

Gergen, K. J. (1991) *The Saturated Self: Dilemmas of Identity in Contemporary Life*, New York, Basic Books.

Gergen, K. J. (2006) *Therapeutic Realities: Collaboration, Oppression and Relational Flow*, Chagrin Falls, Taos Institute.

Giddens, A. (1991) *Modernity and Self-Identity: Self and Society in the Late Modern Age*, Cambridge, Polity.

Gould, R. L. (1978) *Transformations: Growth and Change in Adult Life*, New York, Simon and Schuster.

Greenberg, G. (2011), *Manufacturing Depression: The History of a Modern Disease*, London, Bloomsbury.

Handry, L. B. & Kloep, M. (2012) *Adolescence and Adulthood: Transitions and Transformations*, London, Palgrave Macmillan.

Havighurst, R. (1953) *Human Development and Education*, New York, Longman.

Holstein, J. A. & Gubrium, J. F. (2000) *The Self We Live By: Narrative Identity in a Postmodern World*, New York, Oxford University Press.

Langdridge, D. & Butt, T. (2004) The fundamental attribution error: A phenomenological critique. *British Journal of Social Psychology*, 43, 357–369.

Levinson, D. J. (1996) *The Seasons of a Woman's Life*, New York, Knopf.

Mair, D. (2014) Unpublished Survey of Heads of UK HE Counselling Services, July–August.

Malleson, N (1963) The influence of emotional factors on achievement in university education, *The Sociological Review Monograph*, 7, 42–58.

Mann, S. J. (2008) *Study, Power and the University*, Maidenhead, Open University Press.

McAdams, D. (1993) *The Stories We Live By: Personal Myths and the Making of the Self*, New York, The Guilford Press.

McCaffery, P. (2010) *The Higher Education Manager's Handbook (2nd Edition): Effective Leadership and Management in Universities and Colleges*, London, Routledge.

McLeod, J. (1997) *Narrative and Psychotherapy*, London, Sage.

McLeod, J. (2004) The Significance of Narrative and Storytelling in Post-Psychological Counseling and Psychotherapy, in Lieblich, A., McAdams, D. P. and Josselson, R. (Eds) *Healing Plots: The Narrative Basis of Psychotherapy*, Washington DC, American Psychological Association.

Morrall, P. (2008) *The Trouble with Therapy: Sociology and Psychotherapy*, Maidenhead, Open University Press.

NHS (n.d.) *Online newsletter*. Available from: www.nhs.uk/news/2013/08august/pages/controversy-mental-health-diagnosis-and-treatment-dsm5.aspx (accessed 15th November 2014).

Paton, G. (2010) Spoon-fed students lack resilience needed at Oxbridge, *Daily Telegraph*, 10th December 2010. Available from: www.telegraph.co.uk/education/educationnews/8194038/Spoon-fed-students-lack-resilience-needed-at-Oxbridge.html (accessed 27th September 2014).

Paton, G. (2012) Children no longer allowed to fail, Tanya Byron warns, *Daily Telegraph*, 5th December 2012. Available from: www.telegraph.co.uk/education/educationnews/9725022/Children-no-longer-allowed-to-fail-Tanya-Byron-warns.html (accessed 27th September 2014).

Rana, R. (2000) *Counselling Students: A Psychodynamic Perspective*, London, Palgrave Macmillan.

Royal College of Psychiatrists (2011) *Mental health of students in higher education*, London, RCP. Available from: www.rcpsych.ac.uk/files/pdfversion/cr166.pdf (accessed 27th September 2014).

Shattock, M. (2010) *Managing Successful Universities (2nd Edition)*, Maidenhead, Open University Press.

Stanley, S. (2014) Swimming against the stream? Academic Capitalism, contemplative education and mindfulness. Presentation at Oxford Mindfulness Centre, 25th April 2014.

Wallace, P. (2014) *Counselling in universities and colleges, online training course*. Available from: www.minded.org.uk/course/view.php?id=234 (accessed 14th October 2014).

Theory

Chapter 2

Short-term therapy

Therapy-lite?

Alex Coren

There is a, presumably apocryphal, story told about the psychoanalyst Alfred Adler. A patient explained all their difficulties to him in their first session, after which Adler said, "What would you do if you did not have these problems?" The patient told him and Adler replied, "Well go ahead and do it then". In a version of contemporary therapies' "magic question", Adler's response immediately brought up the issue of time, and duration, in relation to the therapeutic task and the technique of counselling. Why can't therapies be (very) brief? This has perhaps particular relevance to working with students in higher education whose developmental fluidity, and their limited time in educational institutions, is potentially well suited to an Adlerian response.

In this chapter I shall be looking at the history of brief therapeutic counselling in general, with specific focus on counselling in Higher Education settings. I shall outline the development of core psychotherapeutic models that have developed over time and can be used when working briefly with students. Finally I shall attempt to apply these models to an educational context and suggest that the process of gaining or seeking an education may have a personal and developmental function for the individual as well an academic, vocational or pedagogic role. It is both these tasks that need to, and can, be addressed concurrently during higher education and it is here that counselling has an important contribution to make.

History

The idea that students may benefit, or need, psychological attention is one that has been prevalent for some considerable time. The early days of psychoanalysis are littered with references to education and the wellbeing of students. This particularly applies to issues of suicide or self harm, which continue to this day to cause much anxiety in contemporary higher educational institutions. Stekel (1910) talked about the prevalence of suicidal – or self-harming – actions and ruminations, prevalent in the student population, while Freud wrote about the process of learning in general, and curiosity in particular (Freud, 1900, 1905, 1909, 1914). His daughter Anna was extensively occupied with children in education (1955) culminating in the psychoanalytic hubris of suggesting that all teachers should be psychoanalysed before entering the classroom. These ideas contributed to the belief that the process of learning – and for that matter, teaching – are more complex and subtle than had hitherto been thought. We have developed more modest aspirations for counselling in education settings yet it remains true that psychotherapeutic concepts such as self-reflection, mentalisation and thoughtfulness remain pre-requisites for any pastoral intervention in education and can be utilised in brief psychological consultations with students in higher education.

It is significant that most original psychological interventions were brief and highly focused. Over time these were supplanted in favour of the increasing length of treatments and concepts such as "rigour and depth" have come to dominate psychodynamic thinking, making therapy both longer and the clinician more passive and less time sensitive. Increasingly however clinicians are rediscovering the short and active treatments, which previously were both popular and successful. Psychodynamic practitioners have welcomed the opportunity and challenge that this has represented and have creatively applied core psychoanalytic concepts into clinical practice. (See Coren, 2010; Mander, 2000; Smith, 2008; Lemma *et al.*, 2011; Levenson, 2012; Messer & Warren, 1998.) This adaptation is particularly suited to the time frame required in educational settings.

There exists a long and illustrious history of brief psychoanalytic treatment or consultations/conversations as they may be now termed. Freud's treatment of Bruno Walter (1947) lasted five or six sessions while Gustav Mahler was seen by Freud in one four-hour session (resembling some current single-session interventions). Katerina and Lucy R (Freud, 1955) are particularly evocative examples of Freud's early therapeutic technique, which is not dissimilar to contemporary brief interventions with an active therapist seeking to link the past and present with the client's current symptom or distress. Contemporary short-term therapists (see Coren, 2010, 2014; Della Selva, 2004; Lees & Vaspe, 1999; Stadter, 2004), particularly in educational settings, advocate therapeutic activity on behalf of the therapist, the establishment of a therapeutic focus, a confidence in outcome – albeit with limited goals – which is conveyed to the client. Material is proactively elicited and a mutually empowering therapeutic relationship forms the basis of the work. This is not dissimilar to the early Freudians.

However, these more active and engaging approaches met with a great deal of resistance and led to a redirection of therapeutic techniques, aims and outcomes. Historically, issues of transference (essentially the, frequently unconscious, redirection of feelings and desires from one person, often the parent, to another, often the therapist) and resistance (the secondary gain of maintaining the symptom and resisting change including an ambivalence about "getting better") were seen as obstacles, needing time and a specific therapeutic stance to address. Psychoanalysis as a therapy became longer and longer, therapeutically more passive and less overtly challenging or supportive. Therapists became passive in technique, accepting the increasing length of therapies and developing a hierarchy of therapeutic interventions dependent on sessional frequency and intensity, with those most frequent and working exclusively with transference manifestations seen as most privileged.

This has coloured psychodynamic treatments in a manner that has been, at times, dismissive of shorter therapies. The modality embarked on a trajectory where the more psychoanalysis uncovered about psychological development and processes, and the developmentally earlier problems were seen to originate, the longer treatments had to become, a belief that has only relatively recently been challenged. The suggestions that treatments could become briefer and more active, such as from Rank (1973), Ferenczi (1925), Adler (1958), Reich (1952) and Alexander and French (1946) were dismissed and met with a great deal of resistance. For a long period psychoanalytic brief therapies could only be viewed within the paradigm of long-term open-ended therapy, becoming a lesser, and denigrated, aspect of applied psychoanalysis, rather than something that is informed by psychoanalytic knowledge but is essentially different but of equal value. More recently, the attitudes towards short-term therapy have developed (from being peripheral, and second-best to open ended therapy), to having its own body of knowledge and being the treatment of choice in many settings, not least education.

Short-term interventions have established an impressive theoretical body of knowledge and application to clinical practice, for example, Balint (1972), Sifneos (1979), Davanloo (1990), Malan (1976, 1979) and, specifically in educational contexts, Coren (2010). In the next section, the salient features of contemporary short-term therapies and how they are applied in an educational context will be discussed.

Model

Recent years have seen a radical transformation of clinical practice to the extent that short-term therapies are now seen as the treatment of choice for many. Short-term therapy has its own theoretical foundation, clinical application and evidence base. While welcome to many, practitioners and clients alike, it needs to be stressed that this has been due to clinical reasons – both client preference and an increasing evidence base – rather than managerial or financial ones, although clearly in an era of resource scarcity these factors have played a part. Contemporary short-term interventions are designed with their core organising features being both time aware (the therapeutic dyad is constantly alert to time in the process) and time sensitive (where therapist and client note how the possibly limited time might affect the therapeutic dyad). The therapeutic frame needs to incorporate and use time as a central resource. The understanding of the application of such concepts as transference/counter transference, the therapeutic alliance, relationship and process, unconscious communications, developmental theory and the use of self in the "here and now" therapeutic dyad, are central to the work of the short-term therapist. What characterises contemporary short-term therapies are high levels of therapist activity and a central organising framework for the work, frequently termed the therapeutic focus, which links the present problem, the historical past with the "here and now" therapeutic experience. This is the underlying paradigm for dynamic short-term interventions.

Traditionally, short-term approaches have been divided into two therapeutic camps: the conservatives, who believe that short-term work needs to be used judiciously and only in limited situations, and the more radical camp believing that short-term therapy can benefit a wider range of problems and clients (Malan, 1979). This distinction is perhaps no longer valid in that most therapists would hope to achieve something of value for their clients in (very) brief treatments. Selection and assessment of clients has traditionally been the dividing line between clients who may benefit from open-ended therapies and those that would do well in a shorter time. In general, short-term approaches have been advocated for clients presenting with a circumscribed problem, showing motivation and psychological mindedness, a history of being able to establish relationships, the capacity to form a treatment alliance, a capacity to reflect and to recognise that their problems have an emotional or psychological component, whose defences are flexible as opposed to rigid, and who are able to tolerate a level of frustration or anxiety. These have traditionally been viewed as levels of developmental oedipal functioning. Conversely, developmentally pre-oedipal presentations, which would include deficits in the areas of basic trust and emotional regulation, difficulties regarding loss, inability to contain frustration not least in terms of time, exclusive reliance of developmentally early defence mechanisms (projection/splitting etc.) and a tendency to deal with psychological problems by action rather than thought or reflection, were seen to suggest long-term if not open-ended treatment. While this might be a convenient short-hand distinction between different client groups, it is not necessarily helpful in educational settings where counsellors (who have traditionally been drawn to the radical group since most counselling services in educational settings are open access and would hope to offer something of value to all students within the time constraints of education) are mindful that the distinction is not between clients who need longer open-ended therapy and those that don't, but more a recognition that some clients will need longer than others but that all could benefit from a circumscribed number of sessions. I have discussed this at some length elsewhere (Coren, 2010).

Short-term therapy or open-ended therapy (rather than long-term) are not "either or" choices. For oedipal manifestations, separation and dependence are less likely to be issues – making them less sensitive to time-limited work – while pre-oedipal issues of loss, trust and emotional regulation are more likely to require lengthier – or a slightly different model around targeting specific behaviours/traits – but not necessarily open-ended, treatments. The goals of short-term therapy are less characterlogical – one is not aiming to change personality – and more modest. This requires a different clinical paradigm and therapeutic technique and requires the clinician to develop a short-term state of mind.

Technique

There are a considerable number of time-limited therapies, which are developing a sound and rigorous evidence base. These include Intensive Dynamic Psychotherapy (ISTD) (Abbas, 2008; Della Selva, 2004; Malan & Della Selva, 2006),

Accelerated Experiential Dynamic Psychotherapy (AEDP) (Foscha, 2000), Time Limited Dynamic Psychotherapy (Levenson, 1995, 2002, 2012) and Interpersonal Therapy (IPT) (Klerman, 1994). Short-term therapies originating in the UK include Psychodynamic Interpersonal Therapy (PIT) based on the seminal work of Hobson (1982), and Dynamic Interpersonal Therapy (DIT) (Lemma *et al.*, 2011). What all have in common is that they are time-limited, work with an explicit focus, rely on therapist activity and tend to place more importance on the "here and now", including the therapeutic process, as opposed to their historical origin – the "there and then". The question is less "What does this mean?" than "What is going on here?" or "What are we doing to each other?" They share an interpersonal organising therapeutic framework where history is used to shed light on the present rather than the reverse (Coren, 2010). Many are now, to varying extents, integrative, using relational, systemic approaches and more structured approaches, as well as acknowledging more dynamic, symbolic and metaphoric material. They stress the need to challenge attitudes and cognitions in terms of linking and reframing symptoms in relational terms, which lends itself to giving primacy to the therapeutic relationship. To this is added knowledge of narrative (White, 2011) and attachment-based therapies (Wake, 2010), which all cohere on how the therapeutic relationship is used by both therapist and client. Binder (2010) has written with regard to the key therapeutic competencies required for these very brief therapeutic interventions in terms of both the therapeutic process and the skills that the short-term therapist needs to bring to the encounter.

One of the difficulties for counselling in higher education is that most of the therapies alluded to previously are in the region of 12 to 16 sessions although some (ISTD) claim to be considerably shorter but include lengthy individual sessions. Since the average number of counselling sessions in education is between four and eight sessions (not unlike contemporary general practice counselling) a somewhat different model is needed in these contexts.

One of the most popular and helpful models is Malan's Model of the Therapeutic Triangle or the Triangle of Insight (1979). This consists of three variables; the present, including the current unease or symptom, the past or history, and the therapeutic process (the "here and now"), and how these three concepts are actively and affectively manifested in the therapeutic relationship. This core framework has been developed and adapted by several authors and variously named Idiom (Coren, 2010), Interpersonal Affective Focus in Dynamic Interpersonal Therapy (Lemma *et al.*, 2011), Central Maladaptive Pattern (Levenson, 2002), the "Mutual Feeling Language" of the PIT Conversational Model (Guthrie, 1999), and the Central Dynamic Sequence of ISTD (Malan and Della Selva, 2006). This paradigm is also apparent in concepts such as relational templates, core beliefs and cognitive triangles derived from the more cognitive therapies. Attachment (Wake, 2010) and Narrative (White, 2011) approaches as well as concepts such as mentalisation (Fonagy, 2007) and self-reflection all have contributed to the core model of contemporary short-term interventions. A particularly helpful and hopeful therapeutic advance in short-term work is the concept of Epistemic Trust (Fonagy *et al.*, 2013) when allied to mentalisation and attachment, which suggests that it is less the application of a specific therapeutic technique which is mutative in successful therapeutic outcomes, and more the specific qualities of the therapeutic relationship including offering the client hope and an understandable theory that explains the client's distress. These all contribute to the possibility that much of substance can be achieved with students within a short, concentrated and limited time frame.

Working in this way in educational settings has had a major influence on therapeutic technique. Of central importance is the early elucidation of, and mutual agreement on, the therapeutic focus. Since many, if not most, clients present with distress in relationships, either with themselves or others, the focus is frequently a central and generic relational theme with which all material can be linked or associated. Generally the establishment of a therapeutic focus tends to be in the area of the client's core relatedness, in terms of both their current and previous relational history. Allied to this is the need to develop organising therapeutic metaphors and identify the client's affective narratives – the stories, and associated emotional responses, we tell ourselves. These can be seen as internal working models and templates – or internal objects. This has been termed the client's central idiom or way of being in the world. This can span all therapeutic modalities.

The establishment of a therapeutic focus is the central organising feature of short-term work. The focus serves to protect the therapeutic dyad from being overwhelmed by clinical material – it enables "the trees to be seen through the wood" (Coren, 2010). It helps prevent therapeutic drift and links clinical material to the client's central core conflict or anxiety. At best it is alive in the consulting room as well as evident in the client's past history and the presenting problem. In this sense all three paradigms – past, present and "here and now in vivo" – can be addressed at the same time. Ideally the focus is mutually agreed near the beginning of therapy and constantly borne in mind subsequently. The focus is in the area of the client's most predominant frustration or anxiety, is amenable to modification, but framed in relational or emotional terms, and is something that the client frequently has been, at some level, aware of in the past. The mere elucidation of a focus in itself can lead to some relief for the client; for example, a student who consulted her counsellor feeling homesick and was ambivalent about coming for counselling obtained considerable relief when her counsellor suggested they meet for a few sessions to discuss issues around loss (of home and childhood) and attachment (to a new context and a more "adult" life), which were both to become apparent in the counselling relationship.

Foci can be related to content (an issue or difficulty) or process (e.g. affect, self regulation etc.). Occasionally the foci can be related to therapeutic variables: the client's transference to time in relation to therapy (the client may be relieved that they do not have to come for a long time or frustrated that they cannot have as long as they wish) or to their own personal development. The focus is generally in the area of a recurrent interpersonal pattern – based either on a symptomatic concern and presenting problem (e.g. unable to begin academic work) or on a more long-standing or characterological issue (e.g. difficulty entering into or establishing satisfactory relationships). Within this "umbrella" focus there can also be a number of sub foci in relation to the client's life. The focus is a "navigational beacon" (Stadter, 2004), which needs to strike a balance between too rigid an adherence, when the therapy is in danger of becoming formulaic, technical or mechanistic, and the danger of allowing therapy to drift in becoming discursive and meandering, so that little of substance is achieved in the limited time. A useful guide in the timing of the focus is when the therapist has some knowledge of the client's idiom and relational functioning and the client is both aware and concerned about this. In some sense the focus arrives naturally out of the meeting of the client's presenting complaint and narrative, the affective meeting with the therapist and the therapist's philosophy of cure and treatment. The client's "idiom meets that of the therapist" (Coren, 2010). Foci can be distinguished between symptomatic and dynamic (Stadter, 2004), where the former addresses the symptom and how painful and handicapping it is in the client's life, while the latter centers on the underlying intra and inter personal structure of the client's functioning and behaviour and how this affects their relationship with themselves and others. Metaphors and symbols have their part to play in establishing a focus particularly when interacting with personal idioms (e.g. issues of intimacy, control, dependency, separation, trust, anger etc.), which can be divulged in metaphors or narrative stories that may seemingly have little to do with the process of the therapy (e.g. sport, culture, shopping etc.) yet contain themes that are important to decode and work with – often they are illustrative of the therapeutic triangles mentioned earlier and become fruitful metaphors for the treatment. An example here would be "Dorothy" (Coren, 2010, p. 107) and the difficulties she experienced with her supermarket shopping trolley.

While some therapists may be uncomfortable with the need to establish a focus, preferring a more free-flowing, free-associative stance, ideally the focus is the distillation of a client's core relational problem incorporating both symptomatic and dynamic elements. It assists the therapeutic dyad in an overall conceptualisation of the problem, which enables therapeutic drift to be avoided and guides the therapist's interventions.

It is important for the establishment of a focus to be a mutual activity and, in this sense, empowering for the client. This approach also implies that the therapist is more active, more a "real" person rather than a construction of transference (although this in itself may be very helpful in the work in the sense of understanding what – and why – the client has turned the therapist into). The short-term clinician needs to be comfortable in taking up the negative early in therapy – working actively and earlier with resistance and particularly listening for the "cautionary tale" described by Dynamic Interpersonal Therapy (Lemma *et al.*, 2011), which alerts the counsellor to possible therapeutic problems ahead. The adoption of a more "conversational", almost third-party stance, is also helpful in working briefly. In this way a transference neurosis – helpful in longer-term work – can be avoided or kept to a minimum.

The importance of establishing a focus can be both frustrating and problematic for a therapist trained in longer-term work as it involves "selective attention and benign neglect" of therapeutic material. As we have seen, the therapeutic focus needs to incorporate the Triangle of Insight/Therapy (Malan, 1979) – i.e. the current life situation or problem, the client's developmental, relational and social history and the "here and now" therapeutic present – into what is happening in the room. This becomes the organising feature of the work. If a focus cannot be determined, or becomes vague or diffuse, short-term therapy becomes more problematic, although it needs to be mentioned that the lack of a focus might be developmentally appropriate for young students – or adults – and consequently it becomes part of the therapeutic process. While the lack of a therapeutic focus can be a contraindication for brief work it is rare that one cannot be established, although it underlines the importance of regular and high quality supervision for the short-term counsellor who may need regular support in continuing to be actively mindful of the therapeutic focus when distractions are enticing.

Therapeutic activity helps maintain the focus, prevents regression and keeps the emotional tension high in the "here and now". Additionally, significant regression and dependence, which are not helpful in brief work, are minimised by the spacing of appointments (it is not always necessary to meet weekly), with the client frequently choosing how regularly to meet (and the symbolic significance of that decision discussed). Knowledge that the treatment is finite deals with any anxiety regarding any ambiguity in relation to time and its management. The counsellor needs to be active, without impingement, and mindful of empowering the client to be active in taking co-ownership of the sessions. A therapist who is insufficiently active carries with them the danger that the focus will be lost.

A further feature of short-term therapy is that the counsellor models therapeutic optimism that much of worth can be achieved in such a short space of time. In this sense it is important that the clinician actively addresses any ambivalence they may harbour about the value of brief therapy. The short-term counsellor in education needs to believe that it is the treatment of choice for their client rather than a pragmatic, and possibly second choice, option consequent on the high demand and limited resources available.

Particularly in educational settings, the counsellor should guard against counselling becoming a merely cerebral activity – the process must make substantial emotional contact with the client otherwise it becomes yet another intellectual exercise or demand and is dealt with in the same way. The feelings (i.e. the contextual transference) have to be central to the process of counselling as they may be ways characteristic of relational patterns in the client's current life, how they have related to other people in the past and how dysfunctional and unhelpful these ways of relating may be. A premium is placed on early manifestations of transference – to process and setting – and any negative anticipatory material needs to be promptly addressed (e.g. a student who reveals a history of unsatisfactory/untrustworthy relationships in the past or has had poor previous experiences of being helped is likely to find counselling less straightforward).

The issue of transference has specific and discrete meanings and uses in short-term therapies. Here the educational context is of significant importance.

As well as seizing on the individual's developmental drive, students cannot, psychologically or emotionally, stand still. An attempt to do so may well lead them into both psychological and educational difficulties. This brings up the issue, in transferential terms, of whom – or what – the counsellor in educational settings is invited to become. For psychodynamic clinicians in educational settings who are practicing brief therapy, it is helpful to clinically distinguish between the concept of transference as ubiquitous – i.e. it's everywhere – and what has been termed the transference neurosis. The latter has been central to increasing the length of therapies, and is a specific illusion of the therapeutic setting. Counsellors, despite the possibility that students will at times attempt to turn their counsellors into whoever they need them to become, can be quite active in either encouraging or discouraging certain forms of transference manifestations (e.g. commenting on the therapeutic process as it unfolds and alerting the therapeutic dyad to the dangers of dependence are ways in which a transference neurosis maybe minimised).

Short-term therapists do not encourage a transference neurosis to develop and, as we have seen, this is assisted by the therapist being active and focused. Of central importance, however, for a student counsellor is the student's transference to education and their own personal progression. This includes a specific, and perhaps ambivalent, attitude to one's own development, to joining, performing and leaving an institution, to the institution itself and what the counsellor in an educational setting represents to the student. This becomes the cornerstone of therapeutic encounters in education: not who the counsellor is, what the student neurotically invests in or turns the counsellor into, but what the setting, or the counsellor in that setting, may represent or stand for. Transference to the setting becomes a central therapeutic tool. This includes the student's feelings about receiving limited help and being vulnerable in an educational context where self sufficiency and successful performance are privileged, not being encouraged to regress including the development of a sick or pathological role, issues about loss and endings that are in evidence from the beginning, and how congruent a therapeutic experience is with the need to learn and perform in the wider institution. These are the most frequent themes of short-term therapy in education. The therapist consequently assumes an oblique, more third-party role (e.g. by commenting on how the student may be using the counselling in similar ways to how they relate to friends/tutors/family and how they may be uncomfortable with the feelings that this evokes).

One of the aims of short-term therapy is to enable the client to internalise the experience with the counsellor and for a different version, or narrative, of themselves to emerge. Clients are frequently surprised at the emergence of an alternative, and unexpected, narrative of their lives. Short-term therapy in educational settings involves the discovery of alternative scripts (as well as the normalisation of emotional experience, which the student feels only they, and they alone, are struggling with), which provide the student with a different way of viewing and experiencing themselves and their difficulties.

Central to the success of short-term therapy is the ability to establish, maintain and repair any ruptures to the therapeutic alliance. The therapeutic relationship in brief approaches is conversational, active, cooperative and engaging. Safety and trust in a therapeutic relationship can expedite its progress. To the generic therapeutic competencies in establishing a therapeutic relationship needs to be added the short-term therapist's need to establish a therapeutic focus where the relationship becomes the microcosm of the client's relational idiom or template – and a central agent of mutative change – and the therapeutic relationship becomes a form of psycho-education, where the dyad models the nature of the contact that will be established and gives a glimpse of how change can be achieved. The aim of the therapeutic alliance is to lead to the mutual discovery of a therapeutic focus, an agreement in terms of its relevance, and to work together towards addressing it. The aim, in some senses, through the development of a capacity for self-reflection, is for the client to develop the capacity to become their own therapist so to assist in a mode of self-awareness that can persist beyond the end of the limited number of sessions.

Brief consultations are not about "depth" – although the ripples that can be prompted by, among other things, "therapeutic surprise", not least in the creation of alternative narratives – should not be underestimated. Given the partial and circumscribed focus, short-term therapy can be helpful for more disturbed or troubled students who may find a longer-term commitment frightening or inappropriate. It also speaks to those students who are suspicious of open-ended therapies or are not versed in, or comfortable with, western therapeutic traditions of individualised self-reflection. Short-term therapy conveys therapeutic hope; it does not pathologise – the bottle is half full rather than half empty – and it does not procrastinate in the sense that it recognises that life – particularly for a young student – needs to be experienced rather than lived in the consulting room.

Time is clearly central in these consultations. There is not much of it and the restriction needs to be used constructively. Rather than feeling – and conveying this to the client perhaps non-verbally – that limited time is a problem, the short-term therapist utilises the time frame in the service of the focus and the client's core concern. In education, the concept of "topping up" – also termed life-span intermittent therapy – is also particularly useful. Rather than viewing this as a denial of the ending of therapy this can act, particularly in education where the student is a member of the institution for some years during which time they may face a number of developmental obstacles or hurdles, as a cumulative resource where one course of therapy builds on another and the "the whole becomes greater than the sum of its parts" (Stadter, 2004). Students may consult a counsellor in their first year with issues of separation and loss and return in their third year with issues around transitions, leaving and developmental anxieties. In this sense their therapeutic consultations can be linked to developmental life stages, and intermittent therapy can address a focus, perhaps modified and developed over the course of their student careers, which forms a historical narrative throughout their education.

In summary: therapy is brief but not inconsequential. The establishment and maintenance of a therapeutic focus is central as is the transference to time and what it may represent. The therapist needs to be proactive in relation to therapeutic frame, content and process. The therapeutic stance is companionable where the therapist – and client – offers tentative hypotheses and material is linked to the focus and therapeutic triangle. Transference is generally to the therapeutic process rather than the person of the therapist. The goal is to facilitate a "ripple effect" where the client can continue the process of therapeutic reflections without the presence of the therapist.

The need to see so many clients in such a short space of time – putting a premium on beginnings and endings – is a considerable demand on the counsellor and requires its own discipline and supportive supervisory framework. Training, support and supervision are central to enable the clinician to work under what amounts to considerable pressure. Short-term therapy makes great demands on its practitioners since, centring as it does exclusively on beginnings and endings, it involves the regular making and breaking of therapeutic relationships and affective bonds. As we have seen, the need to maintain the therapeutic focus and the high level of activity adds to the pressure on the therapist.

Additionally, evidence suggests that the majority of students (as opposed to what their therapists may think they need) only want brief interventions. Short-term therapies have been applied to educational settings and have successfully led to a specific, and discrete, way of working therapeutically with students (see Cowley and Groves, Chapter 6).

Short-term counselling in educational settings

With the growth of student populations in recent years, there has been increasing demand on student counselling services (see Mair, Chapter 1). Serious consideration needs to be given as to how to respond to this demand, particularly without a corresponding increase in available resources. While the high level of demand for counselling in educational settings, as well as the fact that counselling in these settings is generally open access and needs to take into account the vagaries of the academic year (which can facilitate certain brief interventions), has made short-term interventions the treatment of choice in these settings, care needs to be applied when considering very brief interventions for all clients.

Traditionally the average number of counselling sessions in student counselling has been between four and six. Short-term therapy in other settings, and the evidence base for it, favours between 12 and 16 sessions. This implies that counselling in educational settings is qualitatively (and quantitatively) different from other settings. It may well be that counselling in educational settings is more in the nature of a therapeutic consultation, or conversation. This makes counselling in education a discrete activity necessitating specific skills and expertise. However, what is specific to all short-term approaches is the centrality of time and specifically the need to work within a discrete time frame. Short-term therapy in this sense involves a state of mind rather than adherence to a specific number of sessions.

Being open access, student counselling services have no "filter" and this functions to ensure that all students, and frequently staff, can consult services and expect some form of helpful consultation. Selection on the basis of a psychological assessment is limited but this may actually be helpful since rigorous selection may well function to exclude those students who could be helped by a short-term approach. Originally short term therapists suggested that twenty sessions for mild to moderate presenting problems may suffice while thirty sessions were advocated for more complete presentations. We have come a long way since that. In education a little may lead to, and mean, a lot.

Studying is never only an academic or pedagogic task. When studying we always have a "subjective curriculum" (Jones, 1968), which needs to be attended to, and contemporary short-term practitioners will always be mindful of what this might signify for their student clients. Students are never just studying – they are engaged in personal transformative experiences involving identity formation and individuation for which higher education offers a conduit, or safe structure and framework, for these psychologically important processes to be facilitated rather than stultified. Brief counselling can aid this process. Subjective personal scripts or narratives need to be seen in relation to the student's need to successfully perform in an educational setting. It is these, particularly their symbolic and metaphoric meaning, which the short-term counsellor in education attempts to elucidate and address since they commonly underlie much student distress.

It is perhaps not surprising that short-term counselling has become the treatment of choice in educational settings. Not only does it capture the developmental fluidity of students, be they young adults or more mature entrants into higher education, but it also runs parallel with the student's experience of "being a student" in having a beginning, middle and end. As in education, in short-term therapy this is quite structured, with all three phases needing to be borne in mind concurrently.

Short-term therapy is appropriate for the context in which it occurs. There is a developmental drive in education, not only structurally in that students need to progress through their educational careers, but also in terms of the students psychological development. This mirrors short-term therapy since consultations in education seek to speak to the student's developmental drive, particularly of late adolescence and young adulthood, many of whom, having just left home and their families, do not necessarily wish, or need, to enter into what can be experienced as a regressively frightening (or comforting, which can be equally uncomfortable) therapeutic relationship. At a time in their lives when they need to face and master the world proactively, including the mastery of their studies, offering them the possibility of entering into a regressive therapeutic relationship may well be experienced by the student as a demand that can only be met by either rejection (and many students when offered longer term work will drop out) or a defeated or hostile compliance.

Developmental imperatives such as identity formation, sexuality, competition and separation are among those issues that can be addressed while studying, and arguably intervention at this stage of life may have a more profound impact than the mere number of therapeutic sessions offered. They can facilitate a process of self-reflection and awareness (what we have termed the "ripple effect"), which can enrich and have a transformative effect on the student's experience in education.

Education is about progression and developmental fluidity so the setting and context actually facilitate brief interventions. Young students/adults, having recently left their families – and we must not forget that going to college is one of the most acceptable reasons for leaving home – may not wish to make too great a commitment in any therapeutic relationship. Rather than being seen as a therapeutic problem, which is how it has traditionally been viewed, this becomes, not merely much more understandable in developmental terms, but a therapeutic advantage in short-term counselling in educational settings.

Evidence base

There has been vociferous debate as to what encompasses a successful outcome in student counselling. This hinges on whether student counselling aims at symptom relief – the ability to get students back to academic work and working effectively as soon as possible – or on the student's personal development and wellbeing more generally. The latter is a feature of higher education that is frequently in danger of being lost and is linked to the quality of life rather than objectifiable, quantitative, achievements. This debate is mirrored by the debate between therapeutic effectiveness and efficacy and whether the increasingly quantitative research methodology, privileged in both research and educational settings, is fit for purpose with young students for whom education may come to represent developmental rites of passage, and where more "soft" educational outcomes may be of equal, if not more, importance.

While previous attempts to establish an evidence base for short-term therapies have been deeply flawed (Coren, 2010, p. 206), short-term therapies in higher education are increasingly developing an impressive evidence base not least in the ubiquity with which objective pre- and post-treatment measures are being used (e.g. CORE) in student counselling and wellbeing settings. The increasing use of manualised therapies is also contributing to this and there is growing evidence that many clients who have received short-term counselling have received considerable benefit from it (Clarke, 2008; Ross & Fonagy, 2005; Stadter, 2004). Improving Access to Psychological Therapies (IAPT) is also producing valuable data on the efficacy of short-term treatments (Turpin & Fonagy, 2010). There is growing evidence that short-term student counselling works, not least in the recognition that most therapeutic effect is achieved early in therapy, which argues that therapies are most effective when they are short. The debate is increasingly focusing less on whether clients need long- or short-term therapy, and more on the issue that some clients may need longer than others, often associated with the nature of the clients presenting problem and personality characteristics. While previous research has focused on the difference between process and outcome, we are increasingly seeing the therapeutic alliance – or relationship – as the single most important predictive factor, independent of therapeutic modality, for a successful outcome. This applies to both the more and less structured treatments (e.g. CBT and Psychodynamic modalities). While much current research features treatments in the 12–16 session framework, as we have seen student counselling is far briefer than that, often consisting of four to six sessions. The important facet to bear in mind is that length and duration of treatment needs to be a clinically-based decision rather than, as increasingly occurs, either a "one size fits all" managerial dictat, or where the purchasers of counselling services decide on length of treatments. The latter are unfortunate precedents and are concerning challenges for counselling services.

In the current climate, counselling in general, but also in educational institutions, is in danger of becoming a commodity like any other in society governed by an economic paradigm rather than a discrete form of relationship that does not lend itself easily to market forces. We are all becoming consumers, including the fee-paying student, rather than citizens, which affects both expectations of the "consumer" and that of the "provider" of counselling. In an age where fiscal pressures push and demand ever shorter therapeutic treatments, clinicians, and their managers, should be mindful that clinical decisions are to be made on the basis of clinical need rather than financial audit and the discipline of the market.

This is arguably a current danger in the world of "managed care", where therapeutic modalities are competing with each other for scarce resources and promising more successful outcomes with ever decreasing lengths of treatments. This is where it becomes increasingly important for clinicians in educational settings to be able to present their managers with evidence, not just of the efficacy of their work, but also the subtle distinctions between students who may benefit from differential lengths, and forms, of treatments.

Counselling in educational settings gives people a taste of seeing, thinking, feeling and experiencing themselves in different ways. Attending to the student's personal development is as much a "learning aim or outcome" as their academic progression. Much can be achieved in these short-term interventions but the short-term counsellor must avoid the hubris of assuming it is a panacea for all. Short-term therapy can help the vast majority of students who come for a therapeutic conversation but some students might need longer than others – based on clinical rather than managerial assessment – or something different. There is an inherent danger of assuming that one size fits all and that short-term therapy becomes a convenient way for managing scarce resources and demand. There is also the danger of therapies becoming overtly protocol driven and technical with an emphasis more on standardisation rather than exploration and reflection.

Ending

For students, particularly young adults in education, short-term therapy allows them to proceed with age-appropriate developmental tasks that provide a solid foundation for future development. Counselling in educational settings allows for the student's educational, academic, vocational and psychological developmental needs to be concurrently addressed. Perhaps Freud's definition of mental health, "to love and to work", needs to be reframed for the educational context in terms of "to work and to love". The importance for the student in being able to function and succeed academically needs to be recognised, not merely from the institution's point of view, but also from the student's, for whom academic success may be a major source of self-esteem and pleasure. However, short-term therapy can also ensure that student's psychological health and wellbeing, often at nodal points in their lives, can be facilitated.

References

Abbas, A. (2008) Intensive short term dynamic psychotherapy for personality disorders. *Journal of Nervous and Mental Disease*, 196 (3), 211–216.

Adler, A. (1958) *What a Life Should Mean to You*, New York, Capricorn.

Alexander, F. & French, T. M. (1946) *Psychodynamic Therapy*, New York, Ronald Press.

Balint, M. (1972) *Focal Psychotherapy: An Example of Applied Psychoanalysis*, London, Tavistock.

Binder, J. (2010) *Key Competencies in Brief Dynamic Psychotherapy*, New York, Guilford Press.

Cooper, M. (2008) *Essential Research Findings in Counselling and Psychotherapy: The Facts are Friendly*, London, Sage.

Coren, A. (1997) *A Psychodynamic Approach to Education*, London, Sheldon Press.

Coren, A. (2010) *Short Term Psychotherapy: A Psychodynamic Approach*, London, Palgrave Macmillan.

Coren, A. (2014) Learning and teaching briefly. *Psychodynamic Practice*, 20 (1), 40–53.

Davanloo, H. (1990) *Selected Papers*, Wiley, New York.

Della Selva, P. (2004) *Intensive Short Term Dynamic Psychotherapy*, London, Karnac.

Ferenczi, S. (1925) *The Development of Psychoanalysis*, Madison, IUP

Fonagy, P. (2007) *Affect Regulation, Mentalisation and the Development of the Self*, London, Karnac.

Fonagy, P., Luyten, P., Campbell, C. & Allison, L. (2013) *Epistemic trust, psychopathology and the great psychotherapy debate*. Available from: http://societyforpsychotherapy. org/epistemic-trust-psychopathology-and-the-great-psychotherapy-debate/ (accessed 7th January 2015).

Foscha, D. (2000) *The Transforming Power of Affect: A Model for Accelerated Change*, New York, Basic Books.

Freud, A. (1955) *Psychoanalysis for Teachers and Parents*, London, Norton.

Freud, S. (1900) *The Interpretation of Dreams, Standard Edition. Vol 1V/V*, London, Hogarth Press.

Freud, S. (1905) *Three Essays on the Theory of Sexuality SE Vol X1*, London, Hogarth Press.

Freud, S. (1909) *Analysis of a Phobia in a five year old boy. SE Vol X1*, London, Hogarth Press.

Freud, S. (1914) *Some Reflections on Schoolboy Psychology. SE Vol X111*, London, Hogarth Press.

Freud, S. (1955) *Studies in Hysteria. SE Vol. 11*, London, Hogarth Press.

Guthrie, E. (1999) Psychodynamic interpersonal therapy. *Advances in Psychiatric Treatment*, 5, 135–245.

Hobson, R. F. (1982) *A Conversational Method of Psychotherapy: A Training Method*, London, Tavistock.

Jones, R. (1968) *Fantasy and Feeling in Education*, New York, NYU Press.

Klerman, G. (1994) *Interpersonal Therapy of Depression*, New York, Aronson.

Lees, J. & Vaspe, A. (1999) *Clinical Counselling in Further and Higher Education*, London, Routledge.

Lemma, A., Target, M. & Fonagy, P. (2011) *Brief Dynamic Interpersonal Therapy: A Clinicians Guide*, Oxford, Oxford University Press.

Levenson, H. (1995) *Time Limited Dynamic Psychotherapy*, New York, Basic Books.

Levenson, H. (2002) *Brief Dynamic Therapy*. New York, APA.

Levenson, H. (2012) Time-Limited Dynamic Psychotherapy: An Integrative Perspective, in Dewin, M. J., Steenbarger, B. N. and Greenberg, R. P. *The Art and Science of Brief Psychotherapy*, New York, APA.

Malan, D. (1976) *The Frontier of Brief Psychotherapy: An Example of the Convergence of Research and Clinical Practice*. Oxford, Plenum Medical Books Co.

Malan, D. (1979) *Individual Psychotherapy and the Science of Psychodynamics*, London, Butterworth.

Malan, D. & Della Selva, P. (2006) *Lives Transformed: A Revolutionary Method of Dynamic Psychotherapy*, Karnac, New York.

Mander, G. (2000) *A Psychodynamic Approach to Brief Therapy*, London, Sage.

Messer, S. & Warren, C. (1998) *Models of Brief Psychodynamic Therapy: A Comparative Approach*, London, Guilford Press.

Rank, O. (1973) *The Trauma of Birth*, New York, Harper.

Reich, O. (1952) *The Secret Self*, New York, Farrar, Straus and Young.

Sifneous, P. (1979) *Short Term Dynamic Psychotherapy*, New York, Plenum Press.

Smith, J. (2008) A leap across a basic fault. *Psychodynamic Practice*, 14 (4), 421–439.

Stadter, M. (2004) *Object Relations Brief Therapy: The Therapeutic Relationship in Short Term Work*. New York, Jason Aronson.

Stekel, W. (1910) Paper delivered to the Vienna Psychoanalytic Society. "On suicide with particular reference to suicide amongst young students." IUP 1967.

Turpin, G. & Fonagy, P. (2010) *The evidence base for psychological therapies: Implications for policy and practice. New ways of working for psychological therapies.* Available from: www.iapt.nhs.uk/silo/files/new-ways-of-working-for-psychological-therapists-workstream-one.pdf (accessed 12th January 2015).

Wake, L. (2010) *The Role of Brief Therapy in Attachment Disorders*, London, Karnac.

Walter, B. (1947) *Theme and Variations*, London, Hamish Hamilton.

White, M. (2011) *Narrative Practice: Continuing the Conversation*, London, Norton.

Chapter 3

Counselling in higher education settings

Working with risk, confidentiality and "duty of care" issues

Peter Jenkins

Counselling in higher education (HE) settings seems to be increasingly informed and even framed by concerns about "duty of care". This quasi-legal phrase carries a powerful emotional and policy charge, which can be compared to the influential concept of "workplace stress" in previous decades. Counsellors in HE are encouraged to be mindful of their duty of care to report *all* child abuse (Sher, 2003, p. 140), to work safely with suicidal students (Reeves, 2005, p. 8) and to work to discharge an *enhanced* duty of care to more vulnerable groups, such as students under 18 years, international students and students and staff with a disability or special needs (AUCC, 2010, p. 14). "Duty of care" has, therefore, emerged as a key trope within the wider narrative of counselling within HE, in the sense of it having multiple potential meanings. There are a number of possible reasons for this development having occurred. The recent increase in fees has markedly changed the relationship of student to the university, to one of consumer and potential *complainant*. The scope of counselling has shifted to some extent to include more mental health and preventive work, reflecting a wider intake of students with mental health vulnerabilities, perhaps adopting NHS concerns about the risk of litigation in the process. Finally, a focus on duty of care issues and the key role of counselling in responding to these issues may serve to buttress the role of counselling services during a period of rapid organisational change.

Given that student counselling in universities is part of a rapidly-changing environment, it would not be surprising if counsellors assumed that this shift in language to embrace the theme of duty of care reflected a real change in the legal context in which they operate. Student counsellors work primarily, but not exclusively, with a relatively high-risk client group. This client group is engaged in making a major life transition, from adolescence to young adulthood, and is expected to achieve their desired life goals, while facing major financial (and sometimes relationship) pressures from their peers and family of origin. This chapter will therefore explore the context and relevance of the concept of duty of care to counselling in higher education, with specific reference to high risk situations, such as suicide and safeguarding. The legal context will be assumed to be England and Wales, with similar broad legal principles applying to other parts of the UK, such as Scotland and Northern Ireland.

Organisational context of HE counselling

The specific context of university also brings its own special challenges for counsellors. One author suggests that "Student counsellors must have a relationship with the broader institution and its structures" (Bell, 1996, p. 110). Moore also points to "this sense of dual responsibility", i.e. towards *both* the client *and* the employing organisation. This dual obligation perhaps gives the concept of "duty of care" some added force, as the consequences of decisions by individual counsellors will affect their employing institution, as well as themselves. Counsellors in HE work within a complex organisational setting, with a periodicity of peaks and troughs of client demand, determined by the academic calendar. Within this setting, educational and managerial values may compete for primacy. In the past, counselling work may well have focused on the therapeutic relationship, rather than on organisational imperatives, by seeking to clarify and define key *ethical* boundaries (Davies, 2000; Warburton, 1995). It seems much more likely that current HE counselling services now present themselves as being an integral and, indeed, *essential*, part of the wider organisation, rather than emphasising their role as being separate, discrete and wholly distinct from the parent institution. Or, to quote Bell again, "the context *is* the meaning" (1999, p. 1, emphasis added).

Higher education in the UK is currently going through a rapid period of market-driven change. Government funding has been shifted from block grants, via the Higher Education Funding Council, to student loans and students have been redefined as consumers of education. There has been a fundamental change in the relationship between the student, as an informed customer, and university staff, as service providers. The novelist, Howard Jacobson, accurately captures this shift in stance, with his acerbic comment that contemporary students are no longer "drinking at the fount of knowledge but haggling at the marketplace of entitlement" (Independent, 2006). The sharp rise in tuition fees for undergraduate and postgraduate courses, leading to increasingly high levels of student debt, has encouraged a more assertive and searching attitude by students towards their expectations of university provision overall.

> these are paying for their education – they're customers or consumers, in a way that students weren't in the past. So like all customers and consumers, they want value for money. They're paying for an education that they want to get them somewhere, so they're quite pushy about getting to where they're going – and if things aren't going the right way, they want to know why. If you give them 65% for an essay, some will want to know why it's not in the 70s.
>
> (Adrian Leftwich, quoted in Moorhead, 2010)

University–student contract

This fundamental recasting of the student–university connection into a primarily customer-service provider mould, in turn, has profound implications for the quality of interpersonal relationships between staff and students in the university.

In addition, there are some significant legal implications. If the primary relationship between student and university is one of *contract*, then the potential arises for legal action, on either side, for *breach* of that same contract. Thus, Oxford University was reportedly the first to introduce obligatory "I'll try hard contracts" for students and applicants in 2006, and it was quickly followed suit by others (Farrington & Palfreyman, 2006, p. 292).

This emphasis on the contractual quality of university education has been paralleled by other similar developments that hold a legal dimension, such as the issue of "workplace stress", which is discussed in more detail later in this chapter. Government policy to widen access to university education has led to a conscious effort to make higher education institutions (HEI) more accessible to those students who may previously have been inadvertently excluded, on the grounds of physical disability or mental health condition. In part, this has been driven by legislation, such as the Special Educational Needs and Disability Act 1995, requiring educational institutions to carry out "reasonable adjustments" to meet assessed student needs. This widening of access has, in turn, required closer university collaboration with mental health services, and the appointment of disability service officers and mental health workers.

While this infusion of expertise has been welcomed, it may also have imported very different attitudes by professionals towards the risk of litigation. Smith refers to NHS staff working in HE in a parallel, but slightly different, context, "holding onto important values they brought from their previous professional experience" (1999, p. 134). This factor might partly explain the growing use of the "duty of care" argument within HE counselling circles. Legal action for alleged medical negligence has been a realistic and extremely powerful driver of change within the NHS, with claims running at £1.3 billion for the period 2012–13 (Dyer, 2013, p. 13). Fear of litigation is thus an aspect of professional work in the NHS, which is well-grounded in reality. What is much less clear, however, is whether this fear is applicable to the very different legal context of higher education. Despite this, the related concept of 'duty of care' seems to have taken firm root within HE. It seemed to frame discussion by a student counsellor with a representative of Universities UK, the key HE employer association, expressing concerns about student suicide within HE (BBC, 2010). It was also specifically cited by academics in one recent protest, which challenged their growing role in policing the immigration and visa requirements for international students (Topping, 2014). The concept of duty of care also appears as a key influential motif within professional guidelines for counselling in HE (AUCC, 2010).

Context and background: contract law

The "duty of care" argument is driven by a sensitivity to the perceived risk of being sued for negligence. This is clearly a somewhat realistic fear and policy driver within the contemporary NHS. However, the legal context in higher education is framed primarily by the law of *contract*, rather than that of negligence. Hence "the relationship between the HEI (Higher Education Institute: PJ) and the student is based on a contract" (Palfreyman & Warner, 2002, p. 113). This, in turn, can be divided into first the contract for admission, and second the contract for matriculation, or the teaching and learning process. The shift towards students becoming defined as consumers of education is completely consistent with this legal frame, given that "the university-student relationship is essentially contractual" (Farrington & Palfreyman, 2012, p. 333).

The focus on contract might suggest that students are, even so, increasingly likely to sue for breach of contract, on the grounds of alleged failure by a university to provide adequate academic or related services. There is, however, relatively limited case law confirming that students can win these kinds of cases. One disappointed student sued the University of Wolverhampton, on the grounds of advertised modules being unavailable, seminars and lectures being overcrowded and for the library being understocked (*Austen v. University of Wolverhampton* [2005]). The student received £30,000, but, crucially, this was an out-of-court settlement with no admission of liability, rather than a successful court case. Another widely publicised case, brought by an American law student (*Abramova v. Oxford Institute* [2011]), was dismissed by the judge on the grounds that the claimant "was ready to blame anyone but herself for her misfortunes" (Farrington & Palfreyman, 2012, p. 356).

Beyond the narrow focus on teaching and assessment, as part of the contract between student and HEI, it could be argued that ancillary or support services such as counselling might be considered as part of the implied, rather than expressed, terms of such a learning contract. According to Palfreyman and Warner, "Counselling and pastoral care, as well as academic feedback, could become part of the overall teaching obligations" (2002, p. 118), although this has yet to figure to any significant degree in the emerging case law. Given that student counselling in HE is a completely non-statutory service, it remains a comparatively vulnerable aspect of university non-academic service provision, leading Bell to question "whether an institution should have a counselling service at all" (1996, p. 139). While HE counselling may have a strong record in terms of its outcomes and effectiveness, it constitutes a prime candidate for outsourcing, in the context of the market-driven reforms forcing universities to operate much more as commercial bodies than as publicly-funded agencies (McGettigan, 2013, p. 134). In fact, this has already occurred in Northern Ireland, with regard to student counselling services in both further and higher education (Pointon, 2014, p. 16). Therefore, returning to the issue of duty of care, it may be that HE counselling services are keen to reinforce their protective value to the wider university in this respect, as one element of a strategy for their own continued growth and survival.

Negligence law

If legal action by students for alleged breach of contract is fairly sparse, then this is even more so for successful action for negligence. Bringing a case for negligence requires three conditions, i.e. the existence of a duty of care, between the institution, or lecturer, and the student; breach of that duty; and resultant, foreseeable harm. Again, the UK case law tends to suggest that the courts see this duty of care in narrowly-defined terms, i.e. "to keep the student reasonably safe on HEI premises and when sent on field trips" (Farrington & Palfreyman, 2012, p. 378). Even here, it has proved to be difficult to establish breach of HEI duty of care. One case was brought by a student who was raped while on a study trip in Odessa, but the court found that the university was not negligent, in that it had warned her of the high crime rate in that area (*McLean v. University of St Andrews* [2004]). While it is clear that the HEI owes students a duty of care, in reality, the actual contours of this duty are fairly sharply circumscribed, rather than being open-ended and open to ever-widening expansion. However, an alternative option on this issue of sexual assault, would be via legal action against universities, for breach of their *statutory* duty to end discrimination and harassment against women, under s. 149 of the Equality Act 2010 (Whitfield and Dustin, 2015).

Negligence action by staff

If negligence law has limited application to students as learners, how does this apply to them as *clients within counselling*? Here, the law provides some fairly useful pointers, but only if a clear distinction is drawn between potential client groups. There is a wealth of case law that demonstrates that the university, as an employer, owes a definite duty of care to *staff*. Emerging case law shows that employers who provide staff access to a confidential counselling service will generally enjoy substantial protection against claims for workplace stress (Jenkins, 2008). The key case here is *Hatton* [2002], which set out the legal criteria for evaluating claims for "workplace stress" (see Box for summary). This case, more than any other, effectively signaled the demise of the burgeoning "compensation culture" for alleged workplace stress. It carefully set out the criteria for establishing employer liability, in the case of staff bringing claims for negligence, for failure to prevent "workplace stress". Again, here it may be helpful to look at the way in which the law frames everyday concepts, such as "workplace stress" and the particular role played by workplace counselling in responding to it. A simple "cause and effect" model might assume that an employee can be damaged by excessive, or stressful, working conditions, and that this would then give rise to them bringing a claim for negligence against their employer. However, from a legal perspective, "workplace stress" needs to be more accurately translated into the concept of a "psychiatric injury", such as clinical depression, or post-traumatic stress disorder. This immediately sets a much higher threshold for winning a successful claim for negligence, well beyond that of common anxiety or sleeplessness caused by worries about pressure of work.

Duty of care to staff regarding "workplace stress"

The legal argument for establishing employer negligence needs to prove that the employer was not only made aware of the stressful nature of the work by the employee, but that the employer then failed to redress this, by responding with appropriate support, training and counselling (see diagram below). Experiencing

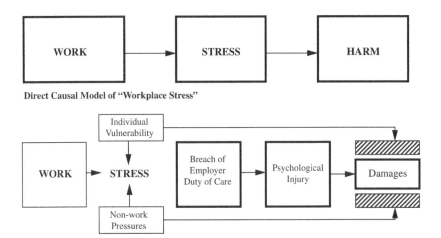

Direct Causal Model of "Workplace Stress"

Duty of Care Model of "Workplace Stress"

Key: ▨▨▨▨   Factors leading to potential reduction in damages

Figure 3.1 Comparison of direct causal model and duty of care model of "workplace stress"

Source: Jenkins, 2008, p. 102. Copyright: Wiley, 2008. Reprinted with permission.

stress at work, on its own, is not sufficient grounds for member of university staff to win a successful legal case for "workplace stress" (see case history).

Furthermore, the *Hatton* case established very clearly that employers who provided access to a confidential counselling service would enjoy substantial protection against future claims for negligence. A university providing a confidential counselling service is, therefore, going a long way towards demonstrating fulfillment of its duty of care to staff. The conclusions of the key *Hatton* case are summarised for reference in the following Box. Having said this, there are other potential avenues for staff to take action over stressful working conditions. In 2004, for example, the Health and Safety Executive served notice that De Montfort University was in breach of its responsibilities over high levels of stress among staff.

Checklist for employer liability for workplace stress

- Is the individual subject to undue pressure of work that is
  - unreasonable by any standard
  - unreasonable judged in comparison with the workload of others in a similar job
  - due to individual vulnerability, which is known to the employer?
- Has the individual received an injury to health, either physical or psychological, that is directly attributable to stress at work?

- Was this injury reasonably foreseeable by the employer?
- Is this injury directly and mainly attributable to the employer's breach of duty of care, in failing to reduce workplace stress (by providing confidential counselling, redistribution of duties, training and so on)?

Source: Adapted from *Hatton v. Sutherland* [2002]

Case history: HE duty of care to staff for "workplace stress" and access to counselling

Mr. Best, appointed as a senior lecturer in 1986, sued the University of Staffordshire in 2003 for alleged workplace stress. He claimed that his health had been damaged by the excessive workload, required in completing his timetabling duties. He broke down in February 1998 with symptoms of anxiety, for which his GP prescribed anti-depressants. He worked only a few days after returning to work later that year and was retired from work, on the grounds of ill-health, in 2000.

His case, alleging breach of employer duty of care, was based on the period prior to his health breakdown in 1998, and was based on the evidence that he had raised his concerns about overwork with the relevant senior staff. The latter had responded by providing him with a computer for use at home and by appointing an administrative assistant, who was then diverted to other tasks. However, he did not raise his health concerns at annual appraisals, on the medical form when applying for promotion in 1998 or with his GP *prior* to his health breakdown.

Mr. Best was aware of the university counselling service, and had, in fact, been on counselling courses, but said, under cross-examination, that he might have been "naive enough" to think that he did not need it. It was pointed out by the judge at appeal, in dismissing his case, that if Mr. Best did not see a need for counselling, then how could his employers be expected to have seen such a need?

Hartman v. South Essex Mental Health Care and Community Care Trust [2005]

Mr. Best's case was heard with a number of other cases at the Court of Appeal in 2005. Applying the *Hatton* criteria, his case failed because he did not raise his health concerns at his annual appraisals, or with his GP prior to February 1998, nor did he make use of the counselling service that was available. His health breakdown could not, therefore, have been reasonably foreseeable to his employer.

His unsuccessful case illustrates very clearly that universities owe a duty of care to staff to avoid causing psychiatric injury, for example, by imposing unreasonable levels of work. However, universities can easily mitigate the risk of successful staff action for negligence, by providing access to a confidential counselling service. This may not completely eliminate the risk of staff litigation, but it can substantially reduce it. Even simply providing a workplace stress helpline for staff, rather than a counselling service as such, "would in fact help to protect the employer against any accusation of not taking reasonable steps to discharge the duty of care" (Farrington & Palfreyman, 2006, 526).

Duty of care to students

If the HEI's duty of care to staff is limited in this way, how does the university's duty of care apply to *students*? The guidance by Joint Information Systems Committee on the duty of care to students in HE is noticeably cautious in setting this out (JISC, 2003, p. 3). It suggests that the HEI duty of care to students includes the following elements:

- duty to provide safe, adequate and properly maintained equipment
- obligations under occupier's liability legislation and health and safety law in relation to halls of residence etc.
- duty to take reasonable care for the health and safety of students engaged in practical study and research, including work placements abroad
- duty to refuse students the opportunity to proceed with studies, or to graduate, or qualify, if they have not proved their competence
- duty to provide accurate references and assessments.

This is a very narrowly-drawn list, but one consistent with the views of established authors writing on the law applying to HE, as previously discussed.

How does the HEI's duty of care relate to counselling students? Here, there is very limited case law to flesh out an answer. This relative absence of reported case law suggests that legal action by students, as dissatisfied clients, brought against university counselling services, or individual counsellors, is still fairly rare in the UK. Stanley *et al.* (2007, p. 8) refer to an out-of-court settlement by Massachusetts Institute of Technology in 2006, following the suicide of a student (Capricciosa, 2006). However, therapist liability for client suicide is already established as grounds for negligence action by third parties (such as parents) in the US, although this principle does not apply under existing UK law. Suicide is a particularly sensitive issue within HE student counselling, and will be discussed in more detail at a later point in this chapter.

Therapist's duty of care

Reported cases of successful legal action brought by clients on the grounds of professional negligence against their therapist are, in fact, decidedly rare in the UK. The legal principles involved can be stated fairly simply. These were confirmed in the key case of *Werner v. Landau* (1961), which was reported following the outcome of the case heard by the Court of Appeal. To establish professional negligence, the client as claimant needs to prove, on the balance of probabilities, as this is heard under *civil*, not criminal law, that:

- the therapist owed a duty of care to the client
- there was a breach of the duty of care by the therapist
- the breach directly caused the client foreseeable harm
- the harm experienced by the client constituted a psychiatric injury.

To briefly run through the criteria, the therapist's duty of care can quickly be established, by reference to professional codes of ethics. A breach could be identified by the evidence of expert witnesses commenting on a therapist's failure to follow established practice, or protocols. The real difficulty for clients lies in establishing that the breach directly *caused* the psychological harm, in what lawyers refer to as proving "the test of causation". Finally, the alleged harm needs to be of a high order, namely a psychiatric condition, capable of being diagnosed by standard reference manuals, such as DSM-5 (APA, 2013) or ICD-10 (WHO, 1992).

Case law on counsellor's duty of care

In the case of *Werner v. Landau* [1961], Alice Landau won her case against Dr Theodor Werner for professional negligence at the Court of Appeal, and was awarded £6,000 damages. Dr Werner, a psychoanalyst, had seen her for 24 sessions of psychotherapy in total, following which he had instituted a period of social contact with her, before then resuming therapy, which he then ended. Following this second and final ending, Alice Landau had made a suicide attempt and had been unable to work (Jenkins, 2007, pp. 79–82, 2014). Expert evidence established that "social contact" in this situation with a client was completely inconsistent with psychoanalysis as a therapeutic method. This contact had constituted a breach of his professional duty of care, which, in turn, had materially contributed to her later suicide attempt.

There are a number of key implications to be drawn from this case, for counsellors working with students and staff in HE. First, this is a very rare case of successful legal action by a client against a therapist in the UK, which perhaps demonstrates the substantial legal hurdles to be overcome by clients considering launching this kind of case. Second, the relevant test for therapist competence is drawn directly from medical case law, in the form of the *Bolam* test. This requires that the therapist exercise no more than ordinarily competent practice, which can be justified by reference to a particular model or "school" of practice. Later case law has elaborated that the law recognises that a plurality of different approaches may exist, so the approach needs to be consistent with the espoused model. The test for competent practice is substantially higher for practitioners claiming to be an expert in their field. Curiously perhaps to a lay person, trainee or student practitioners are assessed against the standard of the ordinarily competent practitioner, rather than against a lower standard. This is based on the "learner-driver" principle, whereby learner drivers are legally required to be competent if in charge of a vehicle.

Duty of care and liability

One key factor relating to the *Werner* case concerns the nature of *liability*. The term "duty of care" carries both an ethical *and* a legal meaning. In legal terms, assuming a duty of care can entail assuming legal liability to a client, if this duty is recognised by the courts. Liability can take different forms, depending on the employment status of the practitioner. If a therapist, for example, is in private practice, then they hold *personal* liability, so that a client would sue them directly. If the therapist is employed or substantially self-employed by a given employer, or is a trainee or a volunteer working "as if employed", then the organisation holds *vicarious* liability. In this case, the client would seek to sue the therapist, together with the employing organisation. In legal terms, the employer has "deeper pockets" and may well be better placed to provide financial compensation, or to make an offer and settle out of court, without any admission of liability. Counsellors working in HE are therefore likely to be covered by vicarious liability if employed, substantially self-employed, working "as if employed", as a trainee on a course, or as a student on placement.

The advantage here is that the university will have easy access to legal representation and will have broad experience of defending legal cases in court. The potential disadvantage is that the interests of the employer and the counsellor are not identical, by any means. The counsellor may have an interest in defending their practice and their professional reputation in court, while the university may well have an interest in seeking to settle out of court, in order to avoid the expense of going to court and any associated adverse publicity. However, settling out of court may still leave some lingering doubts about the counsellor's competence, even with no admission of liability, or fault by the employer. This point underlines the value of the counsellor retaining their own separate legal representation, in order to protect their reputation, as provided by their professional indemnity insurer, or by the Psychologists Protection Society.

Data protection and confidentiality

A further significant legal aspect of counselling in HE concerns client confidentiality. Counsellors are bound to keep client information confidential, according to their code of ethics (BACP, 2013, 2015). This professional obligation is underpinned by common law duty of confidence to keep personal information confidential, where this would be a reasonable expectation. Client confidentiality is also protected by the Data Protection Act 1998, which is one of the primary reference points applying in HE counselling, with most universities having clear policies for staff on processing personal data. The client's right to confidentiality is not an absolute one, as confidentiality can be breached without client consent on a number of grounds:

- where required by law
- for the prevention of crime
- where the individual concerned has consented, or their consent is likely
- in the public interest.

The Data Protection Act 1998 had a major effect on recording of client information by counselling services in HE, with a significant shift away from subjective, process-type recording, and towards the use of briefer and much more factual types of client records (Jenkins & Potter, 2007). Client records in electronic form are accessible to clients, as are "unstructured" manual records held in paper format by the university as a public authority.

Information-sharing with third parties

One of the key issues relating to confidentiality in HE counselling concerns information-sharing with third parties, such as other university staff, or the parents, partners and families of clients. Young people aged 16–17 years have an adult's entitlement to confidentiality, under s. 8, Family Law Reform Act 1969. Young people at university aged 18 have reached the age of majority and are similarly entitled to confidentiality, under both common law and data protection legislation. This can present problems when students are engaged in high-risk behaviours or have health- or life-threatening conditions, such as an eating disorder, or have requested or been admitted on a compulsory basis to psychiatric services. Unless the client consents to information being passed on to parents or to other family members, student counsellors are not required to pass this information on, and would be committing a breach of confidentiality if they did so. One parent described her own anguish and distress about being unable to access information about her daughter's condition and psychiatric treatment in the following manner:

> When we visited my sick daughter, it slowly emerged that the college had been concerned about her for weeks. She had lost a lot of weight, they feared anorexia, she was emotionally unstable and had threatened suicide. She had concealed her problems from us and the college felt it had no right to inform us. If she hadn't caught flu, we might have gone on thinking all was well until it was too late. As my daughter was too ill to be moved, we told her we would come and fetch her home as soon as it was safe. However, the college decided

they couldn't cope with a sick and by now seriously depressed girl, and had her admitted to a psychiatric hospital. We were not informed. . . . We had no legal right to know where she was.

(Dalton, 1999)

Where a third party is seeking information in this kind of situation, for example a worried parent wanting to check if their son or daughter has actually been attending counselling, it may be helpful for the enquiry to be taken by a senior member of the counselling team. In this way, general information about services and agency policy regarding confidentiality might be given, but without breaching the individual client's *privacy* (i.e. the fact of their attendance, or non-attendance, at counselling) or *confidentiality* (i.e. content and process of the counselling sessions).

In policy terms, universities are perhaps surprisingly supportive and protective of counselling confidentiality. According to Universities UK, "this confidentiality underpins the crucial relationship of trust that must be developed if these professionals are to provide effective support" (2002, p. 12). JISC guidance refers favourably to the BAC (sic) Code of Ethics (2008, p. 54), and states emphatically that "HE Employee and Student Counselling Services should ensure total confidentiality of client personal data, subject only to the following exceptions":

- client's express consent for disclosure
- client constitutes a serious danger to themselves, requiring their GP to be informed
- client presents risk of serious harm to a third party
- counsellor would otherwise be liable, under civil or criminal law.

Student mental health and duty of care

The developing language of HE duty of care to students has particular resonance within the narrative about student mental health concerns. The widening of student access to HE since the 1990s has led to greater sensitivity towards, and provision for, students with mental health problems. This been accompanied by a move towards much closer liaison with local mental health services and, to some extent, the recruitment of staff with mental health professional backgrounds to support this commitment to widening access. This process, while clearly welcome at a policy level, has perhaps led to some subtle shifts in language. The concept of "duty of care", broadly described, runs as a defining thread through HE policy documents on student mental health from this time onwards (AMOSSHE, 2001; CVCP, 2000; AUCC, 2010). The distinction between "duty of care" as an ethical obligation, and "duty of care" as a source of legal liability, is often not clearly stated. The Universities UK report on student suicide is unusual in this respect, by being careful to clarify that universities have primarily a "moral duty", rather than a legal obligation, with regard to suicide prevention (2002, p. 12).

The other possible cause of confusion over "duty of care" in HE perhaps derives from the infusion of expertise from the NHS, where professional negligence is a major factor affecting day-to-day practice. One example of this can be found in a recent report on student mental health by the Royal College of Psychiatrists: "The DDA [Disability Discrimination Act: PJ] laid down that there is a duty of care incumbent on higher education, with the potential for legal redress if 'reasonable adjustments' are not made" (RCP, 2011, p. 8). The difficulty here is that the obligation to make reasonable adjustments for students with a disability is a statutory requirement under public law, and not a duty of care, which could give rise to liability and to potential litigation, as might be the case with medical negligence within the NHS. Unlike the NHS, the potential for legal action for negligence within the HE sector is, in fact, very limited, as the following schematic diagram suggests. (This diagram represents no more than very rough estimated proportions of the different types of law and their relative influence within HE, the NHS and Social Care and is not based on any quantitative measures.)

This diagram, if correct, might suggest that legal cases for negligence are likely to play a much smaller role in HE than in the NHS. However, it is clear that the number of complaints made regarding HE has risen substantially over the past decade.

While the volume of complaints has risen for the period 2005–12, with a slight decline for the most recent figures for 2013, the data does not suggest the likelihood of a rising tide of future litigation. Most of the complaints are brought

Higher Education	NHS	Social Care
Statute Law	Statute Law	Statute Law
Contract Law	Negligence Law	Negligence Law
Negligence Law	Contract Law	Contract Law

Figure 3.2 Schematic representation of statute, contract and negligence law across higher education, NHS and social care

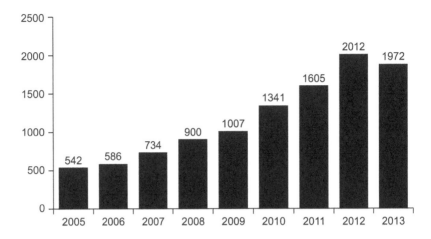

Figure 3.3 Number of complaints received by the Office of the Independent Adjudicator for Higher Education in England and Wales 2005–13

Source: Adapted from OIAHE, 2013, p. 11

by postgraduate students, rather than by the much larger body of undergraduate students, and over two-thirds relate to issues of academic status, or academic misconduct, rather than to alleged negligence (OIAHE, 2013, p. 20).

Working with risk in HE counselling

Given the particular features of the legal landscape in HE, counsellors will still be faced with challenging clients and the need to make accurate assessments of risk. The following, almost routine, catalogue of client distress will probably be somewhat familiar to many practitioners working in a university setting:

> a student persistently unable to learn, . . . a student who repeatedly comes in with vague and medically unfounded physical complaints . . . an unidentified student vomiting repeatedly in the communal bathroom or a student repeatedly alluding to suicide . . .
>
> (May, 1999, p. 16)

Research based on the use of outcome measures for service evaluation, such as CORE, indicates that there are, in fact, significant levels of psychological distress among university students. "(T)he services provided by university counselling services see people with not too dissimilar levels of presenting problems and distress to those seen in NHS primary care services" (Connell *et al.*, 2007, p. 55). While many situations will require a response based primarily on the counsellor's level of therapeutic skill and use of agency service protocols, there may be some that require a more extended working knowledge of the law, such as working with risk of suicide and safeguarding.

Legal aspects of working with risk of suicide

Counsellors in HE are particularly sensitive to the risk of student suicide, given the emotional devastation this can cause for staff, peers, families and friends and the perceived risk of damage to the university's reputation as a safe place to live, work and study. According to Bell, "student suicides are a major pre-occupation in colleges and universities throughout Britain" (1996, p. 108). Research covering England, Wales and Scotland for the period 1994–98 indicates "overall student suicide rates that are similar to those for the general population". However, it is worth noting that the female to male ratio for student suicide was higher for those aged under 19 than for the general population (Universities UK, 2002, p. 9). More recent data for England and Wales, for the period 2007–11, records that suicides by male students in full-time education rose by 36 per cent, from 57 to 78, while female student suicides almost doubled, from 18 to 34 (Groves, 2012). However, while the number of student suicides has increased overall, this has not resulted in successful litigation against universities for alleged breach of duty of care (see Figure 3.4).

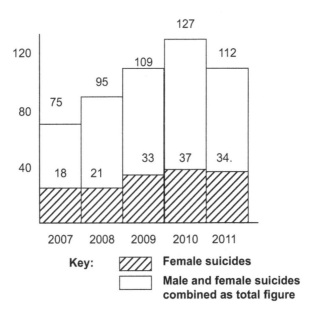

Figure 3.4 Suicides of students aged 18 plus 2007–11, based on ICD-10 classification

Source: Adapted from ONS, 2011

Case study: working with risk of student suicide

Ewan, aged 22, was brought to see a counsellor by a flatmate, who was concerned that Ewan was becoming increasingly withdrawn and isolated. Ewan was reluctant to engage with the counsellor and refused the suggestion of contacting his GP, to discuss the possibility of being prescribed anti-depressants, as being "pointless". He was re-sitting the second year of his BSc Chemistry course, having failed his exams at the end of the previous year, and saw himself as having failed in life generally, and as having disappointed his parents and his own high expectations of himself as a "high flier".

Ewan was seen by a student counsellor on placement at the university counselling service, who was reluctant to press the client to work on a safety plan to respond to his suicidal thoughts. Unfortunately, the client committed suicide over the weekend, before he was due to return for a follow-up appointment with the same counsellor the next week and before the student counsellor was due to have supervision with a more senior counsellor working in the counselling service.

At the subsequent inquest, the student counsellor was called as a witness and was closely cross-examined by the solicitor representing the family of the deceased client. The cross-examination focused on the student's relative lack of experience in working with the risk of suicide. The coroner also requested the counselling records of the deceased client and for a copy of the counselling service policy and protocols regarding confidentiality and working with suicidal clients.

From a legal point of view, suicide was decriminalised by the Suicide Act 1961. It remains a criminal offence to actively assist a person to commit, or to complete, suicide, but there is no specific legal obligation on an individual to *prevent* suicide. Universities UK guidance points out that HEIs have an obligation in relation to suicide "to pay due attention to any potential risks to their student body and to take steps to minimize those risks when at all possible", but correctly identifies this as constituting a *moral* duty, rather than a *legal* requirement as such (2002, p. 12). In practice, this may not mean that there is any appreciable difference in how an HE counselling service manages risk of suicide, but it may be helpful to remove concerns about vulnerability to litigation for breach of duty of care from the decision-making process. The legal consequences of a student or staff member's suicide are likely to be limited to providing information to the Coroner's Court, as a written report, responding via the release of counselling records under a court order, or by the counsellor concerned giving evidence in person. The purpose of the inquest is simply to establish the cause of death, rather than to establish guilt or innocence, or to award damages against the individual counsellor or its employer.

Even within the NHS, with its heightened sensitivity towards perceived duty of care issues, the courts have been very reluctant to open the door to the possibility of third-party action, by the family of the deceased, for professional negligence against NHS Trusts for failing to prevent suicide (Jenkins, 2007, pp. 125–126). The most recent development has been the use of legal action against NHS Trusts under the Human Rights Act 1998, rather than via negligence law, for decisions to discharge psychiatric patients, whether on a voluntary or a detained basis, who then went on to commit suicide (*Savage v. S. Essex NHS Trust* [2008]; *Rabone v. Pennine Care NHS Trust* [2012]). Given the statutory responsibilities of NHS Trusts for mental health care, under the Mental Health Act 1983, it seems perhaps unlikely that this particular application of human rights law will be extended to universities.

University's duty of care for student suicide in the US

The argument over duty of care relating to the issue of student suicide in the UK is sometimes driven by the contrasting example of the law in the US, where there can be a duty of care on therapists and therapy agencies to prevent client suicide. This has lead to substantial out-of-court settlements by universities in the US, to the families of the deceased (Capricciosa, 2006). However, the nature of therapist liability is markedly different in the US and is more extensive than in the UK. It is interesting that some universities in the US have responded to the risk of litigation by reframing suicide as an example of the client's own *personal responsibility* for managing the risk of intra-personal violence, rather than simply demonstrating institutional failure, or negligence, on the part of the university and its support services. Thus, students at the University of Illinois who are perceived to be at risk of suicide are contractually required to attend four counselling assessment sessions, or be withdrawn from their course of study, a policy reputedly reducing the number of subsequent student suicides (Nelson, 2011). Elsewhere, fears of litigation over student suicides have led to the investment of increased resources in student counselling services in the US, such as the recruitment of additional mental health staff who are fluent in languages other than English, and who reflect the growing diversity of the student population (Capricciosa, 2006).

Legal aspects of safeguarding children and young people

Child protection and safeguarding have emerged as major areas of social policy and practice over the past few decades. The legal framework for responding to concerns about the welfare of children under 18 years is set out by the Children Acts of 1989 and 2004 in England and Wales, and by similar legislation in Scotland and Northern Ireland. It is the responsibility of the local authority to investigate situations where a child is suffering or is likely to suffer "significant harm", under s. 47 of the Children Act 1989. The significant harm may be physical or psychological in nature, and includes recordable categories such as physical, sexual or emotional abuse, and neglect. Local Safeguarding Children Boards were set up on a statutory basis under the Children Act 2004, bringing together statutory and non-statutory agencies for information-sharing purposes and to develop good practice in responding to reports of abuse. Reporting child abuse is not currently mandatory in the UK, although a case has been made that mandatory reporting can be held to apply in Northern Ireland (Jenkins, 2007, p. 109). Best practice with regard to child protection in England is set out in statutory guidance, via the document Working Together, which is updated on a regular basis (HMG, 2013). The central motif in this and other related documents is the theme that "safeguarding is everyone's responsibility". This can be interpreted as meaning that there is a *universal* duty of care to report suspected child abuse, on a *legal*, as much as an ethical, or moral, basis. According to Sher, for example, "The Children's Act of 1989 states that everybody has a duty of care to children and this duty overrides their duty of care to their patients" (2003, p. 140). In reality, the Children Act 1989 sets out the duties of statutory bodies under public law, rather than stating a generic duty of care applying to *all* citizens. Failure to report child abuse could lead to disciplinary action against an individual counsellor under the terms of their contract of employment, but is, so far, unlikely to lead to the counsellor or their university being sued for breach of duty of care.

Measures designed to safeguard children under 18 can also apply to adults, aged 18 or over, who are deemed to be vulnerable to assault, abuse or neglect, on the basis of physical or learning disability, mental or physical illness, or reduced capacity to make decisions. Again, the legal remit for safeguarding vulnerable adults applies primarily to statutory agencies, rather than setting out a new duty of care applying to higher education, which are simply required to take "reasonable care" to avoid foreseeable harm. In the absence of any mandatory duty to report suspected abuse, either of children or vulnerable adults, counsellors can legally break confidentiality in order to report abuse *without* client consent, "in the public interest", i.e. for the purpose of preventing harm to others.

Case study: working with risk of child abuse

A university counsellor was meeting on a weekly basis with Sarah, a single parent, to explore issues of low self-esteem, arising from past relationships with her abusive partners. Sarah's attendance for counselling was patchy, due to continuing financial problems, but the therapeutic relationship was perceived by the counsellor to be strong and viable. Sarah arrived late for her session, and explained that she had been let down at the last moment by a neighbour, who had previously agreed to babysit Sarah's daughter, aged nine, that morning. Rather than cancel the session and run the potential risk of being returned to the waiting list, Sarah had left her daughter on her own. In reality, given Sarah's complete reliance on public transport to get to and from the university, this meant that her nine-year-old daughter would be left unattended for at least four hours.

The counsellor, whose previous background was in Further Education, immediately perceived this to be a "duty of care" safeguarding issue, where a vulnerable child had been left in a risky situation. She contacted the local child protection team and gave details of the incident, with the result that the client was interviewed by a social worker and given advice on parenting classes, but no further action was taken. Sarah came in to the counselling service to complain to the service manager for what she had experienced to be a major breach of her trust, refusing to see the counsellor again, or to continue counselling with another counsellor from the university service.

In this situation, the counsellor may have acted on the understanding that there was a legal duty of care towards the child, which required immediate action in the form of contacting Children's Social Care. The concept of duty of care may present the unwelcome prospect of the counsellor being liable to being sued as an individual, together with the employing university. It may be difficult to disentangle how far the decision described here, i.e. to report without client consent might be driven by a wish to cover one's back, rather than necessarily to address the child's potentially vulnerable situation. Access to supervision, or consultation with a more experienced colleague, or even a hypothetical and anonymised "what if" conversation with a social worker from the local child protection team, might all have led to a different outcome, or possibly not. Again, a defensible decision to report might well have been made "in the public interest", but without being underpinned by an overriding concern to exercise a perceived duty of care. Given the complexity of accurately assessing risk to third parties, such as children not present in the counselling room, it seems preferable to try to work here within the existing boundaries of child protection law and practice, without importing additional imperatives, such as a binding duty of care to report abuse.

Conclusion

Counselling in HE necessarily entails a close working relationship with the university, rather than one in any way semi-detached from the organisation. Although discussion of legal aspects of HE counselling seems to be increasingly framed by the concept of duty of care, the primary reference point for law within HE is that of contract. While universities have a duty of care to staff and students, it is fairly precisely drawn for the latter, and perhaps unlikely to undergo rapid or extensive revision in the near future. There is extensive and well-developed case law to demonstrate the university's duty of care towards *staff,* which can largely be discharged by providing access to a confidential counselling service, as is the case with other employers. Individual counsellors and counselling services in HE hold a duty of care towards their clients, i.e. students and staff, the contours of which are based on medical case law. The relative absence of successful cases for professional negligence against therapists might suggest that it is, in fact, extremely difficult for clients to win this type of case in court. While counsellors clearly hold ethical and professional responsibilities towards their clients, to employers, colleagues and to third parties, these duties have yet to take on the finished form of a legally-binding duty of care, for example to prevent client suicide, or to report child abuse.

References

American Psychiatric Association (APA) (2013) *Diagnostic and Statistical Manual (Fifth Edition),* Washington, DC, APA.

Association of Managers of Student Services in Higher Education (AMOSSHE) (2001) *Responding to Student Mental Health Issues: 'Duty of Care' Responsibilities for Student Services in Higher Education,* Winchester, AMOSSHE.

Association for University and College Counselling (AUCC) (2010) *AUCC Guidelines for University and College Counselling Services (Second Edition),* Lutterworth, BACP.

Bell, E. (1996) *Counselling in Further and Higher Education,* Buckingham, Open University.

Bell, E. (1999) The Role of Education in the Role of Counselling in Further and Higher Education, in Lees, J. and Vaspe, A. (Eds) *Clinical Counselling in Further and Higher Education,* (pp. 1–12), London, Routledge.

British Association for Counselling and Psychotherapy (BACP) (2013) *Ethical Framework for Good Practice in Counselling and Psychotherapy,* Lutterworth, BACP.

British Association for Counselling and Psychotherapy (2015) *Ethical Framework for the Counselling Professions,* Lutterworth, BACP.

British Broadcasting Corporation (BBC) (2010) Student suicide. *Woman's Hour,* 23rd September.

Capricciosa, R. (2006) Settlement in MIT suicide case. *Inside Higher Education,* April (4), 1–3.

Committee of Vice-Chancellors and Principals of the Universities of the United Kingdom (CVCP) (2000) *Guidelines on Student Mental Health Policies and Procedures for Higher Education,* London, CVCP.

Connell, J., Barkham, M. & Mellor-Clark, J. (2007) CORE-OM mental health norms of students attending university counselling benchmarked against an age-matched primary care sample. *British Journal of Guidance and Counselling,* 35 (1), 41–57.

Dalton, J. (1999) Dropping like flies in academe. *Guardian,* 10th September.

Davies, L. (2000) Private work in public places: Confidentiality and role tensions in a university counselling service. *Psychodynamic Counselling,* 6 (1), 65–78.

Dyer, C. (2013) Resolving clinical negligence claims. *British Medical Journal,* 347, 13.

Farrington, D. & Palfreyman, D. (2006) *The Law of Higher Education*, Oxford, Oxford University Press.

Farrington, D. & Palfreyman, D. (2012) *The Law of Higher Education (Second Edition)*, Oxford, Oxford University Press.

Groves, N. (2012) Number of student suicides increases, *Education, Guardian*, 1st December.

Her Majesty's Government (2013) *Working Together to Safeguard Children: A Guide to Inter-Agency Working to Safeguard and Promote the Welfare of Children*, London, Department for Education.

Jacobson, H. (2006) The students never fell asleep during my lectures. *Independent*, 4th February.

Jenkins, P. (2007) *Counselling, Psychotherapy and the Law (Second Edition)*, London, Sage.

Jenkins, P. (2008) Organisational Duty of Care: Workplace Counselling as a Shield Against Litigation? in Kinder, A., Hughes, R. and Cooper, C. (Eds) *Employee Well-Being Support: A Workplace Resource* (pp. 99–109), Chichester, Wiley.

Jenkins, P. (2014) *Therapists and Professional Negligence: A Duty of Care?* Newport, Counselling DVDs.

Jenkins, P. & Potter, S. (2007) No more "personal notes"? Data protection policy and practice in Higher Education counselling services in the UK. *British Journal of Guidance and Counselling*, 35(1), 131–146.

Joint Information Systems Committee (JISC) (2003) *Duty of care in further and higher education*. Available from: www.jisclegal.ac.uk (accessed 21st June 2015).

Joint Information Systems Committee (JISC) (2008) *Code of practice for the further and higher education sectors on the Data Protection Act 1998*. Available from www. jisclegal.ac.uk (accessed 21st June 2015).

May, R. (1999) Doing Clinical Work in a College or University: How Does the Context Matter? in Lees, J. and Vaspe, A. (Eds) *Clinical Counselling in Further and Higher Education* (pp. 13–25), London, Routledge.

McGettigan, A. (2013) *The Great University Gamble: Money, Markets and the Future of Higher Education*, London, Pluto.

Moore, J. & Roberts, R. Counselling in Higher Education (HE), in Moore, J. and Roberts, R. (Eds) *Counselling and Psychotherapy in Organisational Settings* (pp. 47–69). Exeter, Learning Matters.

Moorhead, J. (2010) From major to minor, *Education Guardian, Guardian*, 19th October.

Nelson, L. (2011) Dealing with the depressed and dangerous. *Inside Higher Education*, June 29th. Available from: www.insidehighered.com/news/2011/06/29/lawyers_discuss_issues_of_suicidal_students_(accessed 18th December 2014).

Office of the Independent Adjudicator for Higher Education (OIAHE) (2013) *Annual Report 2013*, Reading, OIAHE.

Office for National Statistics (ONS) (2012) *Deaths by suicide for students aged 18 and above 2007–2011*. Available from: www.ons.gov.uk/ons/search/index.html?pageSize=50&sortBy=none&sortDirection=none&newquery=student+suicides (accessed 5th January 2015).

Palfreyman, D. & Warner, D. (2002) *Higher Education Law*, Bristol, Jordan.

Pointon, C. (2014) The changing role of the university counselling service. *Therapy Today*, 25 (8), 13–17.

Reeves, A. (2005) Supporting staff working with suicide. *AUCC Journal*, Autumn, 8–11.

Royal College of Psychiatrists (RCPsych) (2011) *Mental Health of Students in Higher Education. College Report CR 166*, London, RCPsych.

Sher, M. (2003) Ethical Issues for Practitioners Working in Organisations, in Solomon, H. and Twyman, M. (Eds) *The Ethical Attitude in Clinical Practice.* London: Free Association.

Smith, E. (1999) No Client (and No Counsellor) Is an Island: Attending to the Culture of the Educational Setting, in Lees, J. and Vaspe, A. (Eds) *Clinical Counselling in Further and Higher Education* (pp. 125–140), London, Routledge.

Stanley, A., Mallon, S., Bell, J., Hilton, S. & Manthorpe J. (2007) *Responses and Prevention in Student Suicide*, Preston, PAPYRUS/University of Central Lancashire.

Topping, A. (2014) Academics protest over pressure to police students' immigration status, *Guardian*, 2nd March.

Universities UK (2002) *Reducing the Risk of Student Suicide: Issues and Responsibilities for Higher Education Institutions*, London, Universities UK.

Warburton, K. (1995) Student counselling: A consideration of ethical and framework issues. *Psychodynamic Counselling*, 1 (3), 421–435.

Whitfield, L. and Dustin, H. (2015) *Spotted: Obligations to Protect Women Students' Safety and Equality.* Legal Briefing. End Violence Against Women Coalition. Available from: www.endviolenceagainstwomen.org.uk/data/files/Spotted_-_Obligations_to_Protect_Women_Students_Safety_Equality.pdf (accessed 13th August 2015).

World Health Organisation (WHO) (1992) *ICD-10: Classification of Mental and Behavioural Disorders*, Geneva, WHO.

Legal references

Maria Abramova v. Oxford Institute of Legal Practice [2011] EWHC 613 QB

Michael James Austen v. University of Wolverhampton [2005] EWCA Civ 1272

Bolam v. Friern HMC [1957] 2 All ER 118

Erin McLean v. University of St Andrews Outer House, Court of Session 25/2/2004 All 43/01, [2004] Scots CS45

Hartman v. South Essex Mental Health Care and Community Care Trust [2005] EWCA Civ 06

Hatton v. Sutherland [2002] 2 All ER 1

Rabone and another (Appellants) v. Pennine Care NHS Foundation Trust (Respondent) [2012] UKSC 2

Savage v. South Essex Partnership NHS Foundation Trust [2008] UKHL 74

Werner v. Landau, TLR 8/3/1961, 23/11/1961, Sol Jo (1961) 105, 1008

Practice

Chapter 4

Assessment

Laying the foundation for brief therapeutic work in HE

Géraldine Dufour

In this chapter, I look at the complex role of the counselling assessment in higher education (HE). Since most readers will be familiar with the theory and practice of assessment as it is generally covered on professional counselling training courses, I explore here what is specific to assessment in a university context. In therapeutic settings, counselling assessments are used to identify and explore the presenting issue of clients as well as to consider suitability for different forms of psychological support. We will see that in HE there are a number of further requirements such as detecting risk and sign-posting students to additional sources of help. While exploring the multi-faceted role of assessment, I focus on issues of practice as they occur in the context of counselling services in British universities. I illustrate these with examples of clinical work and relevant research findings. Though we will see that there are many benefits to a good assessment, we will see that there are also some potential downsides. One area of difficulty is that by offering assessments, a counselling service might uncover needs that cannot be met and raise unrealistic expectations of the level of service it provides.

What is assessment?

Defining assessment is complex, particularly so because practice differs so much between counsellors[1] and counselling services. Despite this variety it is helpful to think of it as a process rather than a single intervention, a series of steps that help to define the problem from the perspective of both the client and the counsellor. As McLeod (2003) comments,

> The nature of assessment depends a great deal on the theoretical model being used by the counsellor or counselling agency, and a wide spectrum of assessment practices can be found.

(p. 330)

Reeves (2012) further shows that it is not just practice that varies, but even views around assessment itself. There are therapists for whom assessing is anathema, believing it imposes a premature focus onto therapeutic work, whereas working in a non-directive way is seen as less "controlling". Though differing views may have validity according to the setting in which the work occurs, I believe that failing to assess student-clients risks is missing both their needs and those of a counselling service in the HE context.

Why assess for brief work?

In a setting where most therapeutic work is brief in nature, a good assessment of the student and of their needs is worthwhile at many levels. In brief work there is less time for issues to emerge and therefore a thorough assessment assists in finding a focus for counselling. Because of the short-term nature of the intervention it is imperative that as well as being able to assess suitability for counselling, practitioners are able to assess suitability for brief work. A good assessment should help to identify a goal for the work. The inability to find such a focus could be a counter-indication for brief work. Once a focus is established, the counsellor needs to concentrate on the agreed issue(s) and steer the work back if it begins to drift. This will require a careful decision not to address other issues that, potentially, a client may wish to raise after the focus has been agreed – this is known as applying "selective", or "benign neglect" (Levenson, 1995). However, it is worth noting that certain issues, due to their severity, or the risk that they pose, cannot safely be neglected. Consequently for a skilled and competent assessment, the ability to select suitable goals and to be appropriately flexible is central to the practice of brief work.

Assessment is key to the practice of counselling, brief or otherwise, because it helps to clarify the nature of a problem and the severity of symptoms. It also helps with triage, distinguishing between those students who can be helped within the context of a university counselling service (UCS) and those who need to be seen by specialist mental health services outside the university, their GP, or other colleagues within the institution. Assessing a student also helps to identify those whose needs are most urgent. Students approach services for many reasons: assessment helps to clarify the problem they are facing, and the sort of help they require – are their needs psychological, academic, or both? While some students attend counselling with an insight into what might be causing their difficulties, many are simply aware that there is a problem. For instance, many students complain of feeling "stressed". At assessment the role of the counsellor is to establish *why* they are feeling stressed:

- Is it because they are unable to concentrate on their studies?
- What is happening to them when they are unable to concentrate?
- Is their inability to concentrate caused by their emotional state?
- Or is it because studying is too difficult?

If they have identified academic difficulty as an issue, the counsellor needs to explore further what the difficulty is about:

- Does the student lack study skills?
- Is the issue the academic level of their course?
- Do they need more academic support?
- Do they need a screening for Specific Learning Difficulties?

It is important to ascertain if there is anything that can be put in place to help the student practically, sign-posting them to other support services, or perhaps working concurrently with other colleagues in the institution. When a student is struggling, this can be a complex issue requiring several different sources of help. A counsellor needs to be able to adopt many roles: detecting issues, identifying potential sources of help and support while also exploring and attending to the psychological issue that the student is bringing. In that moment they work as a counsellor but also potentially as an advisor, by providing appropriate information. This is why it is so important that counselling services are embedded in the academic institution that they serve. As Caleb (2010) shows, a generalist counsellor, insufficiently grounded within a university context, will struggle to support a student in their academic endeavour. There are many areas that are specific to the university setting, such as referral to disability services for students needing reasonable adjustments. Another complex area is legislation around international students, where attempting to provide advice without appropriate training can incur criminal and financial liability for an individual and an institution. Counsellors need to have a thorough knowledge of other student support services to where they can direct students, as well as awareness of legislation that directly impinges on the provision of support. For instance, the Equality Act 2010 places responsibility on universities to make reasonable adjustments for disabled students.

This dual counsellor/advisor role can be surprising to a counsellor new to HE. It adds an extra dimension to the work of the therapist and connects the student seeking counselling to their studies and the rest of the university.

Triage

As we have seen, "assessment" encompasses different aspects of supporting students. In some services, an effort is made to offer appointments to clients based on their presenting issues and the counsellor's expertise in these areas. Students may also be prioritised because of the severity of their situation and any risk issues. This system of allocation is known as "triage". Triage can be based on different sources of information: a detailed pre-counselling form filled in online by a student, information passed by a referrer or an email from a student. For other services, triage takes place after assessment, and before the client is allocated to an on-going counsellor.

Services vary in the way in which they collect data. Some have pre-counselling forms completed by students. Others rely purely on the information collected by the counsellor at the first appointment. There might also be some additional information sent by other parties such as academic, tutorial, advisory or medical staff. Many UCS also use CORE (see McCrea, Chapter 5) to screen clients, particularly for risk, before they attend counselling.

Mental health issues

Students presenting with potential or diagnosed mental health issues are not uncommon in UCS. If they are young, students attending university go through many changes: leaving home, developing a different sense of self and identity. Early adulthood (18–25) is also an age at which psychiatric illnesses often first emerge (Iarovici, 2014).

In recent years, disability service colleagues have reported increases in students disclosing mental health issues when they attend university, as evidenced in the Equality Challenge Unit (2014) report:

> Since 2007/08 the proportion of disabled students disclosing a mental health condition has increased from 5.9% to 11.1% in 2012/13 (from 0.4% to 1.1% of the entire student population).

(p. 123)

At assessment stage, it is crucial that counsellors are able to identify potential mental health issues to offer students appropriate support. These students might need referring to disability services in case they need reasonable adjustments, or additional support put in place. This is important for a number of reasons: a student with mental health difficulties might not be suitable for a brief counselling model because of the severity of their issues. A disabled student might need specialist support from the university disability service. Failing to set up reasonable adjustments has legal implications under the Equality Act 2010, which can be costly for an institution: they can be fined, and reputation can suffer as a result of negative publicity. Therefore the ability to offer a skilled assessment, where all the needs of the student can be addressed (and when addressed, recorded and actioned appropriately) is key to the institution in protecting itself against litigation, and in retaining students.

Issues of risk

The ability to assess and contain risk is central to the provision of counselling in HE, so a student counsellor will explore issues of risk related to harm to self or others. As well as risk of suicide, a student might be at risk of violence from a partner, or if they are a parent, they might be putting their child at risk.

For students on clinical courses such as medicine, nursing or radiography, the counsellor has to be aware of the risk that a student may pose to others if they are unwell. Many universities now have Fitness to Practice policies and on the very rare occasions when a student might not want to take responsibility for the welfare of those for whom they have responsibility, counsellors need to be aware of the policy in the service and in the university regarding risks to others. For instance, if a very unwell student who is putting others' safety at risk does not agree to leave their placement, a counsellor might have to contact their course director so they can protect those at risk by suspending the placement. (It is important to note that although this is a possibility, it is not one that is frequent. Having worked as a counsellor in HE for over 10 years, I have never had to express concern about a student in order that they be suspended from practice.)

An additional, and much more frequent, risk to which the counsellor must be attuned is academic risk, that could lead to the failure or withdrawal of a student. Therefore in many UCS, students can be prioritised not just on the basis of their psychological needs, but also in relation to their academic situation. Such students would typically include:

- "finalists" in the last few months of their degree
- "freshers" who have recently joined the university
- students at risk of failing where there is a sense that counselling can help
- those causing concern within the institution.

In cases where there is a waiting list, many UCS choose to prioritise students who show the greatest need. Therefore it is essential that assessments are rigorous in identifying risk and the needs of the students who approach the service, as failure to do so can put the student and the institution at risk.

Assessment – the downsides?

In this chapter, I show that there are many advantages linked to conducting good assessments. However, there are also some potential downsides to this process; for example, by identifying demand that is then difficult to meet. Having a counselling service available to students is one way in which a university can effectively demonstrate support for students. It can be difficult to think that such support is limited. Tutors want support for their students. Parents want reassurance that their children are cared for. Students want help when they are struggling. Counsellors want to be able to assist those who approach them seeking help. We can see that there are many expectations impacting on a counselling service. Unconsciously, all involved desire that the service contain and resolve all students' pain and anguish. Zagier-Robert (1994) examines the unconscious wish for unlimited care that gets projected onto mental health services and how therapists use conscious and unconscious defenses to cope with the most difficult aspects of working in the caring professions. This wish for all encompassing support is, however, not one that can ever be perfectly fulfilled. Assessment uncovers need. It can be very challenging for therapists to identify needs that cannot then be addressed. Many counsellors wish that they could work with all the issues they uncover. This can be especially difficult in contexts where the potential for onward referral is limited and counsellors can feel frustrated by the very process of assessment.

Increase in demand

When resources are limited, identifying those who can be helped by UCS and those who require more specialised support is even more critical. Student-led campaigns such as Student Minds (2014) highlight the struggle for students to access health services; this also affects those with mental health issues. Additionally, it is important to note that resources can vary greatly between universities. Attendance rates between services also differ significantly (Dailey & Abbott, 2013). The national average of institutional populations accessing counselling in HE is 4 per cent, yet at some institutions 10 per cent of students may register for counselling. Many factors affect attendance rates. While no conclusive reasons have been established for these diverse rates, it has been noted by colleagues working in Russell Group universities that attendance seems to be higher in their institution (around 8–10 per cent). These universities often have the most well-resourced services and an increase in the availability and the promotion of support might encourage further access; but it is interesting to consider how the social background of students impacts on their openness to counselling. Might there be more access from certain backgrounds, where counselling is encouraged? Art subjects such as music and creative arts also seem to have much higher attendance rates (sometimes as high as 15–20 per cent), as reported by colleagues working in those universities.

External factors also influence attendance rates at UCS. There is a strong belief that increasing difficulties in accessing psychological therapy in NHS services impacts on numbers of students accessing counselling at university (Caleb, 2014). Many Heads of Services report that in their localities, GPs signpost their patients to the UCS rather than Improving Access to Psychological Therapies (IAPT) services due to long waiting lists for such NHS services. Groups such as the Heads of University Counselling Services (HUCS)[2] stress that it is important to remember that UCS exist to complement the work of NHS services, not to replace them. Therefore, it is crucial that at the assessment stage and during counselling, data is collected to demonstrate the severity of distress of those accessing counselling, as well as the level of demand for services. This helps in forming an accurate picture of the level of need and the resources required to meet them. Assessing the severity of issues of those seeking counselling is vital. If people who should be receiving intensive specialist support are seen in UCS rather than NHS services, this can have impact on the availability of resources for other students, especially if they require longer-term psychological support.

"Stages of psychological development"?

It can be argued that during an assessment, counsellors need to discern the level of psychological maturity and mindedness of their clients and whether they are facing difficult developmental issues. Bell (1997) contends, "A thorough knowledge of adolescent development underpins work with students" (p. 196).

Yet, of all the tasks of the assessor, this is, for me, one of the most controversial. For a counsellor to assess someone's psychological development implies a gold standard against which students should be judged. Yet regardless of age, people develop at different paces and in a multitude of ways. As is well documented (King & Bartlett, 1999), therapists have colluded in the pathologisation of others, and especially those who diverge from accepted norms. For instance, not so long ago, therapists typically viewed homosexuals as not having reached the ultimate level of sexual maturation.

Many of our clients are from the so-called "digital generation". I cannot help but wonder how we (often older) therapists really understand youth culture without a certain level of prejudice or misunderstanding. I worry, for example, that we might unnecessarily pathologise young people's use of social media by interpreting their need to stay connected as indicative of inferior level of psychological development.

In a chapter on researching "the child" in developmental psychology, Hogan (2005) stresses the usefulness of the concept of developmental psychology, but critiques the lack of insight and self-reflection displayed by theorists in the field whose assumptions remained unchallenged. She warns particularly against the "search for universal age parameters and strivings to establish normative models of child development" (p. 26). For me this encapsulates the dangers inherent in any student counselling discourse that highlights psychological developments, or lack thereof, in students.

In her book on student mental health, Iarovici (2014) discusses a useful concept that illustrates the evolving sense of identity of young people: "emerging adulthood" (p. 15). She singles out the specific needs of "digital natives" who grew up in an era of constant communication. She points out that their psychological development

> challenges the classical concept of separation-individuation that many mental health professionals learned a generation ago, but again, understanding the culture helps prevent over-pathologizing behaviour that may now be the norm.
>
> (p. 15)

Ecclestone and Hayes (2009) highlight another danger: the "therapisation" of education with assumptions of student vulnerability driving offers of support. Labelling students as "vulnerable" can have a negative effect on their experience and self-belief. They warn that when students are seen as vulnerable they may be over-protected by overzealous parents and university staff.

Pointon (2014) acknowledges that "HE students are already coping with transition, leaving home for the first time, looking after themselves, joining new peer groups and taking on academic demands" (p. 15). From a psychological perspective, whereas there is a risk in denying vulnerability and covering up mental health anguish, there is also a risk in students seeing themselves in the role of victims, and developing a "victim" identity. While some students can genuinely be victimised by HE institutions, there is a danger in viewing all stressful experiences as damaging, as many experiences that are growth-inducing can be stressful at times if we stretch the boundaries of our comfort zone. Equally worrying to see is a rise in a medicalisation of normal human emotions (Ecclestone & Hayes, 2009; Percy, 2014).

So an important task in assessment is to be able to ascertain if a student has been "sent" to counselling to be "fixed". It is perfectly normal for a student to be upset at times. Grieving, for instance, does not require a therapeutic intervention in most cases. A student might also be labelled as trouble(d) because they are fighting what they see as an unjust university system. It is crucial that the counselling service does not collude in treating all students who are labelled as trouble(d). Students have to be able to engage freely in counselling, or refuse to attend, as they see fit. Another important function of the assessment can be simply to normalise emotions that may be felt to be overwhelming simply because they are felt to be inexplicable.

Assessment versus diagnosis

It is important to distinguish between diagnosis and assessment and to note that the term "diagnosis" itself is controversial. For instance, in 2013 the Division of Clinical Psychology released a statement stating that

> there is a clear rationale and need for a paradigm shift in relation to functional psychiatric diagnoses. It argues for an approach that is multi-factorial, contextualises distress and behaviour, and acknowledges the complexity of the interactions involved in all human experience.
>
> (p. 5)

In the UK, the term "diagnosis" and "treatment" are concepts that resonate with a medical model of mental health. Counsellors on the other hand practise from a frame of reference that is more holistic, exploring the whole individual and the relationship between their problem and the environment in which they occur, a model that could be described as "psycho-social". While as counsellors we do not diagnose our clients, we need to know enough about medical symptoms of mental illnesses to encourage students to seek medical help when necessary.

Clarity about the role of assessment at the start of the counselling process is important. Some students might be approaching counselling expecting a diagnosis, adopting a passive patient role receiving treatment from an expert. For this reason many UCS include information on websites or pre-counselling information sheets clarifying the role of the counsellor and communicating an expectation that the client take an active part in the therapeutic work.

The centrality of the context on assessment outcome

I will now outline the context where the counselling assessment takes place and show that it plays a key, though understated, role in the assessment process.

The context of assessment in university counselling services

The exact details of where and how a UCS is located and what is comprised may seem unimportant but there is a parallel process at play here: in the same way that a client cannot be understood without considering the context of their wider life, so too a counselling service cannot be adequately comprehended apart from the context in which it operates.

One of the most direct ways in which the university context affects counselling is the impact of the academic calendar. There are breaks in the university calendar and specific expectations at particular times of the academic year, such as exams or placements. For a student coming to counselling, therapeutic work might not be appropriate depending on where in the academic cycle they present. A counsellor working in a university will vary her interventions depending on the needs of the student at different points within the academic calendar. So in a university the context forms an important part of the frame in which counselling takes place (Gray, 1994) and its demands need to be taken into consideration in the assessment and the counselling of students. Bell (1999) shows that contrary to purist assumptions, therapy is not contaminated by the process of education, but can be enhanced by it; much can be gained by paying attention to a student's relationship to the educational setting, the subject they are studying, how they came to choose it, what it represents for them, both consciously and unconsciously, their relationship to the institution and to the authority of their tutor. A good assessment cannot explore emotional or psychological concerns in isolation, but as they are embedded within a particular context – here, HE.

Clearly, UCS are delivering counselling in a higher education establishment. These institutions' primary task is education, and specifically teaching and research. May (1999) illustrates this well when he asks:

> What does a college or university want from a counselling and psychotherapy service? It is too easy for us to assume that we have been hired to the job we have been trained to do. But the institutional task is not necessarily the same as our own professional sense of the proper work. In the most general terms, the college or university values our work in so far as we appear to support the education, and successful graduation, of students.

(p. 14)

Context is also important because it locates the UCS as a part of a wider system. System theory has much to offer in helping us to think about the dynamics that operate in interconnected systems. It helps understand how a service's relationship to its environment is complex because services are inter-dependent on each other and the rest of the institution. They cannot survive in isolation, but must compete for valuable resources. This helps understand how a counselling service is never totally independent, that it does not function in a vacuum, and that the context will frequently determine the outcome of assessment. Some counsellors may focus solely on the therapeutic relationship that they have with their client, at the exclusion of others. Working in a university means that the context impacts on client and counsellor alike, and therefore plays a key role in determining the outcome of an assessment.

Case studies

The following case studies illustrate typical issues that might emerge during assessment. They feature fictitious students.

George

George self-refers to counselling after the Easter holiday. He is feeling low and very worried that he will not be able to pass his exams as he has been unable to concentrate. He feels stuck in a punishing cycle of failure. He is behind in his studies and feels overwhelmed by the amount of work that he needs to do before his exams. He has lost hope and cannot see how he can tackle his work. He tries to work all day but is frustrated by the quality of his work, feeling he is not achieving what he needs to do in order to pass. There is a strong sense of shame as he compares himself to his colleagues on his course who all seem able to get on with their work. He is worried that he is jeopardising future employment references and fears his lecturers see him as lazy. By the time he arrives for his assessment, he is overwhelmed. The counsellor explores his functioning and level of psychological distress and takes his history, checking for any issues of risk. There is no significant trauma in his past and he is not actively suicidal though at time thinks death would be a release from his current situation. It becomes apparent that George has been suffering from low moods for a significant period of time; he struggles to concentrate, is plagued by guilt and displays many of the symptoms of a depressive episode as described in the WHO (1992) ICD10. With this in mind, the counsellor thinks that this student would benefit from a consultation with his GP to explore possible symptoms of depression, for which medication can be helpful. Though counsellors do not diagnose their clients, they have to be able to suggest that they seek medical support when appropriate. Unless there is a significant cause for concern due to immediate and serious risk to self or others, it is of course the client's choice whether to access their GP for further support.

George is also encouraged to contact his course director as he is struggling academically. The course director will be able to advise him on possible extra academic support to catch up or, if the GP diagnoses a medical condition, advise him on possible academic solutions such as delaying exams until September resits or retaking his module in September without prejudice (as a first attempt) due to ill health.

At this stage, no other potential factors are identified – his difficulties do not seem linked to an underlying specific learning difficulty for example. Having explored his interest regarding his course, it does not seem that a referral to the Careers service is required. Until he started experiencing low moods George had enjoyed his course and was interested in his subject.

George seems to set very high standards for himself so it is possible that his presenting issue is linked to underlying issues of perfectionism. As well as further individual counselling, George might benefit from a referral to two psychoeducational groups offered in the service: "Managing your perfectionism" and "Managing your moods".

At the assessment appointment he is also advised to scale back on his revision schedule, take time off to rest and set a more realistic and achievable revision schedule. He is given advice on self-care regarding sleep, eating and exercise.

George is happy for the counselling service to liaise with his GP and his tutor so he signs an extended confidentiality form allowing the service to communicate with them should they contact the UCS.

George might also need a letter of support for a claim of mitigating circumstances if he opts to take his exams at the September resits. Should he want to apply for mitigating circumstances he would be advised to contact the student union, which can advise him on the claim process.

Kim

Kim self-refers to the counselling service in mid-December before the start of the Christmas holiday. She is a young international student from Vietnam in her first year. She comes to counselling because she is stressed about what is happening with her friends. She is part of a Vietnamese friendship group but feels excluded and isolated by this group. She describes people being unfair to her, gossiping behind her back and making nasty comments on social media. Initially, her counsellor explores this issue, wondering about a potential bullying dynamic. However as they explore the situation in more depth, the counsellor starts wondering if something else is happening. While keeping an open mind, and not dismissing the bullying theory, she starts wondering about the student's mental health and about how much of what she is describing is real. The more Kim talks about her situation, the more improbable it becomes. She describes elaborate surveillance from her friendship group, involving departmental staff, which does not seem plausible. Though Kim's physical appearance does not seem overtly affected, and she describes eating regular meals, she has difficulty sleeping. Trying to find a term that will not frighten

Kim, the counsellor asks her how long she has been feeling this "stressed", exploring her history and level of functioning. As they continue talking, the counsellor realises that Kim has not been attending lectures. The counsellor worries about the implications on the terms of Kim's student visa. As she is concerned about Kim's mental health and about the need for a possible psychiatric assessment, the counsellor suggests a referral to see the mental health advisor (MHA), to which Kim agrees. The counsellor organises an appointment with the MHA who works in the service. She explains Kim's situation and highlights the fact that Kim is not registered with a GP. The MHA arranges a meeting with Kim and, sharing the counsellor's concerns, arranges an onward referral to the early intervention mental health team, who agree to come and assess the client at the UCS. This appointment is arranged with the student's permission, as is liaison with the international student team because of concerns regarding Kim's student visa. Once the mental health advisor engages with the student, the counsellor steps back: counselling is not the most appropriate form of support at this stage due to the nature and severity of the mental health symptoms that Kim is experiencing.

In both of these case studies, the counsellor assesses the psychological needs of the student as well as their needs in relation to their studies and the university. For George those institutional needs are closely linked to academic needs; for Kim they are related to student immigration regulations.

Once a student's presenting issues and level of distress have been understood, an effective assessment directs them towards the best sources of support to meet their requirements, and may require a counsellor to go beyond a purely therapeutic role.

Conducting an assessment

There are different views regarding the conduct of a counselling assessment. Some, myself included, prefer a free-flowing conversation, while others prefer the use of structured questions. Personally, I think the style that we use ought to reflect the needs of the service *and* the practice of the counsellor. As long as key information is captured, the manner in which it is collected is less important. Research shows that counsellors are most effective when they work in a way that feels congruent with their preferred model. Van Audenhove and Vertommen (2000) write that

> Another complicated factor in the intake is that most treatment selection results in the proposal of an appropriate treatment method or technique, while the success of psychotherapy is determined almost as much by the personal characteristics of the therapist and by the therapeutic relationship.

> (p. 288)

My personal model is to have a set of questions that I ask depending on the client presentation, tailoring my enquiries to the client's needs. This of course is a subjective process, though especially pertinent in a context where most of the work is brief and therefore requires a focus on specific issues, thus fitting with the concept of "selective neglect" central to brief work. So, for instance, I do not take a detailed sexual history at all clients' assessment, if that is not linked directly to their presenting issue. Clients can find it intrusive to be asked questions not directly linked to their presenting problem(s). However, there is also a downside to this technique, as it is not uncommon for clients to state that they wished they had been asked something directly by their counsellor, as they felt unable to bring it up themselves. It is important to note that what is asked at assessment can set the tone for the rest of therapy and what can be discussed. Whatever the approach taken, it is crucial not to make assumptions about the client, such as their level of ability or their sexuality.

Presenting issues in UCS

When people think about students attending university, many think of young people perhaps leaving home for the first time. While it is true that many students fit that stereotype, there is now a much greater diversity of students. The student body comprises mature students, students with parental responsibilities, students who stay at home and commute to university. Student profiles also vary greatly between universities. Many factors influence the profile of students in different universities, or even on different courses in the same university. This profile can depend on the subjects being taught, the academic demands of the programmes, the socio-economic background of the student and their ethnicities.

Many counsellors who start working in UCS are often surprised by the severity of the symptoms of those coming to counselling. Research by Wallace (2012) shows that the level of clinical severity of those attending counselling at university is similar to that of those attending counselling in primary care. To the uninitiated, there may be a perception that "student problems" are mainly to do with homesickness or getting drunk. They may dismiss the sort of problems that students face, assuming that the most upsetting issue students experience is dealing with their first relationship break-up. In fact on the occasions when students come to counselling for that reason, it is often because the break-up echoes earlier or more traumatic losses, or highlights some other underlying issue that they are facing.

The university experience as a "trigger"

While I have shown that it is not helpful to think of coming to university as challenging to all students, it would be equally unhelpful to dismiss those for whom being at university creates difficulties. It is a period of transition, which some students will find more difficult than others depending on their past experience and emotional resilience. This is why at the assessment stage the counsellor will take a history of the client's early life, significant events and relationships. For instance a student with attachment issues might find arriving in a new environment problematic because they find being alone a challenge. If a student is leaving home for the first time, they might be re-evaluating their earlier experience and addressing past issues of abuse or neglect.

For others, it might be that their current situation is challenging. It is much harder for a student to separate from their parents who are divorcing or if they are worried about a family member's health or wellbeing. For still others the university experience may disturb a previous equilibrium, as university may feel alien for those who are part of a social or ethnic minority background. It used to be that issues of sexuality would emerge at university. Now many of our LGBT+ clients come out when they are still at school. However, this is not the case for all students; for example, those who come from international or more traditional backgrounds might not have had an opportunity to explore their sexuality. Of course international students can face challenges of their own (see Hunt, Chapter 7).

Culture

All counsellors should pay attention to the cultural context of their clients, whether at assessment or during counselling. Those conducting an assessment in the HE context also need to be aware of the interaction of the client culture with the learning environment. When working with finalist students for instance, it is important to explore whether they are facing issues related to ending. For some students there might be additional cultural issues related to finishing their degree. For example, finishing might mean that they have to face family expectations that now they are ready to get married. While not all those issues will be unpacked at the assessment stage, the counsellor has to be able to check if some attention needs to be given to any particular cultural areas. This is useful on two levels: it shows the client that this is something that can be addressed in counselling, but it also gives a sense of any urgent or risk issues associated with culture. It is not unusual for different issues to intersect. For instance, sexuality might interact with cultural background and the therapist needs to be aware of this at the assessment stage.

Attending to the client and their presenting issue

Having looked at the specific issues that may be explored at assessment, it is worth noting that a first appointment is not a space solely reserved for the exploration of presenting issues or an exercise in history taking. It is also an important opportunity to actually address the client's presenting issue.

Many students are only seen for one session. Connell *et al.* (2008) write, "A large proportion (23%) attended one session only" (p. 6) (and see Cowley and Groves, Chapter 6). Therefore, students should be given some support in managing their issue, if possible, as this might be the only therapeutic encounter they experience.

As therapists, it is useful to keep in mind that for almost a quarter of sessions we might think that we are "just" assessing, whereas in fact we are treating. We need to work with this in mind so that students leave having experienced some level of intervention. This will also help with students' motivation to engage with

---

Box 4.1 Assessment focus

I suggest here areas that a good assessment of a student-client in HE will cover, whether at a stand-alone assessment session, or as part of an on-going process:

- Demographic details (name, date of birth, gender, etc.)
- Contact details (term time address, email and phone numbers including permission to leave a message)
- University details (student ID, course name and level, faculty)
- History, including significant events (loss, parental breakup, illness); past and current relationships; attachment history
- Current health and wellbeing, including disability, support in place and impact on studies. Any needs in relation to the disability (access, support etc.)
- Mental health diagnosis and history
- Previous psychological treatment and outcome
- Medication (current and past)
- Details of those delivering medical or psychological support and contact details including GP information (name of the GP, surgery, address and phone number)
- Current support (from family, friends, partner, at university, or lack of support)
- Current home situation
- Academic situation and history (year of study, any risk of failing)
- Any welfare issues
- Presenting issue(s)
- Underlying issue(s)
- Any other factor that can be relevant to this particular student, their need and situation (sexuality, gender, cultural impact etc.)
- Motivation to change: what is driving the desire to change (see Prochaska et al., 1994).
- Any risk issues (self-harm, suicide risk, previous hospital admission due to self-harm risk to others)
- Potential fitness to practice impact (e.g. with medics, teachers)
- Permission to liaise with other services if necessary (signed consent)

counselling following their assessment. A counsellor conducting an assessment also needs to attend to the immediate needs of the client. There are occasions when a client arrives in a heightened emotional state. If a client is very upset, or angry, this needs to take priority. In those situations, it might mean that assessment should be spread over several sessions. While a lot of information needs to be collected at assessment, this can only be done with the collaboration of the client. A key ingredient to a successful assessment, therefore, is establishing a therapeutic rapport with the client.

Conclusion

Having explored different aspects of the process of assessment in HE, I have shown that a service has much to gain if its counsellors conduct a thorough assessment. For the institution, it helps to identify issues of risk and guide students towards an appropriate source of support. For counsellors, it is one of the key elements to the establishment of a good therapeutic relationship and future engagement in counselling. Yet, much is still to be learned about assessment, making it difficult to base practice on evidence stemming from research.

Hence, it is useful to bear in mind Lemma's (2003) words of caution:

> Our ignorance is strikingly apparent when one surveys the literature on assessment. The word *assessment* might well evoke a scientific frisson, but it is in fact an imprecise process reliant more on intuition than science, limited by the therapist's theoretical allegiances and constrained, especially within public health service settings, by the reality of limited resources.
>
> (emphasis author's own, p. 132)

Continuing to refine assessment helps to improve counselling practice and student engagement. Metaphorically, assessment is the foundation on which the rest of the counselling work is built, as well as the blueprint that will guide that work.

A good assessment holds the key to successful engagement and effective support, ultimately underpinning and facilitating the therapeutic enterprise.

Notes

1 In universities, the custom is to refer to practitioners as "counsellors", regardless of their backgrounds (counselling, psychotherapy, cognitive behavioural therapy, counselling or clinical psychology) and this is the terminology I use here.
2 A special interest group of the British Association for Counselling and Psychotherapy – Universities and Colleges division.

References

AUCC (1999) *Degrees of Disturbance: the New Agenda*, A report from the Heads of University Counselling Services, Rugby, BAC.

Bell, E. (1997) Counselling in Higher Education, in Palmer, S. (Ed.) *Handbook of Counselling,* Rugby, BACP.

Bell, E. (1999) The Role of Education in the Role of Counselling in Further and Higher Education, in Lees, J. and Vaspe, A. (eds) *Clinical Counselling in Further and Higher Education,* London, Routledge.

Caleb, R. (2010) The roles offered by counselling services in further and higher education. *AUCC Journal,* March 2010.

Caleb, R. (2014) Uni counselling services challenged by growing demand. *Guardian,* 27th May 2014.

Connell, J., Barkham, M. & Mellor-Clark, J. (2008) The effectiveness of UK student counselling services: An analysis using the CORE System. *British Journal of Guidance & Counselling,* 36 (1), 1–18.

Dailey, M. & Abbott, T. (2013) BACP universities and colleges annual survey 2011/12. *University & College Counselling Journal,* March 2013.

Division of Clinical Psychology (2013) *Position statement. Classification of behaviour and experience in relation to functional psychiatric diagnoses: Time for a paradigm shift,* Leicester, The British Psychological Society. Available from: www.bps.org.uk/system/files/Public%20files/cat-1325.pdf (accessed 18th January 2015).

Equality Challenge Unit (2014) *Equality in higher education: statistical report part 2: Students.* Available from: www.ecu.ac.uk/publications/equality-higher-education-statistical-report-2014/ (accessed 29th January 2015).

Ecclestone, K. & Hayes, D. (2009) *The Dangerous Rise of Therapeutic Education,* London, Routledge.

Gray, A. (1994) *An Introduction to the Therapeutic Frame,* London, Routledge.

Hogan, D. (2005) Researching "The Child" in Developmental Psychology, in Greene, S. and Hogan, D. (Eds) *Researching Children's Experience* (p. 6), London, Sage.

Iarovici, D. (2014) *Mental Health in the University Student,* Baltimore, John Hopkins Press.

King, M. & Bartlett, A. (1999) British psychiatry and homosexuality. *The British Journal of Psychiatry,* 175 (2), 106–113.

Levenson, H. (1995) *Time-Limited Dynamic Psychotherapy: A Guide to Clinical Practice,* Basic Books, New York.

Lemma, A. (2003) *Introduction to the Practice of Psychoanalytic Psychotherapy,* Chichester, Wiley.

McLeod (2003) *An Introduction to Counselling (Third Edition),* Maidenhead, Open University Press.

May, R. (1999) Doing Clinical Work in a College or University, in Lees, J. and Vasp, A. (Eds) *Clinical Counselling in Further and Higher Education* (p. 13), London, Routledge.

Percy, A. (2014) Student mental health: The situation is more nuanced than it seems. *Guardian,* 16th October 2014.

Pointon, C. (2014) The changing role of the university counselling service. *Therapy Today,* 25 (8), 13–17.

Prochaska, J., Norcross, J. & DiClemente, C. (1994) *Changing for Good,* New York, Morrow.

Reeves (2012) *An Introduction to Counselling and Psychotherapy: From Theory to Practice,* London, Sage.

Royal College of Psychiatrists (2003 and 2011) *College report CR166: Mental health of students in higher education, London, RCPsych.* Available from: www.rcpsych.ac.uk/files/pdfversion/CR166.pdf (accessed 19th October 2011).

Student Minds (2014) *Transitions campaign.* Available at: www.studentminds.org.uk/press-coverage.html (accessed 21st June 2015).

Van Audenhove, C. & Vertommen, H. (2000) Negotiation approach to intake and treatment choice. *Journal of Psychotherapy Integration*, 10 (3), 287–299.

Wallace, P. (2012) The impact of counselling on academic outcomes: The student perspective. *AUCC Journal*, November 2012.

World Health Organization (1992) *The ICD-10 Classification of mental and behavioural disorders: Clinical descriptions and diagnostic guidelines.* Available from: www.who.int/classifications/icd/en/bluebook.pdf (accessed 8th November 2014).

Zagier-Robert, V. (1994) The Self-Assigned Impossible Task, in Obholzer, A. and Zagier-Roberts, V. Z. (Eds) *The Unconscious at Work. Individual and Organizational Stress in the Human Services*, Hove, Routledge.

Chapter 5

Measuring effectiveness in student counselling

Kitty McCrea

"How do we know the student counselling service is worth the £250,000 annual running cost?"

"Could we provide the service more cost effectively by outsourcing it?"

"How do we know if student counselling has an impact on retention and achievement?"

"How do we know if the service is effective in helping students?"

These were some of the more difficult questions put to me by university senior managers as I was interviewed for a head of a counselling post many years ago. I did not know the answers but I understood their importance and once appointed I began finding out. In today's financial and economic climate these questions are more important than ever. The reality is that the future may be bleak for any psychological therapy service that can't provide evidence of its effectiveness.

This chapter reviews the history of attempts by Higher Education (HE) student counselling services to demonstrate the effectiveness of their work. In particular it considers efforts to create robust practice-based evidence through the use of widely-used outcome measurement such as CORE-OM (Evans *et al.*, 2000). It argues that this is the best defence for both the sector as a whole and individual HE counselling services that need to demonstrate that they are providing a cost-effective, ethical service. The implementation of routine outcome measurement (ROM) into a service is a journey, not a one-off event, and here I suggest a five-stage developmental model that involves services and counsellors in an increasingly sophisticated set of skills, based on the framework outlined by Barkham and colleagues (Barkham *et al.*, 2010). This framework (illustrated in Table 5.1) can be used by HE counselling services to identify their current stage of development and potentially their next steps.

This developmental model is illustrated using a case study based on the experience of one HE student counselling service.[1]

Table 5.1 Outcome measurement developmental framework

Stage	Model	Key characteristics
0	No use of outcome measurement	Reliance on client satisfaction questionnaires, often returned anonymously
1	Outcome measurement	Managerially led, administratively resourced, and perhaps paying lip service to the need to collect outcomes data. May use paper forms, in-house or commercial software
2	Outcome monitoring	Use of data to profile client journeys through the service and benchmarking against external key performance indicators. Use of commercial software
3	Outcome management	Use of data to improve service delivery and outcomes; setting internal targets and individual therapist appraisal. Use of commercial software
4	Feedback-informed therapy	Tracking client responsiveness to treatment at each contact in order to identify any clients who are potentially at risk of a poor outcome and maximise clinical effectiveness. Use of second-generation web-based software offering real-time analysis providing immediate clinical feedback and alerts that require clinical attention

Case study part 1: background to the service

De Montfort University (DMU) Leicester provides a counselling service for 22,000 students. There is a "core" team of four staff (one full-time and three part-time). This is supplemented by four sessional staff working between half a day and two days per week and several associate/volunteer staff. Some 600 clients are seen each year. Students can have up to six sessions in the first instance, which can be extended to a maximum of 12 if therapeutically appropriate. The average number of sessions per client is 4.5.

Research, evaluation and audit

There is often confusion around the relationship between research, evaluation and audit (Mellor-Clark & Barkham, 2006). Formal therapy research is typically carried out through randomised control trials (RCTs) with the aim of identifying "what works for whom", the results of which are sometimes known as empirically supported therapies (ESTs) or "evidence-based practice". This is often considered to be the gold standard for research. Evaluation is typically undertaken to demonstrate the effectiveness of service provision and has traditionally relied upon client outcome data without reference to the kind of contextual data (e.g. presenting problems, length of therapy, types of ending etc.) that, it has been argued, is essential in order to clarify what determines effectiveness and ineffectiveness (Mellor-Clark & Barkham, 2006, p. 209). In the HE sector evaluation is often limited to student satisfaction surveys or the use of client-completed outcome measures.

Traditionally, audit has involved simple counting: number of clients seen, number of DNAs, waiting times, number of sessions delivered. In HE this has been the main purpose of the BACP-UC[2] annual survey. Clinical audit however goes several steps further and becomes part of the evaluation process linking inputs to outcomes (as in the CORE System) and provides the link that gives us practice-based evidence. This chapter focuses on the benefits and challenges faced by HE student counselling services in their attempts to secure robust practice-based evidence.

Working towards an evidence base

For the past 16 years (1998–2014) a number of higher education counselling services have attempted to demonstrate the effectiveness of their work using the paradigm of practice-based evidence. Practice-based evidence can be defined as the evaluation of client outcomes "carried out in routine clinical practice" (Barkham *et al.*, 2010, p. 23) and is a now well-established complement to the dominant RCT model inherited from medical research. While it can be useful to demonstrate the efficacy of specific treatments (and the current dominance of CBT approaches shows how influential such evidence can be), a randomised control trial conducted with selected patients with one identified diagnosis and one treatment model is never going to be entirely relevant "to real life in a university or college counselling service: it doesn't address the range of clients, the multiplicity of their concerns, the impact of the institution or the process of learning" (Parker, 1999, p. 142). Practice-based research, however, provides the opportunity to evaluate treatment approaches in specific clinical settings and can therefore help to "elucidate the significance of contextual factors for the results" (Holmqvist *et al.*, 2015, p. 3). These include number of sessions offered (typically short-term in higher education services), types of presenting problem, impact of university life, age, gender and so on.

Nevertheless, many counsellors and service managers in higher education still seek a kind of Holy Grail that will tell them which approaches work best for a student population. Even if there were such evidence it still wouldn't tell us which services are able to deliver that therapy effectively.[3]

However, managers in higher education rightly need to know whether counselling is cost-effective – "i.e. does it achieve what it sets out to do within the resource limits laid down and does it do it better than using other forms of pastoral care or than doing nothing?" (Parker 1999, p. 142).

The launch of the CORE System in the UK in 1998 (Mellor-Clark, 1999) gave higher education counselling services the opportunity to pilot a system, which would potentially allow them to build an evidence base to demonstrate their effectiveness. Typically, services would annually send their collected paper outcome measures to a research centre for batch-processing, receiving the results back some months later. While initially attractive to services and counsellors, this "hands off" approach ultimately set back the cause of outcome measurement among HE counselling services because of several disadvantages. These included a lack of engagement with the data due to the time that elapsed before results were returned, the relatively high cost of the process, and an inability to "drill down" into the data to explore outcomes in more detail (Mellor-Clark & Barkham, 2006).

CORE-PC, a software package for personal computers, was launched in 2001 to counteract the problems experienced by the remote analysis of data. It enabled services to take control of their own data management and to support in-house analysis and reporting. Designed to support pre- and post-outcome measurement, the aim was to promote a "research-practitioner" model so that services no longer had to rely on external expertise to analyse their data (Mellor-Clark & Barkham, 2006).

Case study part 2: the introduction of CORE PC

De Montfort University (DMU) was one of the early adopters of the new CORE PC software. CORE was introduced to help improve the management of the service, particularly with a view to being transparent and accountable. Following a pilot at a smaller campus, CORE PC was rolled out across the university in the autumn of 2003. However, the re-introduction of CORE into the service was a challenging process for a number of reasons – previous negative experiences of using CORE when data had to be sent away for analysis being one of them, but it was also difficult for the team to accept the change to a managed service that was willing to open itself up to scrutiny.

By 2005 there were more than 30 HE counselling services using CORE PC and an informal network was established with the aim of forming a practitioner-led research network with CORE System measures acting as a "hub" to which an additional "spoke" to capture student counselling specific variables could be added. In 2010 CORE System benchmarks for higher education were published, and continue to provide the best evidence base so far for the effectiveness of student counselling, using a range of key performance indicators that can also be compared to equivalents in Primary Care. These include waiting times, severity levels at assessment, pre- and post-counselling outcome measure completion rates, assessment outcomes, planned and unplanned endings and improvement rates. See Table 5.2 for a summary of the key performance indicators.[4]

With the availability of CORE PC software a small band of enthusiasts attempted to establish an HE Practice Research Network, defined as an agreement by members "to pool data relating to clinical outcomes, using the same measure or

Table 5.2 2010 Key performance indicators for HE services[5] (CORE IMS, 2010)

Indicator	Overall mean	Highest performing service	Lowest performing service
Waiting time from referral to first assessment (days)	9	0	22
Pre-therapy CORE-OM completion rates (%)	92	100	71
Pre- and post-therapy CORE-OM completion rates (%)	41	82	18
Clients accepted for ongoing therapy following assessment (%)*	77	100	51
Differences in clients' and practitioners' ratings of risk (%)	16	0	26
Client-initiated termination of therapy by undeclared discontinuation (%) – unplanned endings	52	21	78
Clients meeting criteria for recovery and/or improvement (%)	75	89	60

*In this case, "highest" performing service is something of a misnomer, since interpretation of what is "good" depends to some extent on how services are expected to meet the needs of clients.

Source: Reproduced with permission of CORE.

set of measures" (Parry et al., 2010, p. 313). Such a pool of anonymised data from a common methodology would potentially provide a significant source of material for reflection on individual and service performance and eventually resulted in the publication of the CORE HE Benchmarks (CORE IMS, 2010). These developments between 2005 and 2010 moved many services from Stage 1: Outcomes Measurement – the traditional, managerially-led and administratively resourced, largely passive collection of outcome data – to Stage 2: Outcomes Monitoring – the active use of outcome data to profile client characteristics and outcomes and benchmark service data against external key performance indicators. One of the key elements of change driving this was the ability of relatively well-resourced university counselling services to provide access to CORE PC for each of their counsellors, who were then able to enter client data themselves and thus begin to engage more fully with client profiles. This helped services move away from simply paying lip service to the need to collect data but failing to engage with it in a meaningful way.

The development of practice-based evidence as a complementary paradigm to the traditional approach of evidence-based practice is particularly important in the context of student counselling as the evidence base for counselling in higher education is otherwise very limited. Writing in 1999, Eileen Smith, then head of the counselling service at the University of Hertfordshire, lamented the lack of any explicit reference to the role of counselling in the influential Dearing Inquiry into Higher Education (HMSO, 1997) and at the same time noted "the relative paucity of respectable evaluation and research studies in counselling" (Smith, 1999, p. 136). Specific studies looking at the effectiveness of student counselling were even harder to come by. Early studies (e.g. Rickinson, 1997) tended to be very small scale, based on single services and, on occasion, the work of single practitioners. A comprehensive scoping review commissioned by BACP in 2006 with the aim of assembling the best quality published research into student counselling reported that "the evidence base associated with student counselling is characterised by low quality and/or research designs that are inappropriate to the research questions" (Connell *et al.*, 2006, p. 6). Not surprisingly, there was a strong recommendation that future student counselling research would benefit from better co-ordination.

Historically, most student counselling services relied on feedback satisfaction questionnaires from students attending counselling – many still do. While results from feedback surveys tend to show a high degree of satisfaction with the service, response rates are typically low relative to student throughput (Connell *et al.*, 2006) and suffer from the inherent flaw that the majority of such questionnaires returned are from those who have continued to a planned ending and thus are more likely to be satisfied with the service they have received. Moreover, client satisfaction questionnaires are often completed and returned anonymously with the intention of making it impossible to link client feedback to their individual counselling record or to their counsellor. This anonymity severely reduces the usefulness of the data. As Lesley Parker, then chair of the AUCC research committee put it: "Evaluation questionnaires become useful only if the results are used to improve a counsellor's practice with individual clients, or to consolidate or change what a service or institution offers" (Parker, 1999, p. 146). Too often they are used as lip service, to honour the client's perspective and reassure counsellors (and the institution) that they are doing a good job.

In an attempt to improve the data available, the AUCC invited student counselling services to contribute to an annual survey, reporting on a common data set such as numbers of counselling session delivered, staff to student ratios and counsellor-identified problem/ severity levels (BACP, 2014). While helpful in terms of raising the profile of the work done by student counselling services, such surveys focus on inputs rather than outcomes and are therefore limited in both scope and objectivity.

Stage 3: outcome management – using data to improve service delivery

Despite the availability of the HE CORE sector specific benchmarks, relatively few university counselling services using CORE have moved from Stage 2: outcome monitoring, to Stage 3: outcome management. The biggest obstacle for services in making that leap is the issue of data quality. Poor data quality was cited as a reason by many of the 15 services using CORE PC who declined to anonymously pool their data towards the benchmarking exercise. Yet those who contributed still only managed to achieve post-counselling outcome measures for around 40 per cent of clients. Poor data quality of course is a common shortcoming of practice research network data (Parry *et al.*, 2010) and remains an ongoing concern. However, as the case study illustrates, it is possible for services to overcome these hurdles by setting internal targets for key performance indicators such as outcome measure completion rates, improvement rates, planned endings etc.

Case study part 3: improving data quality

The increasing counsellor "buy in" has been demonstrated by big improvements in the quality of our data over 10 years. The first two rows in Table 5.3 shows the percentage of clients seen who completed a pre- (OM1) and pre- and post- (OM2) outcome measure. The improvement rate figure can only be based on the OM2 percentage however. Therefore in 2003/4 we had 71 per cent of clients for whom we had no data on whether they "improved" or not.

Table 5.3 Improving data quality

Measure	2003/4	2013/14
OM1 (pre-outcome measure)	85%	100%
OM2 (post-outcome measure)	29%	81%
Clinical and/or Reliable Improvement	74%	75%
Planned endings	45%	75%

Once counsellors could see the benefit to the client, the greater their motivation to collect as many pre- and post-outcome measures as possible.

The most striking improvement in the case study was an increase from a 29 per cent pre- and post-outcome measure completion rate in 2003 to 81 per cent in 2013. This was achieved following an upgrade to CORE Net, a web-based software system, at the beginning of that academic year (see case study part 6).

Case study part 4: setting targets for service improvement

As a team we set targets to try and maintain or improve the quality of our data and our work. Our collective targets are 80 per cent in the key performance indicators – OM1 and OM2 (pre- and-post outcome measures), Improvement Rates, Planned Endings and Sessions Attended.

We aim to get 80 per cent planned endings. One way of achieving that is to follow up clients who cancel or DNA and see if they wish to continue or are happy to finish (balancing a respect for client autonomy, with showing that we are "holding them in mind"). Students can miss sessions and then feel bad about that and think for a variety of reasons that it is no longer okay to resume sessions!

We have also found that using regular CORE measures to progress check the work has helped to increase client "buy in" to the work and contributed to the increase in planned endings.

Case study part 5: how CORE Net helped us to improve our data quality

In autumn 2013 we moved to CORE Net, which has improved functionality and was very "client friendly". Moving to CORE Net has helped increase the OM2 rate even further through use of the quick and short CORE 10 measure, which takes about a minute to complete on screen. This is now used regularly during therapy and sometimes session by session depending on what the client and counsellor find most useful. With CORE Net, the last measure collected is counted as the post-outcome measure whenever that was collected (as long as there are at least two measures). This therefore includes clients who left before a planned ending.

"Scoping in" the majority of our clients rather than a minority as we did when we started using CORE makes the improvement rate data far more meaningful. We are not just capturing the success stories of clients who have "neat" endings and in that sense a current 75 per cent improvement rate means a lot more than the 74 per cent we recorded when we first started.

This use of outcome data to improve service delivery is only possible if contextual data is also collected so that it is possible to drill down into the data to answer increasingly sophisticated questions. For example, My Sister's Place used the evidence from their data to move from open-ended therapy to a 12-session model (Twigg, 2012). Their analysis of CORE data "showed that the majority of clients showed significant change between 7–10 sessions" (p. 2) and that this had remained steady over five years of data collection. The data also "clearly showed that clients attending for 20 or more sessions demonstrated little improvement and even deteriorated" (ibid, p. 2). This kind of analysis is only possible if numbers of sessions attended are related to client outcomes.

Stage 4: Routine outcome measurement: feedback-informed therapy

Ten years ago a small group of university counselling services formed a pilot group using the CORE system to systematically assess, monitor progress and evaluate outcomes in counselling provision. One of their aims was to explore the active, collaborative and therapeutic use of outcome measures with clients and the group agreed to use an outcome measure mid-therapy to track client progress and understand more about the effect on the therapeutic alliance of using outcome measures in this way. Recognising the clinical benefits of using outcome measures with clients has a major impact on counsellor commitment to collecting data, as our case study illustrates.

Case study part 6: the therapeutic use of CORE in contracting and building the counsellor-client alliance

Using regular CORE measures to progress check the work has helped to increase client "buy in" to the work and contributed to the increase in planned endings.

We expect all counsellors to ask for feedback about the opening session. As well as checking out feelings/thoughts and expectations of counselling we ask for specifics about how the initial appointment went for them and their thoughts about having more sessions, exploring any ambivalence. The counsellor–client "fit" is also important taking account of various factors such as gender.

CORE can then build on this. The counsellor and client may look at the summary tracking chart in sessions 2, 3, 4 etc. and collaboratively try to understand the story behind the chart. The greater the number of points on the chart the greater the sense there is of the counselling "journey". What sense can be made of the lines going down (reduction of problems) or up (increase in problems or flat lining – no change)? What is happening with risk?

Whatever the chart shows helps increase awareness. If things are getting better, then "Well done" and "What are you doing to make it better?" (Keep doing those things!) If things are getting worse then it can reinforce the need for the client to take positive action and not ignore problems. With nothing changing – what would need to happen for things to go in a more positive direction? Is counselling helping or not helping right now?

CORE can help as a kind of therapeutic "sat nav" in addition to counsellor experience! In short-term university counselling it is important to find a collaborative focus fairly early on in the work and that can sometimes mean prioritising what is most important to work on right now.

In the United States, over the same period, a group of researchers were exploring the clinical value of monitoring clients' progress using formal outcome measures at every session (Lambert, 2007; Lambert & Shimokawa, 2011). This research indicates that rates of deterioration for clients whose therapists received feedback from session by session monitoring were half of those whose therapists did not. The research suggests that the use of formal feedback tools can help therapists overcome natural limitations in their ability to predict how well clients will do in therapy (Macdonald & Mellor-Clark, 2014). Feedback

> typically involves a client completing a symptom questionnaire prior to, or at the beginning of, every session of therapy. Scores are then plotted on a graph, and progress towards the client goal of symptom reduction is monitored and can be regularly discussed in therapy.
> (Macdonald & Mellor-Clark, 2014, pp. 249–250)

Client progress can be tracked very simply using pen and paper and a simple tracking chart (see Figure 5.1 for an example of a tracking chart).

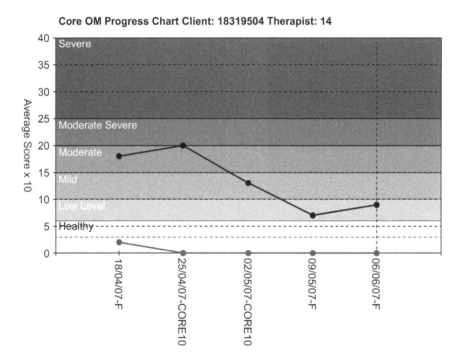

Figure 5.1 CORE progress tracking chart

Source: Reproduced with permission of CORE IMS, Rugby

Benefits and challenges of introducing routine outcome measurement (ROM)

The evidence in favour of establishing routine outcome measurement in psychological therapy services is well documented.

Client benefits

Client benefits include greater client involvement in the progress of therapy and a means of helping them to see that they are making progress, even when change is slight, increasing motivation and hope and strengthening the therapeutic alliance.[6] There is also evidence that for some clients it is easier to communicate sensitive and potentially shameful issues such as risk (Youn *et al.*, 2012).

Crucially, potential exists to improve outcomes for clients: evidence suggests that clients whose therapists receive feedback on their clients' progress using routine outcome measurement are 3.5 times more likely to achieve reliable change than those whose therapists receive no such feedback (Boswell *et al.*, 2013).

Service benefits

Practice-based research using ROM in HE counselling services provides a complementary paradigm to traditional RCTs, allowing empirically-supported treatments to be evaluated in the actual clinical context of higher education.

Data quality is improved as routinely collecting outcome measures at every session means that as long as a client has attended at least two sessions there will be a measured outcome (even though there may be an unplanned ending).

Case study part 7: using CORE measures therapeutically with clients

Most clients like CORE! They may say, "Can I have a copy of my chart as an email attachment or as a print out or can I take a photo on my phone?" They pin the chart on their bedroom wall or show it to their partner, friends or family. Of course this is most likely when positive change is indicated, but "no change" charts can serve as a useful reminder to take positive action. Maybe a client is stuck and not able to get over a relationship break up. No change could represent ruminating and a reminder of the need to make changes as well as grief over the loss.

The visual impact can be powerful and having a copy can serve as a reminder and reinforcement of what helps. Other common reactions are:

1. *"I am doing okay" (at or near the cut-off point between problematic and healthy functioning). Having the concept of a cut-off can be very helpful in looking at*

> *"how am I doing" in relation to what has been shown to be healthy levels of functioning and risk.*
> 2. *"That confirms what I thought"– a visual representation of their sense of change. If however there is a difference between an inner feeling and what CORE shows, this is a focus for discussion.*
> 3. *"Have I really changed that much!" The pleasure of seeing the journey from a) to b) as the client may not always recall how things were when they first started counselling.*

ROM provides a means by which services can actively work to improve outcomes for clients, and also a means by which services can identify the strengths and weaknesses of individual therapists. For too long this has been the elephant in the room and can no longer be ignored. Evidence from practice-based research clearly shows that it is the differences between therapists that are significant, rather than the differences between types of therapy (Barkham *et al.*, 2006, 2008). It is hardly surprising that a study of nearly 700 clinicians indicated that all of them had areas of strengths and weaknesses (Youn *et al.*, 2012). Practice-based evidence allows service managers, supervisors and therapists to undertake practitioner performance and appraisal, although this requires "the same kind of courage that we often see in our clients, to confront important issues rather than finding clever ways of ignoring or avoiding them" (Mothersole, 2006, p. 190). Case study part 9 illustrates how one service approaches this in a positive and collaborative way.

Case study part 8: using data to reflect on individual performance

It is a positive motivational message for the team to see how well we are doing in terms of clinical and reliable change rates and to examine what helps us sustain that as well as making sense of the clients who do not show improvement. This can then help us drill down into individual reflective practice. We do not set individual targets, but CORE provides us with appraisal data relative to both our internal and the HE sector benchmarks. These allow us to explore reasons for variations between therapists, which can then be fed into personal development plans.

Research benefits

Practice-based evidence offers the potential to evidence the effectiveness of a particular treatment or approach with students in a higher education setting, and the therapeutic gains for clients with multiple issues. (Holmqvist *et al.*, 2015).

The CORE HE benchmarks show that students attending HE counselling services are typically recorded as presenting with between two and 10 problems, ranging from Anxiety/Stress (experienced by over 50 per cent of clients) to Psychosis (0.5 per cent).

Practice-based evidence can help to identify therapist variables. HE counselling services typically now have a heterogeneous approach so that the team includes therapists offering a variety of approaches. Moreover, therapists tend to have multiple competencies gained from continuous professional development, and many describe themselves as using an integrative approach. In the CORE HE National Database, integrative work is by far the most commonly used type of therapy (37 per cent), with psychodynamic and person-centred approaches being less than half that at 15 per cent and 13 per cent respectively. A related issue is length of therapist training and experience. In RCTs, experienced therapists are selected with similar levels of training and experience. Real life in a counselling service is not like this. HE counselling services typically require their "core" team to be BACP Accredited (or similar) but also employ sessional staff and unpaid trainees whose levels of training and experience may vary considerably. Interestingly, the few studies that have been done so far often suggest that training and experience is of limited importance (Homqvist *et al.*, 2014).

HE counselling services typically offer short-term interventions and these have been getting shorter over the years as services find creative ways of reducing or eradicating waiting lists while still meeting client needs. The average number of sessions attended per client is around 4.5 (CORE HE National Database), although the range per service will typically be between one and 12 sessions. While some services are refining their contracting with clients and offering single-session work, often many clients who were expected to attend more sessions only attend one and then drop out between assessment and first therapy session. Although it is important for services to be able to keep treatment length down in order to reduce waiting lists, it is also crucial to ensure that clients get enough therapy to make a difference. But how much is enough? Early research on the "optimal dosage" of therapy suggested that there was a direct relationship between the number of sessions and client improvement, i.e. the more sessions a client had, the better their outcome (although the rate of change could be expected to slow once higher numbers of sessions were reached). Further analysis suggested that "14% of clients improved before attending the initial session, 53% were improved following 8 weekly sessions, 75% by 26 sessions, and 83% after 52 sessions" (Lambert, 2013, p. 185). Other studies support the view that clients in treatment tend to make most improvement early in therapy. However, as Lambert points out, the limitation of these studies is that they relied on pre- and post-outcome measure data, rather than session by session ratings, making it difficult to identify the exact time to recovery or improvement for individual clients.

Later studies suggest that there is not a standard "dose" of therapy that is optimal, but that the optimal dose depends on the rate by which individual clients change over the course of their therapy. In other words the speed of recovery determines the number of sessions attended, rather than there being a fixed dose – providing a "good enough" dose of therapy for individual clients (Barkham *et al*., 2006). Moreover, it looks as if equal amounts of change occur over the course of therapy, but at different rates for different clients. So for example, "some clients require only 4 sessions to achieve recovery, and others more than 20" (Lambert, 2013, p. 186). This finding will strike a chord with many counsellors working with students and underlines the importance of not having standard, fixed numbers of sessions offered to every client. As Lambert (2013) points out, this is "akin to establishing a set minimal time to keep a broken leg in a cast, rather than removing the cast when sufficient healing has taken place" (p. 186). Nevertheless services will still have to grapple with the issue of how long to continue treatment when clients have not yet responded, and it may well be appropriate (and ethical) to set limits to that. Interestingly (given the common practice in HE counselling services of offering more widely-spaced sessions over a longer period of time to clients who do not respond to brief work) the evidence suggests that "spaced sessions produce slower recovery", with session frequency having a significant influence on outcomes (Lambert, 2013, p. 186).

A significant benefit of session-by-session measurement is that clients who make gains early on in their counselling can be encouraged to end therapy sooner than planned, thus freeing up space for clients on the waiting list (Lambert, 2013, p. 188). This is also likely to reduce unplanned endings to the benefit of both the client and the service.

The problem of client drop-out has already been noted several times in this chapter. It is a major problem for most psychological therapy services, regardless of sector, and HE services are no exception. Unfortunately drop-out in the HE context is too often seen as an inevitable factor associated with the client group rather than as a serious problem of service quality, which needs to be addressed. As Holmqvist *et al*. (2015) point out, client drop-out is "a large problem both for the individual, for the service, and for society at large" (p. 6). In fact, services are often not aware of the extent of the problem until they start trying to collect outcome data. In the HE sector the average drop-out figure across services (unplanned endings) is around 52 per cent – very similar to that in Primary Care (HE Benchmarks, 2010; Primary Care Benchmarks, 2011). Practice-based evidence offers the opportunity for services to understand the extent of the problem, then identify common features in clients who drop out (e.g. presenting problems, severity levels, therapist, age, gender, etc.) and then consider ways of addressing the issue. Services that have done this demonstrate that it is possible to considerably reduce drop-out rates in this way.

Obstacles to implementing routine outcome measurement in HE Services

Taken alone, each of the benefits described seem to be compelling arguments for why HE counselling services should adopt outcome measurement and preferably feedback informed therapy. Taken together, the evidence seems overwhelming.

However, there are many obstacles and challenges to be faced along the way, and this helps to explain why over the last decade relatively few HE services have moved up the developmental framework I proposed at the beginning of this chapter and also underpins the reluctance of many HE services to engage with the process at all. Recently there have been a number of papers exploring these obstacles and challenges and the following summary is sourced from these (Boswell *et al.*, 2013; Holmqvist *et al.*, 2015; Mellor-Clark *et al.*, 2014). In line with those authors I have divided the obstacles into practical ones and philosophical ones, although in practice they often overlap.

Practical obstacles

Time

Many therapists fear that using routine outcome measures with clients will be a further administrative burden. This is understandable given that counsellors are usually required to complete a range of administrative tasks associated with seeing clients and are often allocated little or no time for these tasks. From a clinical point of view some therapists view time taken in client sessions to complete outcome measures to be an intrusion into the therapeutic space and something that will take up valuable therapy time. In reality, once counsellors start using outcome measures such as CORE in a collaborative, conversational way and make it part of the therapy (as described in our case study) they tend to realise the therapeutic potential of using such a tool. However, it is understandably hard to convince colleagues who have had no experience of using outcome measures. Often, therapists fear that clients will not want to complete outcome measures, and certainly not at every session. Such resistance may be based on the negative experiences of some therapists working in IAPT and AQP (Any Qualified Provider) services where clients are required to complete multiple measures at every session (Griffiths *et al.*, 2013). However there is plenty of evidence to support the view that the skilful introduction of outcome measurement with clients actually helps to improve the therapeutic alliance and that clients often welcome the opportunity to track their progress in this way (Boswell *et al.*, 2013; Holmqvist *et al.*, 2015; Unsworth *et al.*, 2011).

Cost

Cost is another factor that deters some HE counselling services from implementing routine outcome measurement or moving to session by session measurement. While the CORE measures are all "copyleft", i.e. they can be freely downloaded, copied and used as long as they are not altered in any way, a licence for software to fully utilise the data is a significant cost for many services operating on tight budgets in a squeezed financial environment. One of the motivations behind attempts over the years to formalise a Higher Education Practice Research

Network has been the economies of scale that could potentially provide access to sophisticated software for all their members at much reduced cost. Unfortunately this has not yet been possible to achieve for a range of reasons, including lack of funding, the difficulty of releasing busy counselling staff able to lead such a project and the challenges involved in getting HE counselling services to agree on a common data set.

Data quality

Many services that have implemented routine outcome measurement and invested in software to assist the process have been disappointed by the results of their efforts in terms of data quality. Often this only becomes apparent when the service manager needs to produce an annual report and finds that there are significant problems with data quality and completeness. This problem is reflected on a larger scale with the data donated by services for the HE Benchmarking exercise. As has already been noted, many services declined to donate data because they were aware that their data quality was poor; others donated, but there was a large amount of missing data, which hindered the compilation of accurate benchmarks (CORE IMS, 2010). As Mellor-Clark and colleagues (2014) explain in a recent paper, this has led CORE IMS to review their implementation model for services adopting CORE Net. The new implementation model puts more emphasis on helping services prepare for implementation, including establishing the readiness of staff to use routine outcome measurement, and the setting of initial data quality targets with monthly and quarterly reviews in the first couple of years. A re-implementation model is proposed for services already using CORE Net who may be struggling (Mellor-Clark, 2014). HE counselling services already using CORE software, paper forms or other software to collect outcome measure data may wish to review their own progress and reflect on what they have found to be the barriers to success in implementing routine outcome measurement.

Organisational issues

Some HE services want to streamline client management systems at the same time as introducing software for routine outcome measurement. This is understandable given the policy in many universities to reduce the number of databases in use and a growing aspiration among services to reduce or eradicate paper records altogether. CORE Net, although primarily an outcome management system, now also provides many elements of a client management system such as the ability to record client contact details, allowing clients to complete a registration form online, provide an appointment booking system and more. However, while all of this has the potential to streamline and improve administrative functions and potentially save counsellor time, it is challenging for any service to introduce so much change at once. Sometimes the main focus of implementation in the service is on the client management aspects of the task because these seem larger and more daunting, and the outcomes measurement aspect becomes secondary, ultimately affecting data quality.

Philosophical obstacles

As Meyer (2012) points out, for many counsellors outcome measurement is felt to run counter to their values and their belief that much of the value of the work undertaken with clients cannot be measured. A frequently voiced concern is that a single, nomothetic (i.e. a standard set of questions and norm referenced scoring) measure such as CORE, the OQ, TOPS and ORS does not and cannot accurately reflect client outcomes. Of course there is no such thing as a perfect assessment tool and it is important to take into consideration a wide range of sources of information regarding any individual client in the particular context in which the counselling takes place, including the counsellor's clinical judgement (Boswell et al., 2013). The CORE measures, like the OQ, the TOPS and the ORS/SRS, have strengths and weaknesses. For instance, "an intrinsic strength of the CORE-OM is its coverage of a broad scope of symptoms as well as well-being and aspects of social and general functioning together with a robust coverage of risk (to self and to others)" (Holmqvist et al., 2015, p. 8), making it preferable as an outcome measure compared to say the symptom specific PHQ-9 and GAD-7. While the CORE-10 is recommended for use as a session-by-session measure (Barkham et al., 2012), it contains no well-being questions and only one risk item. As Evans (2012) points out, "we need to look carefully at what may be lost when we take measures designed for cross-sectional coverage and psychometrics and use them for sustained, session-by-session intra-individual measurement of change" (p. 133).

Evans's paper (2012) raises a number of other issues and concerns regarding the use of session-by-session measurement, reflecting the kinds of concern that are often expressed by counsellors trained in the psychodynamic and person-centred traditions, especially those used to working longer term with clients. He is concerned that the use of outcome measures may take the place of clinical judgement, "of focusing so heavily on one small source of information that we might throw out the baby, not the bathwater" (p. 133). One way of ensuring that the "nongeralizable individuality" (Evans, 2012, p. 133) of every client is recognised is to combine a traditional nomothetic measure such as CORE or OQ with an ideographic measure that allows clients to identify and track progress on problems/concerns which are unique to them. The Personal Questionnaire (PQ) (CORE IMS, 2013), is an example of an ideographic measure. The principle idea of the PQ is that every client should be rated on his or her own set of problems, as opposed to a predetermined criteria.

Another concern is the suitability of standard outcome measures for some clients, including those with severe and enduring mental health problems, such as Borderline Personality Disorder. A development that has the potential to provide a practical complement to existing feedback systems, especially in work with clients who may be less likely to show empirically meaningful change on mean item or clinical score levels is TRIM: Tracking Responses to Items in Measures (Cross *et al.*, 2014). TRIM has not yet been evaluated in formal research but is already proving of interest to counsellors in HE services seeking an extension to the traditional method of tracking overall scores.

Finally, Evans (2012) raises an interesting methodological issue around using the same measure for use session-by-session as is used for the pre-post outcome measure. He argues that an independent outcome measure should be administered pre- and post-therapy, in order to ensure that the findings cannot be explained by other factors.

Conclusions

Routine outcome measurement is an established and appropriate way for individual clinicians and services to evaluate their work and demonstrate that they are doing the best for clients. It is particularly important in HE short-term work where there is a need to be able to demonstrate to stakeholders the value of counselling and allow comparison with other providers, e.g. EAPs. There is no doubt that, whatever its shortcomings, practice-based evidence will continue to complement evidence from RCTs as well as other kinds of evidence, including qualitative studies. Generic measures such as CORE can be supplemented by sector specific measures such as the CIAO and by ideographic measures such as the PQ, thus ensuring that both the individual client and the context are sufficiently honoured and accounted for.

HE counselling services may wish to reflect on the stage they have reached in terms of the developmental model described here and what their next steps could be. For the sector as a whole there is the ongoing challenge of how best to collaborate in order to maximise the benefits of practice-based research. At present, the aim of an HE Practice Research Network becoming a formal reality is some way off, but still provides the best long-term solution to ensuring a robust evidence base for student counselling.

Abbreviations used in the text are outlined in the following box.

Box 5.1 Abbreviations used in chapter

AQP	Any Qualified Provider
AUCC	Association for University and College Counselling
BACP	British Association for Counselling and Psychotherapy
CBT	Cognitive Behavioural Therapy
CIAO	Counselling Impact on Academic Outcomes
CORE	Clinical Outcomes in Routine Evaluation

DNA	Did Not Attend
EAP	Employee Assistance Programme
EST	Empirically Supported Therapy
GAD-7	Generalised Anxiety Disorder
IAPT	Improving Access to Psychological Therapy
OM	Outcome Measure
OQ	Outcome Questionnaire
ORS	Outcome Rating Scale
PCOMS	Partners for Change Outcome Management System
PHQ-9	Patient Health Questionnaire
PQ	Personal Questionnaire
PRN	Practice Research Network
RCT	Randomised Control Trial
ROM	Routine Outcome Measurement
SFA	Short Form A
SFB	Short Form B
SRS	Session Rating Scale
TOP	Treatment Outcome Package
TRIM	Tracking Responses to Items in Measures

Notes

1 Case study kindly supplied by Trevor Butlin, Team Leader for Counselling and Well-Being, De Montfort University, Leicester.
2 Formerly AUCC – Association of University and College Counselling.
3 For a thorough account of the pros and cons of RCTs and evidence-based practice see Green and Latchford (2012).
4 Readers should note that these benchmarks are based on data from services mostly collecting outcome measures at pre- and post- only, not session-by-session.
5 See case study part 8 for examples of this in practice.

References

BACP (n.d.) *Impact Evaluation Tool (CIAO).* Available from: www.bacpuc.org.uk/research_tool_t.php (accessed 24th November 2014).
BACP (n.d.) *UC Annual Survey.* Available from: www.bacpuc.org.uk/research_survey_t.php (accessed 28th October 2014).
BACP (2012) *The Impact of Counselling in Further and Higher Education. Briefing on Recent Research Finds,* Lutterworth, BACP.
Barkham, B., Bewick, B., Mullin, T., Gilbody, S., Connell, J., Cahill, J., Mellor-Clark, J., Richards, D., Unsworth, G. & Evans, C. (2012) The CORE-10: A short measure of psychological distress for routine use in the psychological therapies. *Counselling and*

Psychotherapy Research: Linking Research with Practice, DOI:10.1080/14733145.20 12.729069.

Barkham, M., Stiles W., Lambert, M. J. & Mellor-Clark, J. (2010) Building a Rigorous and Relevant Knowledge Base for the Psychological Therapies, in *Developing and Delivering Practice-Based Evidence*, Chichester, John Wiley & Sons.

Barkham, M., Connell, J., Stiles, W. B., Miles, J. N. V., Margison, J., Evans, C. & Mellor-Clark, J. (2006). Dose-effect relations and responsive regulation of treatment duration: the good enough level. *Journal of Consulting and Clinical Psychology*, 74 (1), 160–167.

Boswell, J. F., Draus, D., Miller, S. & Lambert, M. (2013) Implementing routine outcome monitoring in clinical practice: Benefits, challenges and solutions. *Psychotherapy Research*, DOI: 10.1080/10503307.2013.817696.

Connell, J., Cahill, J., Barkham, M., Gilbody, S. & Madill, A. (2006) *A Systematic Scoping Review of the Research on Counselling in Higher and Further Education*, BACP, Rugby.

CORE IMS (2010) *Benchmarks for higher education counselling services*. Available from: www.coreims.co.uk/Support_User_Benchmarking.html, (accessed 24th November 2014).

CORE IMS (2011) *Benchmarks for primary care counselling services*. Available from: www.coreims.co.uk/Support_User_Benchmarking.html (accessed 24th November 2014).

CORE IMS (2013) *Personal Questionnaire (Information Sheet)*, Rugby, CORE IMS.

Cross, S., Mellor-Clark, J. & Macdonald, J. (2014) Tracking responses to items in measures as a means of increasing therapeutic engagement in clients: A complementary clinical approach to tracking outcomes. *Clinical Psychology & Psychotherapy*, DOI:10.1002/cpp.1929.

Evans C. (2012) Cautionary notes on power steering for psychotherapy. *Canadian Psychology*, DOI: 10.1037/a0027951.

Evans, C., Mellor-Clark, J., Margison, F., Barkham, M., McGrath, G., Connell, J. & Audin, K. (2000) Clinical outcomes in routine evaluation: The CORE-OM. *Journal of Mental Health*, 9, 247–255.

Green, D. & Latchford, G. (2012) *Maximising the Benefits of Psychotherapy*, Chichester, John Wiley & Sons.

Griffiths, S., Foster, J., Steen, S. & Pietroni, P. (2013) *Mental Health's Market Experiment: Commissioning Psychological Therapies through Any Qualified Provider*, Chester, Centre for Psychological Therapies in Primary Care.

Holmqvist, R., Philips, B. & Barkham, M. (2015) Developing practice-based evidence: Benefits, challenges, and tensions. *Psychotherapy Research*, 25 (1), 20–31.

Lambert, M. (2007) Presidential address: What we have learned from a decade of research aimed at improving psychotherapy outcome in routine care. *Psychotherapy Research*, 17 (1), 1–14.

Lambert, M. (2010) *Prevention of Treatment Failure: The Use of Measuring, Monitoring, and Feedback in Clinical Practice*, Washington, DC, APA.

Lambert, M. (2013) The Efficacy and Effectiveness of Psychotherapy, in E. Bergin and S. Garfield (Eds) *Handbook of Psychotherapy and Behaviour Change*, New Jersey, John Wiley.

Lambert, M. J. & Shimokawa, K. (2011). Collecting Client Feedback, In Norcross, J. C. (Ed) *Psychotherapy Relationships That Work (2nd Edition)*. New York, Oxford University Press.

Lambert, M. J, Hansen, N. B & Harmon S. C. (2010) Outcome Questionnaire System (The OQ System): Development and Practical Applications in Healthcare Settings, in Barkham, M., Hardy, G. E. and Mellor-Clark, J. (Eds) *Developing and Delivering Practice-Based Evidence*, London, Wiley-Blackwell.

Macdonald, J. & Mellor-Clark, J. (2014) Correcting psychotherapists' blindsidedness: Formal Feedback as a means of overcoming the natural limitations of therapists. *Clinical Psychology and Psychotherapy*, DOI:10.1002/cpp.1887.

Mellor-Clark, J. & Barkham, M. (2006) The CORE System: Developing and Delivery. Practice-based Evidence through Quality Evaluation, in Feltham, C. and Horton, I. (Eds) *The Handbook of Counselling and Psychotherapy (2nd Edition),* London, Sage.

Mellor-Clark, J., Barkham, M., Connell, J. & Evans, C. (1999). Practice-based evidence and need for a standardised evaluation system: Informing the design of the CORE system. *European Journal of Psychotherapy, Counselling & Health*, 2, 357–374.

Mellor-Clark, J., Cross, M A., Macdonald, J. & Skulsvik T. (2014) Leading horses to water: Lessons from a decade of helping psychological services use routine outcome measurement to improve practice. *Administration and Policy in Mental Health and Mental Health Services*, DOI: 10.1007/s10488-014-0587-8.

Meyer, D. (2012) Building evidence that counts. *AUCC Journal*, November pp. 31–34.

Mothersole, G. (2006) The use of CORE System data to inform and develop practitioner performance assessment and appraisal: An experiential account. *European Journal of Psychotherapy and Counselling*, 8 (2), 177–191.

National Committee of Inquiry into Higher Education: Chairman Sir Ron Dearing (1997) *Higher Education in the Learning Society*, London, HMSO.

Parker, L. (1999) Evaluation of Clinical Counselling in Educational Settings: Preparing for the Future, in Lees, J. and Vaspe, A. (Eds) *Clinical Counselling in Further and Higher Education*, London and New York, Routledge.

Parry, G., Castonguay, L. G., Barkovek, T. D. F. & Wolf, A. W. (2010) Practice Research Networks and Psychological Services Research in the UK and USA, in Barkham, M., Hardy, G. E. and Mellor-Clark, J. *Developing and Delivering Practice-Based Evidence,* London, Wiley-Blackwell.

Rickinson, B. (1997). Evaluating the effectiveness of counselling intervention with final year undergraduates. *Counselling Psychology Quarterly*, 10 (3), 271–285.

Smith, E. (1999) No Client (and No Counsellor) Is an Island: Attending to the Culture of the Educational Setting, in Lees, J. and Vaspe A. *Clinical Counselling in Further and Higher Education*, London, Routledge.

Twigg, E. (2012) *A study of excellence: Use of the CORE System in My Sister's Place Counselling Service. CORE IMS.* Available from: www.coreims.co.uk/site_downloads/MSP_study_of_excellence.pdf (accessed 27th October 2014).

Unsworth, G., Cowie, H. & Green, A. (2011) Therapists' and clients' perceptions of routine outcome measurement in the NHS: A qualitative study. *Counselling and Psychotherapy Research: Linking Research to Practice*, DOI: 10.1080/14733145.2011.565125.

Youn, S. J., Kraus, D. R. & Castonguay, L. G. (2012) The Treatment Outcome Package: Facilitating practice and clinically relevant research. *Psychotherapy*, 49, 115–122.

Chapter 6

The Cardiff Model of short-term engagement

John Cowley and Vicky Groves

Until 2006, the counselling service at Cardiff University was typical of most, providing an average of four or five sessions for clients. We were constantly wrestling with heavy demand, and decisions about how soon after May we would write to students apologising that they may not be seen until September and perhaps suggesting they contact their home GP to ask for support over the summer. An ongoing task for any head of counselling service is managing a waiting list in a safe and timely manner. The Heads of University Counselling (HUCS) mail base revisits this question on a regular basis. Heads of service rarely have the luxury of time to carefully think about how to most effectively deliver services in a significantly different way. Even if one is lucky enough to have additional resources granted, the pragmatic solution is to quickly replicate existing processes. Clients get seen, which is key, and the intention is always to "think about changes in the summer" as a way of postponing a thorough review of service provision.

In 2006 a number of circumstances coalesced, both internal and external, prompting the service at Cardiff to pause and reflect carefully on whether there was a better way to deliver services that were more equitable and in a more targeted way. Until then, students were seen and prioritised according to perceived risk. High-risk clients took a disproportionate amount of counselling hours while students at high risk of failing their studies and not fulfilling their career ambitions remained in limbo on ever lengthening waiting lists. One group was at risk of failing because of their mental health issues, the other at risk because of anxiety about speaking in seminars. The common problem was that they were both at risk of failing, albeit by different means.

A chance training event by the university solicitors on the subject of duty of care was the catalyst for considering a more planned and potentially radical departure from what already existed. Like many other services over the years we had been increasingly drawn into, and to a certain extent were colluding with, the lack of availability of talking therapies in the NHS. In addition, counsellors often express enjoyment of longer-term work. In 2006, counsellors were suspicious of the value and desirability of brief interventions. This was perhaps a legacy of so many being in private practice. It was common to hear counsellors say: "I enjoy long-term therapy with clients." It was, however, rare to hear clients in HE say:

"I want to be in therapy for a long time." We needed to ask: "Whose needs are being met?"

Explicit in the solicitors' presentation was the idea that counselling services existed to provide an educational service as opposed to providing what should rightfully be catered for by the NHS. Faced with the prospect of once again seeking additional resource funding and recognising the uncomfortable feelings about "begging" for more and getting only limited funds, we resolved to take a more planned approach to any future request. Reviewing what we were doing thoroughly and systematically was essential. If it proved to be the most effective way of delivering services, then so be it. If there was a different way then we could explore it and weigh the risks and opportunities against the established conventional wisdom.

A small group of senior counselling colleagues were asked to meet monthly during the academic year to explore the brief: "If you were to begin to design an effective counselling service in HE to provide students with an educational service what would that look like?" No constraints were placed on the group's thinking and for the most part the head of service opted to remain uninvolved in the research and discussion for the first six months other than to receive updates and be involved when requested. The rationale for this approach was primarily recognising that predominant "group thinking" of other heads of services could restrict creativity in the early stages of the project.

The intellectual challenge of focused reflection on current practice and the prospect of designing a new model of delivery was professionally exciting for the counselling team. From the perspective of a service head it was essential to know if there was a different and more helpful way to deliver services that both the client and the university valued.

Along with the original brief the project team was also asked to review all aspects of the existing service, focusing specifically on the questions: "Are we relevant?" and "Are we research-based?" If changes were to be introduced, the project team was instructed to develop a variety of approaches that counsellors in the team could choose from, rather than to produce a prescriptive model.

In the existing service, there was inconsistency in the length of support offered to students: long-term therapy was offered by some members of the counselling team, and a briefer model provided by others. This inconsistency was due to staff not having an awareness of, or a sense of responsibility for, the waiting list. The bulk of responsibility for managing the waiting lists was left to support staff, who carried the additional weight of also managing risky clients. The project team agreed that this seemed neither equitable for clients, nor appropriate for support staff.

Based on the message from the university solicitor and the head of the service about duty of care, the project team's starting point was to re-think the service's primary task as a counselling service within a university. This led to agreement that the emphasis for the service should be to focus on enabling students to study effectively, to enhance the educational objectives of the individual and the institution, rather than providing therapy for self-development or as ongoing support throughout a student's university journey.

The primary task statement became: "Our core business is to provide equal access to counselling services, thereby enabling our clients to be free enough from psychological distress to maximise their potential for successful study or work."

With the focus clearly mapped out, the project team drew up several "Ideal World Wish Lists" – for the service, the client and the wider university. These wish lists became the guidelines, and were referred to frequently throughout the project.

Wish list for the service

The project team's ultimate wish was expressed as "Could we dare to dream of not having a waiting list?" This seemed impossible, when students were currently being told they might not be seen within the current academic year if they applied for support after the Easter recess.

The project team felt that the service's therapists needed to carry the burden of waiting list management and that they should also be responsible for risk management among clients, moving these responsibilities away from the support team to appropriately qualified staff.

The project team wanted to know if it was possible to make good use of resources and psycho-education in both individual sessions and in workshop format, whether these approaches would provide a valuable support, and/or be enough input for some individuals with milder presenting difficulties. In 2003, Neil Frude founded the "Book Prescription Scheme" for mild to moderate mental health difficulties, which went on to become a joint project between the local NHS Psychology Department and Cardiff County Council. Thirty-five well-known self-help books, covering many difficulties, were made available in every community-based library, and a "Book Prescription Pack" was made available to psychologists, GPs and counsellors/therapists. The scheme was developed as a cost-effective way of getting low-intensity treatment to individuals with mild difficulties, and has now been duplicated in many cities across the UK.

While it is acknowledged that further research is needed on psycho-education's effectiveness, Lukens and McFarlane concluded that these approaches could be successful when used either as primary or adjunctive treatment: "as part of a strategic program for prevention, or as an experiential training tool for patients and their families in a range of settings" (2004, p. 221). The project team was therefore hopeful that an increase in self-help and guided self-help materials would support the service's students.

It was felt that, while the current service contributed to some students staying at university, an improved service could contribute more to student retention and also help students study more effectively, whilst improving students' employability. This improved service needed to be "fit-for-purpose", current and prospective. It also needed to be future-proof; able to respond to changing needs of individuals and, potentially, to influence the shape of services to come.

Wish list for the client

The project team's aspiration was, again, focused around reducing waiting times and meeting a commitment to offer all students access to a prompt, reliable and equitable service, including providing the same number of sessions to each individual. In addition, the project team was keen to explore whether it was possible to offer a greater variety of therapeutic approaches, giving the client choices in their therapy.

Wish list for the university

It was recognised that lengthy waiting lists in the current service were pushing the stresses of managing distressed students back to tutors and academic schools. The project team was committed to working to prevent this, and to reducing staff anxieties about supporting distressed students. This meant striving to strike a delicate balance: providing scope in the service to offer something immediate, but at the same time avoiding the (false) impression of the service as an emergency service for the university. Caleb (2014) states, . . . "it is not the role of university wellbeing services, however excellent, to replace the specialised care that the NHS should provide to students with mental illnesses".

With the aspirations of the project team clearly defined for the service, the client and the university, and the new direction promoted by the "primary task" statement in mind, the "Cardiff Model" was formed: a stepped care framework advocating equality of access.

The Cardiff Model

The Cardiff Model comprises an initial 90-minute "therapeutic consultation" (TC), a 15-minute follow-up appointment four weeks later and the opportunity of some brief ongoing 50-minute counselling sessions thereafter. The decision was made to use Solution-Focused brief therapy (SFBT) techniques as much as possible during the TC with the therapists drawing on their own theoretical approach for ongoing counselling. Counsellors would explore difficulties with clients in a 90-minute session, and then work together to identify strategies for making improvements, drawing on the client's inner strengths and resources, and providing self-help resources for clients to take away and try out in their own time. A brief "Follow-Up" appointment would be offered four weeks later as an opportunity for checking on progress made, and evaluating the success (or not) of the strategies, tools and resources given. If further support was needed, further counselling sessions would be available: four sessions would be offered as standard, but these could increase to up to ten in exceptional circumstances.

Solution-Focused Brief Therapy emerged in the 1980s as a forward-thinking, future-oriented, goal-based therapy focusing on solutions, rather than the development of problems, i.e. focusing on if and when the problem does not occur, or occurs less frequently (Berg & De Shazer, 1993). It emphasised the importance of building solutions rather than solving problems: "As client and therapist talk more and more about the solution they want to construct together, they come to believe in the truth or reality of what they are talking about" (ibid, p. 9).

The Cardiff Model consequently incorporates SFBT tools in the 90-minute consultation appointment, aiming to promote the understanding that a single session is enough for some people.

The project team acknowledged that SFBT would not be right for all clients, and were keen to embrace this by incorporating the possibility of brief ongoing sessions, utilising therapists' own core modality, to those needing more support. It was clear early on in the development of the model, taking into account the existing economy, that it would not be viable to offer long-term therapy to clients. Caleb (2014) states that "most services have to restrict what they offer to individual students so that they can support the high number that need them".

In order to offer equality of access (every student having the opportunity of some sessions, and the same number of sessions), the direction of the service had to move from the previous long-term counselling that had sometimes been offered, towards brief therapy. The project team's definition and understanding of this was "a defined number of sessions that are . . . focused in a purposeful way" (Wells & Giannetti, 1993) and guided by the premise that "change is possible". The aim was to empower clients, moving them out of feeling stuck in a problem or situation, into a direction of finding solutions, and using available resources in the most effective way possible.

McKeel (1996) suggests that

> brief therapy is an effective approach for most clients, including clients with severe and chronic problems. Studies comparing brief therapies with longer-term therapies show no difference in success rates between the two approaches.

While working at Cardiff, Dubrow-Marshall compared outcomes for clients who received short-term brief therapy (one 90-minute therapeutic consultation, plus four ongoing 50-minute sessions) and those who received a single 90-minute session incorporating solution-focused techniques, and concluded that there was no marked difference in positive outcomes between groups (Dubrow-Marshall, 2009).

While the premise for the model was the idea that single-session or short-term brief work could be "enough", it was agreed that "chunking" would also be supported: clients re-entering the service some time later, having consolidated/processed the therapy and steps they achieved in their previous session/s, for some further brief ongoing work.

The Cardiff Model, by its own design, aims to eliminate lengthy waiting lists. It seeks to empower clients to make significant and meaningful changes with limited interventions, thereby making good use of clients' own internal resources.

Prior to accessing "formal" support, students can be directed to attend a widely promoted daily drop-in service, offering a brief (10–15 minute) meeting with a therapist to gain a coping mechanism, ask a question, take away a self-help resource and/or be sign-posted to appropriate further services. In this way, the Cardiff Model provides a forward-thinking stepped care service for students, offering choice.

Development of the model

With the Cardiff Model guiding a new understanding of the role of counsellors in the service, the project team felt it important to share the primary task statement with the counselling team early in the model development process, to stimulate thinking about the role each counsellor could play in championing equality of access and consistency of service, and about offering the same number of sessions to all. If individual counsellors chose to form their own waiting lists comprised of the clients they assessed, then they would own responsibility for managing these.

The project team felt it to be imperative that all the counselling team were involved in the design and background to the model, not least because some therapists previously offered long-term support and preferred to work in this way. At the same time, the team was conscious that it would be important to provide SFBT training for staff, so that counsellors used SFBT as much as possible in the TC with an acknowledgement that the aim of this was to expand the individuals' repertoire of tools, rather than an aim to change therapists' theoretical backgrounds and counselling philosophies.

Support staff, too, would need to have a voice and input into the development of the model, particularly as any changes would potentially impact considerably on the 'back shop' running of the service.

The project team set up one-to-one meetings with all staff, as well as an away-day at the end of the project, where all members of the counselling team were asked to offer their views on whether or not to instigate the various potential new steps:

- therapeutic online self-referral tool
- therapeutic consultation
- psycho-educational tools
- follow-up appointment
- brief ongoing therapy
- daily drop-in service.

Staff were asked to vote on whether to initiate all of these new steps, or just some of them. The full team consensus was to try all of the steps, with a reassurance from the head of counselling – "If it doesn't work we can always go back to the old model".

The project took place over one academic year and, during this time, the project team reviewed and visited other university and Primary Healthcare Therapy services, including a Primary Care Service in Birmingham that was, at the time, employing a "Two plus One" model (Barkham, 1989). The project team also reviewed the available literature on single-session therapy, and the work of Talmon (1990, 1991) became pivotal to the development and structure of the model.

Talmon (1990) states that

> one session is enough for 78% of clients; those with specific problems, those needing reassurance about their reactions to troubling situations, and those stuck in a strong reaction to past events or needing support to deal with a life problem
>
> (p. 31)

Talmon (1991) and his colleagues contacted a sample group of 200 of clients who DNAd their second appointment and found, to their surprise, that the stated reason for not attending was that one session had been enough. Many of the clients contacted talked at length about how helpful and fundamental in producing change their single session had been.

This led the project team at Cardiff to opt for a 90-minute therapeutic consultation as the first step in the model, with the view that this might be enough for many clients.

Talmon (1990) describes routinely contacting clients by telephone prior to the first meeting:

> The pre session conversation and the time between the initial call and first session are important parts of single session therapy.
>
> (p. 18)

His research demonstrated that clients who were offered emergency appointments with a quick turn-around had a high DNA rate, whereas those clients who waited "usually 2–3 weeks after the call" (p. 18) for an appointment were more likely to improve; in fact, up to a third no longer needed an appointment.

The project team at Cardiff knew from experience that trying to contact students to book appointments via telephone was not viable: busy, active student lives meant that individuals were invariably in lectures, unavailable or out with friends and unable to talk when phone calls were made. As a result, the decision was taken to create online documentation as part of the Cardiff Model: an online self-referral form, which would be intended to help individuals to focus on their reason/s for applying for counselling, and to think about the ways in which they were currently managing their difficulties. Solution-focused questions would help clients to look at coping skills and also to take responsibility for the focus of their therapy, encouraging motivation for change and preparing individuals for change.

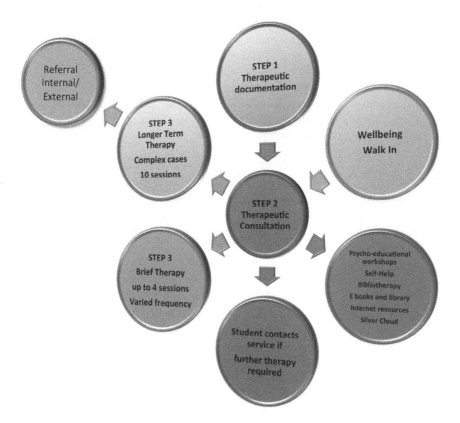

Figure 6.1 The Cardiff Model

Step 1: therapeutic documentation

All clients contact the service by completing the therapeutic online self-referral form. Once submitted, this is read by a member of the counselling team and the client is scheduled for a 90-minute TC within two to three weeks. If risk is indicated, the client is contacted on the day of receipt of the referral, and risk factors are explored.

Just as Talmon's phone calls had helped many of his clients (one third) to improve, so too did the use of therapeutic documentation trialled by the counselling team in Cardiff. It was found that a significant number of clients would contact the service to cancel booked appointments the day before a session was scheduled to happen or on the day of the appointment itself, declining further input or a face-to-face appointment, stating that completing the self-referral form had helped in itself.

Research was subsequently carried out in the form of electronic questionnaires, asking students why they had not taken up the offer of one or more counselling appointments. The most recent data (2013) indicates that 26 per cent of those who applied for support and then declined appointments did so because they felt sufficiently helped by completing the self-referral questionnaire.

This knowledge – that the gap between a client submitting their documentation and having their first appointment could induce change – was incorporated into the Cardiff Model insofar as the TC is offered two to three weeks after receipt of the referral; this gap is purposeful.

Step 2: therapeutic consultation

A TC of 90 minutes duration is offered either face to face or online. As this may be the only session the client needs or wants, the aim was to offer a meaningful length of time to combine an assessment and a therapy session.

Dubrow-Marshall states that

> another important change in perspective offered by Talmon was that the first session did not only have to be an intake session with an emphasis on assessment, but that substantial change could be promoted from the outset.
>
> (2009, p. 3)

Taking this information forward, the project team decided to combine the 30 minutes we had previously used as an assessment with a therapy hour. This established 90 minutes as the length of a TC, giving the client a meaningful amount of time in order to absorb that change was possible for them.

This 90-minute appointment has proved sufficient time for building a strong therapeutic alliance between therapists and clients. The counselling team were in no doubt that Carl Rogers' fundamental "Core Conditions" of congruence, unconditional positive regard and empathy were necessary and important to the development of the therapeutic relationship. Indeed, when discussing this, McCanny (2009) quotes Carl Rogers, stating that

> little change could take place until the client felt that the counsellor had their best interests at heart and felt understood and believed.

However, the power of SFBT in rapidly building a powerful, trusting, working relationship during just one session lies in celebrating each individual client's internal resources, their strengths and abilities and helping them to further recognise and develop those abilities. McKeel (1996) sums this up when he states:

> Studies of the perceptions of clients highlight the importance of therapists' relationship with their clients and that SFBT is successful when it is both solution-oriented and client-oriented.

During the TC the counsellor utilises solution-focused techniques and the intent is for the client to leave the session with a collaboratively-formed goal and strategies or tasks to perform, which will help them work towards attaining that goal.

However, after utilising a model of post-TC follow-ups for four years, the decision was taken to discontinue this step, after discovering that it yielded the highest rate of DNAs of all the steps in the model. Research undertaken (all clients who DNAd over the course of one academic year were contacted) revealed that one session had been enough for the majority (75 per cent) of those students and, when questioned about what had led them not to attend, several made comments to the effect of not wanting to waste either their time or our time by coming in when all was well, indicating that one session had been sufficient for their needs.

It therefore seemed appropriate to amend the original model; to stop scheduling 15-minute follow-up sessions after four weeks and to leave it in the hands of the client themselves to make contact if they required further input. It was anticipated that this would also further empower clients to make decisions about their care.

The amended model, therefore, asks clients to get in touch by an agreed "next contact date" (usually four weeks) following their TC, to advise if they require further input from the service for a follow-up session. The purpose for this gap is to give students the opportunity to incorporate suggestions from the TC, to try out agreed strategies, to monitor mood and functioning and then to decide whether the TC was sufficient input, or whether further support is required.

It felt important that, within the 90 minute TC session, therapists would hold in mind a notion that "This might be the only time I meet this client; this might be all the input they need". This influences both the therapist and client to maximise the use of every moment spent together, resulting in a truly "active" session, with both parties working hard. Counsellors are also encouraged to work with clients in the TC to instil the idea that "change is possible".

The project team agreed that, at the start of a TC, the Clinical Outcomes in Routine Evaluation (CORE) (Barkham, 2007) questionnaire should be completed and reviewed, to get a picture of where the client was "starting from". As this measure is problem-orientated, the guidance from SFBT training was that, after review, the questionnaire then be put aside, to reflect a purposeful move from problem-oriented to solution-orientated work.

The project team decided that the CORE measure should be followed with a question about any "pre-session" change – i.e. looking with the client at any changes that had happened *since* submitting their self-referral form, writing about their difficulties and becoming more focused on what they are bringing to counselling.

In his 2007 paper, George outlines four basic areas for use in SFBT:

- What does the client want?
- What is the client already doing that is useful?
- How will the client know that she/he has got it?
- Watch out for more: Goals/Homework/Experiments.

The project team at Cardiff designed the 'main body' of the TC around these questions.

What does the client want?

Bakker *et al.* (2010) describe goal setting as a fundamental part of the first session:

> During the first conversation the client is asked to state their goal in positive, concrete and achievable behavioural terms: 'What needs to come out of this therapy? What do you want instead of your problem?' They may also be asked, 'What are your best hopes'?
>
> (p. 297)

When creating the model, the project team was aware of the importance of any (collaboratively-set) goals being realistic and achievable, and therapists were encouraged to set small goals or to break down one goal into "climbable steps", which clients could progress towards.

It was observed that individual climbable steps could often be collaboratively identified by asking clients a "Miracle Question" during the TC, e.g. "Imagine that tonight, while you are asleep, a miracle happens and the problem that brought you here today is resolved". The therapist then asks: "What would you notice when you woke up? What would be different that tells you the miracle has happened?", and then continues to build up a picture by using further sequential questions: "and then . . . ?"; " . . . and what next . . . ?"

The project team identified that by working through the miracle question, the client's goals would often become clearer and better understood, and that this process would also often highlight steps the client had already started to make toward their goals.

George *et al.* (2006) state, "the answers to the miracle sequence . . . have a therapeutic value in themselves" (p. 26).

The next question is linked to this.

What is the client already doing that is useful?

Having written about their difficulties and the way they are managing, clients may well have started trying alternate ways of coping or problem solving. Looking for exceptions can be useful here. In his paper, George (2007) talks about this being appropriate for clients who are problem oriented; when the problem occurs less frequently or doesn't occur or "impacts on the client's life less despite happening" (ibid, p. 4).

McKeel (1996) states that

> exception questions typically prompt clients to talk about exceptions and improvements regarding their problems.

How will the client know that she/he has got what she wants?

The focus here is on what the client will be doing differently once the problem/ difficulty is overcome, or when it is managed differently. Often the "Miracle Question" and asking clients to think about their "preferred future" will inform this.

Watch out for more: Goals/Homework/Experiments assigned by the client

The client is encouraged to watch for times when they are able to manage their difficulty or when it doesn't occur.

The project team anticipated that, when clients were asked to talk about their "preferred future", they would begin to set their own goals and, therefore, their homework would develop, organically, from this.

While it is recognised that this is very different from homework-setting within, for example, CBT, where the therapist would be very active and instructive in setting tasks, the project team hypothesised that the value would be similarly high.

Other SFBT techniques are also encouraged during the TC, as appropriate, for example:

- **Scaling questions:** providing the therapist and client with a framework to measure any improvement/s. For example, asking a client to rank on a scale of 0–10 (where 0 is "No difficulty" and 10 is "Difficulty at its worst") "What number are you at today?" can help clients to acknowledge their resources, notice when change occurs and identify how they themselves helped things to improve.

  Clients can also use scaling outside of therapy, to measure subjectively how things are improving; for example, "If my mood is 6 right now, what can I do to move it to 5?"
- **Coping questions:** acknowledging how clients are coping and managing, showing empathy and highlighting what clients are achieving. George (2007) discusses how it is important to acknowledge what the client has already tried. Talmon (1990) also describes how the main goal of therapy is to "help people help themselves" (p. 60). The project team wanted to promote this goal by incorporating various self-help and guided self-help packages into the service, offering psycho-educational material, online programmes, a library of books and e-books to lend to students and by purchasing computer-based therapeutic programmes such as *SilverCloud* (2014) – an online support service providing opportunities for students to access support out of hours in the privacy of their own homes.

  At the end of the TC it is intended that clients leave with collaboratively-planned and clearly-defined goals. Each client is asked how long he/she feels it will take to complete their chosen task(s) and a "next contact date" is booked for the client to get in touch with the service to advise whether they will require further input from the Service (in the form or brief ongoing counselling) or not.

Step 3: ongoing brief therapy

For those clients requiring ongoing therapy, therapists utilising their own therapeutic approach have the flexibility to offer up to four 50-minute sessions. On rare occasions (and with supervisory input), this can be increased to a 10-session maximum.

The counselling team were keen to offer choice to clients about the frequency of their ongoing sessions, by asking at the end of a session: "How long would you like to try out the tasks we've agreed / give those ideas more thought?" The aim was to give clients both ownership and autonomy.

It is interesting to note that the majority of students opt for fortnightly sessions, or even for appointments once every three weeks. Contrary to the popular belief that a lack of fixed frequency, or a frequency of less than once per week, may interfere with the quality of the therapeutic relationship between counsellor and client, the project team was convinced that this flexibility actually gave clients ownership of their therapy and in fact could strengthen the therapeutic relationship.

Feedback and outcomes

Each step of the Cardiff Model has been researched continuously since its creation, by routinely asking students for feedback and by comparing pre- and post-CORE outcome measures.

The Cardiff team's findings vary (dependent on the counsellor) with between 49 per cent and 58 per cent of clients attending a single session, similar to that of a 2008 study on Single Session Therapy (SST) by Perkins and Scarlett, who report that "about 60% made significant clinical improvement after one session of therapy" (p. 154). Importantly, the study also reported that changes made were sustained – i.e. changes were not short-lived: "benefits of SST were maintained 18 months after the initial consultation" (ibid, p. 154).

Case study: when single session therapy is all a client may need

Mia is a first year student attending therapy for the first time. Responding to the therapeutic documentation question: "What brings you to therapy now?" Mia writes that she is anxious most of the time and is missing lectures and finding it difficult to sleep. Her self-referral form reveals that she has a good support network: flatmates, friends and parents who try to help and with whom she regularly talks about her problems. She has no current or previous suicidal ideation, and she has not sought help for her difficulty from a GP.

Beginning of the session

Mia hands Sue, the therapist, the CORE-10 form, completed in the waiting room. Sue reviews the form, noting each individual score that is high, i.e. scored 3 or above, and the total score of 35 out of a possible 40, indicative of a severe difficulty.

Mia feels that anxiety is taking over all aspects of her life and affecting her daily routine. She explains that she has always been "prone to anxiety" but describes that her symptoms have been exacerbated significantly recently. The trigger for this seems to have been a meeting between Mia and her tutor, and specifically a conversation in which her tutor told Mia that she had high expectations for her achieving a good degree.

When looking for any pre-session change it is difficult for Mia to see that anything has altered; she feels very "stuck" in her problem.

"I usually spend hours working on my essays but I feel 'frozen', like nothing will be good enough for my tutor."[1]

Mia's best hope for the counselling session ("What does the client want?") is to leave feeling that she has something to try. In the longer term, she describes hoping that her anxiety will reduce.

Responding to the "How will the client know she/he has got it?" question, Mia can see some of her "preferred future": she will be sleeping for a full night, she will attend all of her lectures and she will be able to focus and concentrate on her studies again.

Introducing "scaling" reveals that Mia could not feel much worse than presently; rating herself 9 out of 10 in terms of her difficulty and stating that she doesn't think she should stay at university and that she is "letting everybody down".

Using coping questions and looking for exceptions, Sue asks Mia how she has been managing her symptoms so far, to gain an understanding of what she has found that helps her to manage and to identify times when her anxiety is less severe. Mia reveals that she is finding as many tasks as possible that keep her busy and away from thinking about university work; she is going out with her friends, shopping in town, cleaning her bedroom or cooking for her flatmates.

Mia is confused when Sue pays her a compliment, and offers a reframing of the situation by saying:

"You have shown real strength Mia. Despite feeling very down, you have managed to keep busy and active. I am hopeful that we can work together to tap into and re-direct some of that strength."

Sue introduces the "Miracle Question", and Mia immediately visualises her preferred future: working and studying hard, and eventually achieving a "good" degree. Sue then highlights the similarity between this preferred future and the tutor's comment, and Mia starts to giggle. She acknowledges that if she could "calm the worry thoughts" down, she probably "wouldn't get so worked up".

This is a self-identified goal, and Sue explores with Mia how she might start to work towards "calming her thoughts". The idea of introducing breaks seems reasonable to Mia, and she begins to build a plan of how she might try balancing her work with rest and social activities. Sue shows some curiosity about whether this would help Mia to sleep better, and Mia shares this curiosity.

Sue introduces a simple breathing exercise and a thought-challenging "wise mind" technique, showing Mia how to realistically challenge and balance any negative or anxious thoughts she might have about her abilities. Mia decides that practicing these techniques will be second and third goals.

Toward the end of the session, Sue uses the Scaling Question again, and Mia's score is down to 5 out of 10. Sue then asks, "What might you do/try to do when you get home that might move the score down to 4.5 or even 4?" Mia states simply that she plans to "Try out some of the things we have explored". Mia also borrows the book *When Perfect Isn't Good Enough* by Martin Antony (2009), which she intends to read, and also agrees to try a mindfulness drop-in group run by the service once per week (goals 4 and 5).

Mia feels four weeks will be enough time for her to read the book and to attempt her other four goals, so Sue books a "next contact date" for four weeks' time, asking Mia to get in touch by this date if she would like any further support/sessions. Mia agrees that Sue is free to call her on the telephone to do a CORE-10 feedback measure if she has not been in contact by this time.

Mia is clearly more positive as she leaves the therapist's room, and Sue is excited to find out if she will need to return.

Four weeks later, Mia has not been in touch and Sue makes contact via telephone. Mia is delighted to report that she is studying again, attending university and has a meeting scheduled with her personal tutor to discuss catching up the work from the previous lectures she has missed.

Sue takes time to validate and celebrate the progress Mia has made, before moving on to asking about any further changes she might like to make. Mia describes that she is sleeping better but that her routine has not completely returned to normal. Sue mentions the previous discussion about balancing work with rest and socialising, and Mia states feeling hopeful that the Mindfulness Group, that she is planning to attend for the first time that night, might be helpful with this.

Taking her CORE-10 scores over the phone reveals a reduction in Mia's score, which is now at a non-clinical level. Mia decides not to have further input from the service at this time, describing feeling confident to carry out the next steps herself, without any further assistance.

Conclusion

The introduction of short-term therapy to Cardiff University has been transformational for the service. In particular, the initial 90-minute TC has been both challenging and a pleasant surprise. This dramatically changes the focus and, to a certain extent, increases the need for immediacy from the counsellor. It removes the luxury of anticipating more sessions in which to engage the client, and heightens counsellors' expectation that this may be the single opportunity to effect enough change for the client.

This alone was not sufficient to be transformational for the service. The single session, solution-focused approach, is contained within a coherent model of service delivery. The Cardiff Model, which was awarded the BACP Innovation award in 2010, demonstrated a model of service delivery that could be introduced into the HE sector, holding and supporting students in distress and providing equality of access. The shift in mission and delivery model was not initially universally popular with clients who had previously used the service, and who were used to unlimited access. Neither was it popular with some local NHS providers. For some more complex issues, which (rightly) should have been regarded as appropriate for NHS interventions, the ability to say "go to the University Counselling Service" was no longer present.

Prior to the introduction of the Cardiff Model, there had been a steady rise in numbers of students seeking counselling of approximately 100 annually. The difficulty of meeting demand resulted in a negative perception of what counselling might offer, and frustration from personal tutors who were having to support more difficult students while they waited six to eight weeks for counselling to begin. Even at times when the waiting time was seasonally lower, the perceived wisdom was that students would wait too long and it was felt that it was therefore not worth referring the student. The "bad press" relayed by word of mouth among students masked the evident need of those students who would have benefitted from help.

During the first year immediately following the introduction of the Cardiff Model, the number of referrals increased as they always had. The difference was that using the same staff resource, but using the Cardiff Model, the majority of students were seen in two weeks and there were no waiting lists. We regarded this as a success and staff and students were delighted.

The consequence of this newfound confidence in what was being delivered changed both the perception and positive reputation of the counselling service in the university quite rapidly. Of course it is the most desirable state for any counselling service to be regarded positively and have short waiting times. The result of this perfect combination began to drive up numbers of students referring themselves or being referred by personal tutors.

In year two, numbers rose steeply and there was some impact with waiting times rising to three weeks. It became clear that further innovation was required to manage demand. This was achieved through the introduction of more online tools and self-help resources. The creative use of online counselling, workshops and an increasing use of sessional staff to meet peaks in demand all played a part in managing increasing demand effectively.

No model is perfect and this model presented challenges, in particular the 90-minute initial session. These difficulties were not so much issues for the client, but for the counsellor, who was required to deliver a great deal in 90 minutes. There were certain challenges in benchmarking using CORE because the process did not neatly fit the traditional model of "assessment; wait; then on-going counselling". Our approach was premised on the therapeutic process beginning with the registration tool; it was both an assessment and held therapeutic content. These differences were problematic if we sought to benchmark externally or contribute to sector data surveys.

A further professional hurdle emerged when counsellors submitted for accreditation. The reason for this was a belief that therapy can only be effective if the client comes back, or that therapy cannot be successful in a single session. The evidence of our daily practice would suggest, for this client group at least, that for many, the initial intensive input is sufficient.

The Cardiff Model as a concept could not remain static, but must continue responding to need. Over time it became clearer that by providing a range of self-help interventions before the TC, rather than at the end of the session as homework, the need for students to require on-going counselling may be further reduced.

The IAPT programme (Increasing Access to Psychological Services) in England successfully trialled short-term Cognitive Behavioural (CBT) interventions including one-to-one and structured programs for common conditions such as depression and anxiety. In early 2014 the service introduced a Student Wellbeing Team, whose focus remains on providing short-term interventions in the form of advice, self-help materials, structured interventions and more. It is too early to evaluate its long-term success. However, it has without doubt enhanced the Cardiff Model by enabling interventions that may remove the necessity to engage with counselling. Equally it provides the ambivalent client with a taste of what they may receive if they engage with the newly-renamed Counselling, Health and Wellbeing Service.

The challenge for counselling and wellbeing services within the HE sector is to support the maximum number of students with just enough input to enable them to successfully complete their studies. A secondary task is to manage institutional anxiety surrounding mental health, psychological and emotional distress. Short-term or single session therapy addresses the economic issue. The Cardiff Model places the activity in a coherent and equitable model of service delivery. The outreach work and visibility of the Wellbeing Team helps to manage institutional anxiety.

What is abundantly clear from our experience is that so many more students would access counselling and wellbeing services if it were easy to see some-one quickly. Rather than regarding waiting lists as a problem caused by service inefficiencies they can be understood as a symptom of many unhappy, unwell or distressed students who would benefit from support. Supporting students fully to achieve their potential is in everyone's interest. The Cardiff Model has increased opportunities to offer support, but the challenge remains to continue innovation and reach even more students.

Note

1 Sue has found there are discernible themes and patterns that arise when using the Cardiff Model. Sue includes here the case of "Mia" to reflect some of the themes/outcomes she has come across. To safeguard confidentiality, Mia's case combines some of the features of other single session work to create an anonymous but composite example.

References

Antony, M. (2009) *When Perfect Isn't Good Enough (2nd Edition)*, Oakland, New Harbinger.

Barkham, M. (1989) Exploratory therapy in two-plus-one sessions. *British Journal of Psychotherapy*, 6 (1), 81–88.

Barkham, M. (2007) Researching best practice with CORE, in *Core: A decade of development*. Available from: www.coreims.co.uk/site_downloads/CORE-A-Decade-of-Development.pdf (accessed November 2014).

Bakker, J. M., Bannink, F. & Macdonald, A. (2010) Solution focused psychiatry. *Psychiatric Bulletin*, 34, 297–300.

Berg, I. K. & De Shazer, S. (1993) Making Numbers Talk: Language in Therapy, in Friedman, S. (Ed.) *The New Language of Change: Constructive Collaboration in Psychotherapy* (pp. 5–25), New York, Guilford Press.

Caleb, R. (2014) Uni counselling services challenged by growing demand. *Guardian Professional*. Higher Education Network. 27th May, 2014. Available from: www.theguardian.com/higher-education-network/blog/2014/may/27/students-mental-health-risk-cuts-nhs-services (accessed November 2014).

Dubrow-Marshall, L. (2009) The use of single session therapy in a university counselling service. *AUCC Journal*, November, 28–31.

George, E., Iveson, C. & Ratner, H. (2006) *Problem to Solution (2nd Edition)*, London, Brief Therapy Press.

George, E. (2007) Treading lightly. *Counselling at Work*, February, 55, 2–5.

Lukens, E. & McFarlane, W. (2004) Psychoeducation as evidence-based practice: Considerations for practice, research, and policy. *Brief Treatment and Crisis Intervention*, 4 (3), 205–225.

McCanny, G. (2009) *Solution focused therapy*. Available from: www.counselling-directory. org.uk/counselloradvice10033.html (accessed 15th October 2014).

McKeel, A, J. (1996) *A selected review of research of solution-focused brief therapy*. Web document updated version of McKeel (1996) A Clinician's Guide to Research on Solution-Focused Therapy, in Miller, S. D., Hubble, M. A. and Duncan, B. L. (Eds) *Handbook of Solution-Focused Brief Therapy* (pp. 251–271). Available from: www. solutionsdoc.co.uk/mckeel.htm (accessed 3rd October 2014).

Perkins, R. & Scarlett, G. (2008) The effectiveness of single session therapy in child and adolescent mental health, part 2: An 18 month follow-up study. *Psychology and Psychotherapy: Theo, Res, Pra*, 81: 143–156. doi 10.1348/147608308x280995, Wiley Online Library (accessed 24th November 2014).

Reading Well Agency (2013) *Reading Well commissioning guide*. Available from: http:// readingagency.org.uk/adults/impact/research/reading-well-books-on-prescription- scheme-evidence-base.html (accessed 1st November 2014).

Rogers, C. R. (1942) Counselling and Psychotherapy, cited in McCanny, G. (2009) *Solution focused therapy*. Available from: www.counselling-directory.org.uk/counselloradvice 10033.html (accessed 3rd September 2014).

Silver Cloud Health (2014) *Silver Cloud: Making space for healthy minds*. Available from: www.silvercloudhealth.com/ (accessed 21st June 2014).

Talmon, M. (1990) *Single Session Therapy*, San Francisco, Jossey-Bass inc.

Talmon, M. (1991) Therapists say a single session may be enough. *New York Times* 2nd May, B14, Health section. Available from: www.nytimes.com/1991/05/02/health/therapists- say-a-single-session-may-be-enough.html (accessed 21st June 2015).

Wells R. & Giannetti, V. (1993) *Casebook of the Brief Psychotherapies*, Nato Science Series, New York, Plenum Press.

Chapter 7

Lost in translation?

Working therapeutically with international students

Pat Hunt

Introduction

International students studying in universities in the UK form a substantial proportion of the student body and represent an important source of income for the HE sector. For such students, studying abroad, especially if English is not their first language, brings many emotional and psychological challenges and international students can be particularly susceptible to loneliness, social isolation and anxiety. How can university counselling services effectively support these students, especially within a short-term time frame?

This chapter explores cultural transitions and the inevitable components of loss and change that international students face. It draws on findings from a research study conducted at the University of Nottingham into the needs of international students. There is a particular focus on the needs of Chinese students and lessons that can be learnt from therapeutic work with them, drawing on learning from setting up a counselling service in Ningbo, China and from the experience of working with Chinese students at the University of Nottingham. Each section of the chapter begins with a short vignette and these are generic composites drawn from a number of international student's situations rather than specific examples. Any resemblance to individual students is accidental rather than real.

The number of international students in UK universities has increased markedly in the last few years. In the academic year 2013/14 the proportion of Chinese students on full-time postgraduate courses at UK universities (23 per cent) was almost as great as the proportion of British students (26 per cent) (*Guardian*, 2014). At the University of Nottingham (UoN) in the same academic year there were international students from 192 different countries. International students bring to the HE sector and to university counselling services an extraordinary diversity of ethnicity and also of personal experience. To give a small snapshot of this, within the last few years in the University Counselling Service at the University of Nottingham (UCS) we have worked with students affected by the conflicts in the Arab spring – Libya, Egypt, Kuwait, Tunisia; the Kenya uprising; in Nigeria, natural disasters, murders, rape, air disasters, terrorist attacks; war in the Middle East and Eastern Europe. International students can face significant challenges arising from such experiences when studying so far from home. In the face of such human tragedy and trauma what can we offer within a short-term therapeutic frame? In my experience the positive impact of the existence of a counselling service as part of the university community should never be underestimated. For students coming from all over the world the presence of somewhere to be able to talk about their experience and the enormity of things happening in their lives, and be offered a therapeutic intervention offers them containment, reduces their level of anxiety and gives them a chance to make sense of their experience. In this way the potential negative impact of tragedy and trauma on their academic study is reduced. With such a richness and diversity of international student population in UK universities it is important to begin from a position of humility in terms of what can appropriately be offered within counselling services. We have so much to learn not least in relation to language.

Lost in translation? Language dimensions

In a reception appointment with a student from the Middle East the counsellor began by trying to follow word by word what the student was saying. Her brow furrowed with the effort of concentration. The strenuous attention to words became the focus of her mind and the overall meaning of what was being conveyed was getting lost. She decided to try to allow the words to flow over her and see what happened. Immediately the dynamic changed. Meaning emerged and it became clear how much the student was struggling with the demands of his academic course.

Language and words are so central to the work of psychotherapy and counselling that it can seem impossible to try to conduct therapeutic work across different languages. Solutions to this dilemma include bringing in translators and employing multi-lingual counsellors. This is done successfully in a number of universities. However, with international students coming from so many different countries it is not possible to offer translators for everyone. A central component of therapeutic work is the client articulating, both to the therapist and to themselves, the problems that they are experiencing. Very often they are doing this for the first time and the process of articulation makes things understandable to the student that they have not previously understood and it may be the first acknowledgement to themselves of the difficulties that they face. These are important first stages in the therapeutic process, which can be fulfilled even when the client is not speaking in their own mother tongue. However, conducting therapeutic work in a language that is not the client's mother tongue can have practical consequences, which need to be born in mind in short-term work. Experience suggests that during the first two or three sessions the primary focus for the student may be adapting to the culture of counselling/therapy, which is unfamiliar, and also language attunement. Some extra sessions may be needed to allow for this adaptation. Lago (2006) stressed that the therapeutic process with its accent on listening, acceptance and building a therapeutic alliance provides "the opportunity (for clients) to speak, practise, experiment with and thus create and develop their 'word' and their symbols of meaning" (p.71) and he emphasises that this is true also for those whose first language is not English.

Barty (in Lago, 2011) highlights the powerful vehicle that language provides for the expression of self and comments that international students for whom English is their second, third or one of many languages can feel "a loss of 'self' in the loss of fluency and range" and "reduced in their ability to express themselves, with the potential for shame" (p. 187). She also notes, however, that there can be a sense of having a different self in a different language and that this can be a liberating experience. In my view a component part of the development of a therapeutic alliance is the emergence of a shared and commonly understood language. This might involve the use of key phrases, which the client has used to describe herself or a vital experience, and the repeated use of this phrase plays out in a creative way to bring resolution of prior trauma. In a parallel way, working with students for whom English is not their first language can be liberating and healing for the client who discovers that communication through English phrases brings meaning, resolution, reduced anxiety and the relief of being understood.

Non-verbal language has the potential for mis-communication across cultures. Patterns of facial expression, body signals, emotional displays, uses of space and concepts of time are subtly nuanced in their expression in different cultures and for different individuals. There are differing cultural expectations about deferring to a person perceived as being in authority – for example, thinking it rude to speak first without being invited to do so. International students can be confused about the pattern of taking turns in speaking in sessions. Eye contact is different across cultures and what one person might take as a display of sincere interest might feel rude or intrusive to another. Some people turn their head away to think best how to phrase something, but others turn their ear to the speaker to show they are listening carefully, and these differences can be misinterpreted. Interestingly, Hall (1976) has conducted research demonstrating that when two people talk to each other their movements and non-verbal communication often become synchronised. He goes further to state that this "syncing" is perhaps the most basic element of communication, and is the foundation upon which all subsequent speech interaction and behaviour is built. This finding has considerable implications for the quality of communication that occurs in working with international students in University Counselling Service settings. It suggests that the degree to which a sense of synchronisation is achieved between the therapist and the student in the ebb and flow of the therapeutic exchange is a vital factor, and that this can lead to the development of a common language within which the client feels that they are understood.

Cultural transition

A student from an Eastern European country came for a short series of sessions presenting with problems of difficulties in adjusting to the UK environment, and also self-harm, which had been a problem in his teenage years but had re-emerged as a problem since arriving in the UK. He had had a difficult early life with estrangement from his father who left the family home when he was three. Self-harm developed as a coping mechanism when he was bullied at school, and had stopped when he managed to bring the bullying to an end on his own. He engaged well in the sessions and a strong therapeutic alliance quickly emerged. For the first time he was able to talk about his early childhood and the bullying he had experienced. A greater internal resilience emerged and the urge to self-harm reduced. In the penultimate session he stated that the sessions had been of central importance to him as they represented stability – stability that he had not experienced before in his life, and stability that he could internalise.

The need for stability is evident for all students, and the reasons for this are particularly highlighted by international students as the transition – cultural and geographical – that they make is affected by whether or not they have a secure base. Bowlby (1992) describes the provision of a secure base as

> the provision by both parents of a secure base from which a child or an adolescent can make sorties into the outside world and to which he can return knowing for sure that he will be welcomed when he gets there, nourished physically and emotionally, comforted if distressed, reassured if frightened.
>
> (p. 11)

For international students part of their secure base is their culture: culture is part of the basis of confidence and resilience and it operates like a second skin (Bick, 1987). As international students lose their culture through coming to study in the UK they can lose their second skin, part of their secure base, with a resulting loss of confidence and resilience and capacity to cope. Many international students ride this transitional process well, relishing the experience of an exciting new culture and and are not undermined by the loss of second skin. But not all do. Other students experience intense loneliness and isolation in the process of cultural adjustment.

Bick (1987) describes the function of the skin in early childhood as a boundary containing the early development of the child's personality, and that as the child grows a "second skin" develops, which may have components of culture and language incorporated into it. This continues to fulfil the function of creating a boundary that supports the child's developing personality. This second skin of language and culture plays an important role in the development of identity. If a student has a secure internal sense of their identity and a secure base this is likely to give them sufficient resilience to be able to flourish. Students who don't have an internalised secure base can develop compensatory over-attachments to other students, tutors, hall wardens and other university staff and these attachments can become problematic. When the cultural scaffolding of a student's home country is taken away it can have quite marked consequences, for example in a student's experience of their sexuality. Norms and acceptance of sexualities vary widely in different cultures, and it is not uncommon for an international student to become questioning and confused about their identity when studying in the UK due to the different cultural influences that they are being exposed to.

Lago and Shipton (1994) identify four stages of culture shock among international students newly arrived to the UK. In the first stage everything is new and exciting, but there can be an immediate sense of loss and social isolation which is disorientating. High expectations may be dashed and the sense of disorientation can lead to the second stage of apathy and disintegration. The student may become depressed and consider withdrawing from the course at this stage. If this can be survived a third stage of reintegration emerges as the student recognises the value of their individual and cultural differences and, sometimes, becomes critical of the host culture. Finally in the fourth stage autonomy and independence can emerge with the final outcome of the development of a sense of competence and confidence within both their home and the new culture. Critical stages that may require a therapeutic intervention are the experience of disintegration and depression in the second stage. Not every student reaches the final stage.

The iceberg concept of culture has been widely used (e.g. Lago, 2006) to illustrate the fact that many cultural differences are hidden. There are some aspects of cultural difference that are very evident e.g. language and history, and this is the part of the iceberg above the water. Other aspects of cultural difference such as educational methodology, gender expectations, operation of hierarchy, parental norms and sexual norms operate below the surface of conscious awareness, below the water line on the iceberg, and have a huge impact even though we are less consciously aware of them. Students accustomed to operating within the norms of their home culture are often not aware of the strength of their own cultural scaffolding until they arrive in the UK and realise that their home culture no longer holds them in check. The differences in culture of which they are least aware can leave them vulnerable, isolated and challenged in their own identity. For international students learning that they are not perceived in the new culture in the way they had anticipated can be a difficult experience. Many international students respond to this situation by quite naturally forming groups and it is common to see groups of international students moving around campus together. The sense of the collective in the group helps to offset the loss of culture and develop a new alternative culture that they can inhabit.

For the student from Eastern Europe in the vignette at the start of this section, what supported him as an individual was to discover a place of stability within the therapy sessions and therapeutic alliance. This was a form of second skin, which he could use to build his identity and personal integrity forged from the integration of his home culture, which he had left, with the new culture he was inhabiting. This emerged in ways that helped him to become more resilient. It is in this sense that short-term therapeutic interventions, and indeed the presence of the University Counselling Service, can offer a temporary second skin, which offers containment and the student can internalise and continue to use while they are studying in the UK.

The work of reception and administrative staff is key here as their work is a central part of the experience of stability for international (and home-based) students. Administrators and receptionists are the first people students contact and experience of this initial contact is vital. This is especially so for international students who may be affected by language limitations, stigma, uncertainty and anxiety as they contact the service for the first time. A warm, understanding, empathic reception as they arrive in the service can be tremendously reassuring in overcoming such barriers.

Sense of collectivity and group work

A male postgraduate student from Iraq presented to the service with problems of social isolation and depression. He was offered the opportunity to come to the eight-week therapeutic group, which the service runs for male postgraduate students, facilitated by two male counsellors both experienced in therapeutic group work. Initially he said very little in the group and seemed socially isolated here as well. In week three the notion of transference was introduced and the way in which past experience can be re-played within the group. This created the opportunity for him to explore, within the containment and relative safety of the group, the basis of his isolation. He talked about his childhood in Iraq, the deaths of several family members in politically motivated circumstances, the impact on his developing sense of self growing up in a family outlawed by the regime in power and the bullying he had endured at school. His awareness that he was not alone in these experiences grew as his openness prompted two other group members, who were also international students, to talk about the problems of growing up in their home country. The dynamic in the group changed, a sense of identification emerged and the student from Iraq became from that moment a more active, engaged member of the group whose story had allowed others to explore their own relationship to their unique history of trauma/oppression.

Therapeutic groups draw on the element of collective identity, and years of experience at UCS have evidenced the positive therapeutic work that can be done in short-term groups drawing on this strength. This is particularly attractive and relevant for international students who come from areas of the world where collective identity is more important than individual. Eastern concepts of self see "a human being as an integral part of the universe and the society. People are fundamentally connected. Duty towards all others is a very important matter. Collectivism is stronger." By contrast a Western sense of self is described as "an individualistic nature and an independent part of the universe and the society. Individualism is stronger" (Bibikova & Kotelnikov, 2014).

Several examples confirm the concept that "collectivism is stronger" for many international students. The way in which international students naturally group together can offset the loneliness and disorientation that are parts of the experience of transition to another country: the group offers coherence and security in the face of uncertainty and change. The ability to make meaningful interactions with others has a powerful impact on students' wellbeing, reducing homesickness and loneliness and helping them to cope with the stresses inherent in the move to a new culture. When we are thinking about working individually with international students concerning the problems they are experiencing, cultural factors mean that they cope differently with academic problems. The "we" is always present, even in individual academic problems, as part of the psyche. Collective identity is a strong positive component as it represents the joint enterprise for international students to be able to study in the UK. Financially there is a strong collective element as students are often government, family or employer sponsored. The implication of this is that the student is not studying in the UK just as an individual, but is here as a member of a collective, reporting back to extended family members, Skyping family and remaining embedded in family. When students from countries with strong collective identities talk about themselves it is important we hold the "we" in mind if we are to understand their situations and problems clearly.

Yu (2011) noted that Malaysian students appear to be very likely to seek social contact with other students from their home country when they are dealing with stress as collective identity is stronger. Malaysian students studying at the University of Nottingham naturally form groups and support each other. Most government-funded Malaysian students will have attended a Departure Training Programme prior to leaving home, at which they probably will have been instructed to look after each other, help each other maintain and uphold Malaysian values and standards of conduct (S. Nadarajan, 2014, personal communication).

Kohut (1979) makes an elegant differentiation between "self" and "identity", defining *self* as a depth psychological concept that refers to the core of the personality formed from the interplay of the child's earliest objects, and *identity* as the point of convergence between the developed self in late adolescence and early adulthood and the sociocultural position of the individual. Attractiveness of group membership to overcome the sense of social isolation, collective consciousness that operates in Eastern countries is very different and working groups are preferred. A study at the University of Bournemouth (Brown & Holloway, 2008) showed that while cross-national interaction was associated with improved cultural awareness, the major patterns of interaction were monocultural bonds evidenced in co-national friendships.

Limitations and attractions of brief therapeutic work with international students

A postgraduate student from Sri Lanka came to UCS because she was experiencing problems in her relationship with her husband. He was in their home country, and although he had encouraged her to pursue her own education and study in the UK the physical, geographical and cultural separation between them was causing estrangement. She had become quite desperate and had developed a fear that he was having an affair. Her mental state had deteriorated under this pressure

and she had experienced suicidal thoughts. These thoughts were accompanied by
experiences of shame and guilt, and she did not know what to do. She was deeply
distressed at her first appointment.

Many students come from countries where mental health problems carry both
a sense of stigma and shame, and for whom the offer of short-term appointments
may not necessarily be welcomed. At the other end of the spectrum at the start
of most academic years we receive one or more requests from students from the
USA and Canada for long-term therapeutic work because they have been in therapy for most of their educational career. With the current high level of demand
on university counselling services it is not usually possible to respond positively
to these requests. How to offer appropriate interventions in response to this vast
range of background experience and therapeutic culture is not easy. Nevertheless,
however, there is a constant in the length of the therapeutic hour, which allows
clients time for exploration both at the surface of the conscious mind and also
engagement with unconscious areas of the mind where problems often lie.

Malan (1990) outlines three conditions for undertaking brief focused or time-
limited therapeutic interventions: that the client's life problem can be clearly identified and offers a focus for therapy, that the client has the motivation to work
within this focus and that the possible dangers of offering only a certain number of
sessions have been considered and either there are none to be seen or it is reasonable to think that they can be avoided. He also comments that his experience has
shown that it is best to work with a time limit set from the beginning. The majority of work conducted with international students in higher education settings is
likely to be brief and time limited for reasons that have been explained in other
chapters in this book, and in considering Malan's conditions there are positive
comments to be made about this. The time limit is usually set from the beginning
and this gives international students a realistic expectation of what help is being
offered to them. For those who do not know what counselling and psychotherapy
are, some educational elements are facilitative at the start of the sessions and set
expectations at a realistic level. A clear time frame falls into this category – it is
clear how much time there is, clear when the sessions will end, clear that developing dependency on the sessions is being minimised and the development of a
capacity for autonomy maximised. International students are often highly motivated clients and approach their counselling sessions with commitment, and this
helps in the process of identifying a focus for therapeutic work. The existence of
the counselling time frame parallels their experience as an international student,
which is time-boundaried, and a carefully worked therapeutic ending can help the
student when the time comes for them to leave the UK and return home. However,
the short-term time frame can have negative consequences – if English is not the
first language, additional time components are sometimes incurred to establish
communication and understanding; stigma and shame can operate as resistance
and time is needed to respond sensitively. Language difficulties may result in
central problems not being articulated at the outset when the therapeutic focus

is being identified and risk factors may be hidden by the limitations of language, shame or somatisation. Malan's condition that "the possible dangers of offering only a certain number of sessions have been considered" (p. 243) may need to be re-evaluated and a different time frame established. At the University of Nottingham we retain the capacity to offer additional and long-term sessions on a case by case basis so that clients can be offered this when needed, and many other HE services do the same. This is illustrated in the vignette.

Barty (in Lago, 2011) insightfully describes that in working with international students therapists need to have "sharply attuned antennae to notice the effectiveness, or ineffectiveness, of any intervention used" as "there may be less common ground than assumed to support an intervention that might otherwise appear to be appropriate" (p. 189). Also, it is "likely to be more fruitful for a counsellor to start from the stance of not knowing" – the position of humility suggested at the start of this chapter. There is a disjuncture in what we think works in the therapeutic alliance and what really works in a cultural context, and because of this it is not usually possible to deliver a Western-based therapy to non-Western students in a straightforward way. Subtle adaptations are needed in clinical practice, and the key is that these will be suggested to the therapist by the individual international student rather than being prescriptive or formulaic.

For the student in the vignette at the start of this section, additional sessions were indicated and needed due to the level of risk, and other areas of support in the university were involved. International students are encouraged to register with the university health centre when they arrive at university, and for this student it was vital to work in an integrated way with a GP. One of the university mental health advisers was also brought in to offer an interventionist approach where this was needed. With this integrated support in place the student became less distressed and her suicidal thoughts diminished.

Working with Chinese students

A final stage PhD Pharmacy student from China presented with problems of procrastination and low mood. She described herself as a top student at school and university, and with a sense of shame she described her prolonged avoidance of working on the final stage of her thesis. Her parents had wanted her to do a highly esteemed UK pharmacy degree and then, as the only child, come back to China and run the family shipbuilding company. She got a first and progressed to a Masters degree. Her parents again said that she should come back to run the company, but she chose to begin a PhD. During her first appointment she articulated for the first time her dilemma that she did not want to run the family shipbuilding business but neither did she want to dishonour her family.

Within the short-term time frame it was possible to give her space to talk about her tremendous love for her father; her desire to live up to the virtues embodied in filial piety; the father/daughter dynamic; her fear of disappointing and dishonouring him and her own sense of disappointment in not feeling able to fulfil his dream; how she might tell her parents and articulate her own wishes; how to anticipate the future dynamic of her parents' and her own disappointment and how to live with this. Her initial presentation had been tentative with two missed appointments before she came for the third, and she described that she had found it hard to come because she feared two things – that she would become depressed and she didn't have time for this, and that a counsellor would be strict with her and expect her to uphold her parent's values. This revelation highlighted the transference at work and the therapist was able to use this to help her express the deep sense of loss pervading her situation. The transference also facilitated working through to an understanding that she had internalised her parents values, their disappointment that she – their only child – was not a boy, and that as a consequence she was expecting everyone to be completely disappointed in her, and that this was the basis for her disappointment in herself. As she understood this her internal world shifted a little, she recovered her capacity to work and was able to complete her thesis.

Wu (in Lago, 2011) highlights the centrality of family in traditional Chinese society, stating, "Today, for most Chinese people, family is still the most important social support system" (p. 343). Family and the parent–child relationships come into most conversations, and the vignette emphasises the kinds of conflicts that can emerge when the values of family are juxtaposed with the experience of Western education.

This section is focused on the needs of a particular group of international students, namely Chinese students, and the lessons that can be learnt from offering short-term therapeutic interventions to them. At the University of Nottingham we have had the privileged experience of working closely with Chinese students, both those who come as international students to Nottingham and those who study as home-based students in the University of Nottingham's Ningbo Campus (UNNC) in China. Internationalisation is a key element of the University of Nottingham strategy, and in 2004 Nottingham gained approval from the Chinese Ministry of Education, under the new Sino-Foreign Education Co-operative Law, to establish and run a campus independently within the Chinese mainland. By 2009 UNNC was home to a thriving community of 4,000 Chinese students and in that year we were asked to set up a counselling service on the campus. The founding principles of the service were that it would be for staff and students of the university and aim to offer both short and longer-term therapeutic interventions. As counselling is an emerging profession in China we had no idea whether the service would be used by Chinese students and staff. We were working into the unknown. In fact, the service was used by Chinese staff and students, as well as international (non-Chinese) staff and students, from its first year of opening. It is interesting to note that in 2011 a notice issued by the Chinese General Office of the Ministry of Education called for universities to establish psychological counselling services and courses in mental health education throughout China (Education & Policy Department, 2011). Counselling is still an emerging profession in China. There are government directives to provide counselling and yet the structures needed to support therapeutic work including professional training, codes of ethics and practice and clinical supervision are not well developed.

Results from studies including Lu (1990) have shown that homesickness is a common psychological reaction among Chinese students studying in Britain. Other studies have emphasised the way in which Chinese students studying in the UK adapt, to varying degrees, to their new learning and living environment. Gu and Maley (2008) conclude from their study of Chinese students in the UK that "despite various intercultural challenges and struggles, most students have managed to survive the demands of the learning and living environment, and to adapt and develop" (p. 38). This is a helpful normative frame within which to consider the needs of Chinese students who have more difficulty adapting.

There are ingredients deeply embedded in Chinese culture that are richly resonant of therapeutic work. The traditional Chinese written character for listening is extremely beautiful, incorporating three elements: using both ears with full attention in the act of listening; using both eyes with full vision to see every possible aspect; and using whole heart or whole body attention to note every non-verbal element in the act of listening (I. Huang, 2013, personal communication). This is of course very close to the key principles of listening within therapeutic work. At the start of this chapter I highlighted an important attitude when working with international students, which is the need for us to learn from them. This is of the essence in working with Chinese students as it is not possible for us to make definitive statements about how students from China conceptualise themselves and their world. Experience suggests that instead of trying to understand them by reading extensive literature about Chinese culture (we may want to do that for our own interest of course!) it is more effective to have an attitude of openness, curiosity and naivety, leading to a state of unknowing, from which emerges our capacity to engage with the student's individual experience. This then becomes central to the therapeutic alliance and the sessions.

In the academic year 2013/14 the most common presenting problem among the Chinese students who accessed UCS at the University of Nottingham was perfectionism. Perfectionism has been described as a student becoming "so intent on getting it right that they lose sight of any sense of pleasure or achievement therein, and the process of education has given way to the supremacy of the goal" (Wraight 2008, p. 11). Successful Chinese students will have become used to marks in the 90–100 per cent range during their schooling in China and will probably be thought of as talented, gifted and special. Their first experience of marks in UK higher education where a very good mark is 75 per cent can create a sense of failure, and that they are no longer special within a high achieving student population. Students who have a perfectionist personality style are particularly vulnerable to this sense of failure and over the course of time this can become all encompassing and devastating. "One failure is total failure, small failure is massive failure and average achievement levels are also failure" (Wraight, 2008, p. 10). An intense experience of shame is invoked and a crisis can be precipitated as the student's raison d'etre for being in the UK shatters around them. A perceptive comment by Percy (2014) is relevant here:

> Unrealistic perfectionism is a key driver for more serious problems such as depression, anxiety, self-harm and eating disorders. Despite being more connected in a virtual way, many students feel more isolated as they believe they have to hide their true self and present a perfect image to others.

In this situation most Chinese students will not immediately think of turning to the University Counselling Service. A University of Nottingham study (Yu, 2011) reports on a mental health needs assessment, which was conducted with Chinese and Malaysian students studying at the university. Key findings include the realisation that "international students have greater support needs and need more targeted information in comparison to UK students" while "stigma relating to mental health is a major barrier for many international students" (p. 4). The report outlines the way in which Confucian thinking has profoundly affected Asian society for over 2,000 years including advocating internalising stress and avoiding expression of direct feeling (Yu, 2011). A consequence of this is somatisation and the expression of physical symptoms rather than mental health presentation: for example, a headache is experienced rather than depression. Traditionally mental health problems are a source of shame and "loss of face", but experience of working with Chinese students and staff at the University of Nottingham's Ningbo, China campus counselling service has shown that this is changing and that there is great diversity. Yu (2011) found that the Chinese students in the study expressed a sense of shame and embarrassment if friends found out that they had been receiving counselling. A common perception was that an individual who experiences personal distress or unhappiness should keep it to themselves and not burden others with their problems. Others said they would need to be explicitly directed to seek help from UCS or the Health Centre by tutors or friends. Some Chinese students reported that they found it easier to attend a workshop on perfectionism as these are similar to educational courses, there is some social contact and they feel less embarrassed to talk than in individual support. It can be helpful for university counselling services to offer workshops on perfectionism and other common presenting problems, and our experience in Nottingham is that these are well attended by international students including Chinese students, and that students quite often contact UCS for ask for an individual appointment following the completion of the workshop.

Chinese students may have particular expectations of counselling and may bring a range of meanings to what in more Westernised contexts is known as the relatively well-defined terms of "counsellor" and "counselling". Confidentiality, the disclosure of personal information with someone who is not family and the therapeutic relationship may need to be explained as the process unfolds. In a short-term therapeutic intervention where perfectionism is a central presenting problem, listening to the student's expression of their difficulties can entail:

understanding the primary source of shame that they experience and the difficulties in having come to feel that their value and specialness lies in their high
achievement; articulating some of the pressures that they may have experienced
in their formative years as part of the one-child generation in an upwardly aspirational country; identifying the bubble that they live in where perfection is the
norm and falling short of one's own and everybody else's expectations is a tor-
ment; experiencing friends and peers as supportive at times but also competitive, punishing and excluding; wanting to be the perfect client; and expressing the
longing to do things perfectly or not at all. All of this can be liberating and also
daunting. At first it will be difficult for the student to accept that they are not going
to be the best, but with effective work this can become possible and the student
can discover how to be more creative and begin to enjoy learning again.

Lost in translation – going back home

*A female PhD student from Nigeria, who had successfully conducted innovative
scientific research, presented to UCS during the final stages of writing up her
thesis. She described her difficulty in getting off to sleep at night and how she
woke frequently worrying about things. She was finding her relationship with her
supervisor difficult as she felt he was rushing her and setting unmanageable dead-
lines. She said that she had found herself retreating to her room, not socialising or
communicating with her peers. As she talked it became clear that she was worried
about returning home and was anticipating the sense of loss that she would feel in
leaving her attachments in the UK to people and to her studies, and also the freedom and status that she experienced in this cultural context. She expressed her
fear that all the development she had made while in the UK would get lost because
of the different expectations of her as a woman in her home country.*

The cross cultural transition of returning home at the end of the course is a transition that international students often do not anticipate and yet it is an important
stage to negotiate and a reaction of reverse culture shock can emerge at this final
stage of a student's sojourn in the UK. Returning home to a familiar culture may
be problematic due to external changes that have occurred at home while the student has been away or employment opportunities not being available as expected
and hoped for. However, for many students it is the degree of change in their
internal world that has taken place while they have been studying in the UK that
leads to the greatest experience of culture shock as they prepare for the transition
home. The differing societal expectations between the UK and their home country
can loom very large and daunting at the moment of completing their studies. The
difference can be quite extreme for some students, for example returning to an
arranged marriage, or to a culture where homosexuality is illegal.

What work can UCS do to facilitate the transition for international students
back to their home country? Counsellors and psychotherapists are very used
to the ending phase of therapeutic intervention, which often involves, even in

short-term work, engaging with current and previous processes of loss and transition triggered by the experience of loss, which is the ending of the therapy and of the therapeutic alliance. In this ending phase much can be done to help prepare international students for the coming transition by acknowledging the reality of a transition not just an ending, by normalising the feelings involved, and by preparing students for the realities of the changes to come. At this point the challenge for the student is to discover how to integrate their international experience and transform what they have started to believe about themselves and their abilities and retain this as internal strength as they return to their home culture. For some years the University of Nottingham International Office offered a session to international students at the end of their course to help them prepare for the future, and as part of this I was invited to conduct a fantasy journey for the students present. The fantasy journey guided them in their imagination through the real journey to come, the changes ahead, the return home to family and friends and to the realities and possibilities that awaited them. The feedback from this was almost uniformly positive, with students reporting a reduced sense of uncertainty and apprehension and an increased sense of their capacity to make the transition ahead of them. A fantasy journey can, where appropriate, be incorporated into the final session of short-term counselling work.

Transitional objects are important at various developmental stages of our lives. Donald Winnicott (1964) introduced the concept of a transitional object having observed that these are chosen by a child to help her face steps of development and exposure to external reality by choosing or creating a symbol. International students can choose a transitional object to support their journey back to their home culture that captures something of their experience in the UK, a metaphor, the way in which they will hold this experience in their heart, and something that will capture and evoke the memory of their experience in the UK. In a parallel way international students will internalise from therapy what they choose to take away that is of value to them, and will continue to be meaningful to them as they return to their home culture.

Conclusion

The chapter has focused mostly on what gets lost in language translation and cultural transition for international students studying in the UK. However it is also worth considering what doesn't get lost. In a therapeutic exchange in short-term work with international students there is often a powerful and intense communication. There is no British etiquette to work around and move beyond. International students for whom English is not their first language are often careful, economical and perceptive with their choice and use of English words and this opens up therapeutic depths remarkably quickly. Powerful counter-transferences operate, and responses evoked from the therapist by the student can emerge quite spontaneously, bringing insight to the problem being outlined. A Saudi Arabian student came for a short series of sessions, and at the start of each session as the door of the therapy room was closed she slowly and carefully unwound the head veil she was wearing, took it off her head and hung it on the coat hook on the door. This gesture seemed to pave the way for her to be able to articulate a traumatic experience from her childhood. She spoke slowly and carefully, no words were wasted, and she evoked in me a sense of the truth of what she had experienced being quite literally uncovered. It was possible to work at depth straight away. She used the sessions remarkably well, and some post-traumatic symptoms she had been struggling with reduced. At the end of each session she carefully wound the head veil back onto her head and then left the room.

In this chapter I have outlined an approach in working with international students that begins with a receptivity to learn from them, and includes the capacity to tolerate within ourselves a level of uncertainty and unknowing. This enables us to respond with an attitude of openness, curiosity and the capacity to engage imaginatively with their experience. This will lead to the development of a good therapeutic alliance, which transcends cultural difference, and can facilitate an ability to use the therapeutic intervention well and as they recover they are able again to fully engage with their academic studies.

Acknowledgements

I would like to thank members of the University Counselling Service team at the University of Nottingham for their help in the writing of this chapter – those whom I have been in conversation with will recognise their contribution. I would also like to thank my colleagues at the University of Nottingham, Ningbo China counselling service for their collaborative work on the section on working with Chinese students. Finally I would like to thank Michael Hunt, Kate Tindle and David Mair for their valuable comments.

References

Bibikova, A. & Kotelnikov, V. (2014) *East versus West*. Available from: www.1000ventures. com/business-guide/crosscuttings/cultures-east-west (accessed 29th October 2014).

Bick, E. (1987) The Experience of Skin in Early Object Relations, in *Collected Papers of Martha Harris and Esther Bick*, Perthshire, Clunie Press.

Bowlby, J. (1992) *A Secure Base: Clinical Applications of Attachment Theory (2nd Edition)*, London, Routledge.

Brown, L. & Holloway, I. (2008) The adjustment journey of international postgraduate students at an English university – an ethnographic study. *Journal Of Research in International Education*, 7 (2), 232–249.

Education & Policy Department (2011) *Principal requirements for development of mental health education in Chinese universities*. China, General Office Ministry of Education. Available from: www.moe.edu.cn/publicfiles/business/htmlfiles/moe/s3020/201103/115721.html.

Gu, Q. & Maley, A. (2008) Changing places: A study of Chinese students in the UK. *Language and Intercultural Communication*, 8 (4), 224–245.

Hall, E. T. (1976) *Beyond Culture*, New York, Anchor Press/Doubleday.

Kohut, H (1979) *In the Search for the Self: Selected Writings of Heinz Kohut 1978–81* (Ed. Ornstein, P.H.) London, Karnac.

Lago, C. (2011) *The Handbook of Transcultural Counselling and Psychotherapy*, Maidenhead, Open University Press.

Lago, C. (2006) *Race, Culture and Counselling: The Ongoing Challenge (2nd Edition)*, Maidenhead, Open University Press.

Lago, C. & Shipton, G. (1994) *On Listening and Learning*, London, Central Book Publishing.

Lu, L. (1990) Adaptation to British universities: Homesickness and mental health of Chinese students. *Counselling Psychology*, 3 (3), 225–232.

Malan, D. (1990) *Individual Psychotherapy and the Science of Psychodynamics (8th Edition)*, London, Butterworths.

Nisbett, R. (2004) *The Geography of Thought. How Asians and Westerners Think Differently . . . and Why*, New York, Free Press.

Percy, A. (2014) *Student mental health*. Available from: www.theguardian.com/higher-education-network/blog/2014/oct/16/student-mental-health-situation-is-nuanced (accessed 17th October 2014).

Royal College of Psychiatrists (2011) *The mental health of students in higher education*. Available from: www.rcpsych.ac.uk/publications/collegereports/cr/cr166.aspx (accessed 21st June 2015).

Shaw, C. (2014) *International students are turning to proofreading agencies to get support*. Available from: http://www.theguardian.com/higher-education-network/blog/2014/apr/09/international-students-proofreading-academic-writing-support (accessed 22nd September 2015).

West, C. (1993) *Race Matters*, Boston, Beacon Press

Winnicott, D. W. (1964) *The Child, the Family and the Outside World*, London, Penguin.

Wraight, M. (2008) Why tamper with perfection? The development of a workshop on perfectionism. *AUCC Journal*, 2008, 10–13.

Yu, H. (2011) *Investigation into the mental health support needs of international students with particular reference to Chinese and Malaysian students*. Available from: www.nottingham.ac.uk/studentservices/documents/investigation-into-the-mental-health-support--needs-of-international-students-with-particular-reference-to-chinese-and-malaysian-students.pdf (accessed 21st June 2015).

Chapter 8

Working with depression and anxiety in a short-term setting

Denise Meyer

Stress, anxiety, low mood and depression have always been the "bread and butter" issues brought to counsellors in university settings – as issues in their own right, and in their many guises linked with student life, such as homesickness, presentation or exam anxiety, self-esteem issues, or drug and alcohol problems. The university counselling sector has a long tradition of working effectively in a brief, focused way with these issues, taking into account developmental factors and the educational context (Bell, 1996). In this chapter I will argue that challenges within the sector in recent years – increased demand, restricted resources and increasing complexity and severity of presentation – are making it more and more difficult to offer effective interventions for all presentations of anxiety and depression solely within the traditional model of a short series of one-to-one counselling sessions. I make the case for a multi-modal approach, which retains the key strengths of the traditional bespoke individual therapeutic engagement while extending available resources through skilful integration of a range of other forms of intervention, including psycho-educational, therapeutic or peer support groups and guided online self-help. The guiding principle for this approach is a re-focusing on our key mission in this sector – the support and enrichment of student *learning*.

Short-term counselling – choice or necessity?

Following the lead of their student clients, university counsellors have traditionally been skilled at working in a short-term or time-focused way, offering a "light touch" intervention suited to the developmental needs of clients whose life stage is characterised by strong motivation to resist dependence and whose engagement on a course of study provides a powerful context for rapidly transformative therapeutic engagement (Bell, 1996; Coren, 1999).

However, there have always been clients who did not fit the developmental profile of those who were expected to benefit from short-term interventions. In the service I worked in during the 1990s, the 4–6 session average was often the product of numerous very short (1–6 session) engagements balancing out much longer-term engagement with a minority of students with more severe or complex presentations. Students with more severe depression or who were at risk, for example, were often offered longer-term support.

However, in most university counselling services the current 4–5 session average no longer represents a "natural balance" reflecting client-directed needs, and instead reflects a general sector-wide imposition of service limits in the face of substantially increased demand (Wallace, 2014a). In the past decade, there has been a widely documented increase in numbers of students seeking emotional support as well as a significant increase in the severity and complexity of diagnosable mental health problems among the student population. The factors contributing to this phenomenon have been widely documented and discussed (see Mair, Chapter 1), but the bald outcome is that students with more complex or severe presentations are no longer a distinct minority among those who present for psychological help – and these students can no longer routinely be offered longer-term support in the traditional in-house, one-to-one counselling format.

Questions have been raised about the ethics of raising the expectations of psychological help for vulnerable students in the face of reduced time resources (Hallett, 2012), and I would agree that complete clarity about the level of help available is essential – university counselling services cannot, and should not, be offering to replace full courses of NHS treatment for diagnosed mental health conditions. However, I would argue that even students with more complex needs, such as specific phobias or serious depression, can benefit from intensive shorter-term episodes of individual therapeutic work, as long as this can be offered within a wider containing framework of support along with access to NHS treatment. The key to making best use of the limited resource is to build on the traditional strengths of work in our sector – its "embeddedness" in the specific context of *education* – and, by identifying common factors, to find ways to deliver interventions that can meet the needs of higher numbers of students simultaneously.

Depression and anxiety – the common factors

Depression and anxiety have long been the issues most commonly presented at counselling services (Wallace, 2014a) and this picture is certainly still borne out when talking to leaders in the sector today: Head of Counselling at the University of Birmingham, Dr David Mair (November 2014, personal communication), said recently, "We typically see 1,000 students a year; very few present without anxiety or depression being a significant part of their presenting problem". At the University of Cumbria, where the mental health and wellbeing service uses the PHQ-9 and GAD7, screening tools for depression and anxiety respectively, rates of diagnosable anxiety and depression are significant and increasing – 81 per cent of those presenting with anxiety in 2013–14 were in the diagnosable moderate to severe category (with 44 per cent registering as severe), up from 68 per cent the year before; for those presenting with low mood and depression, 82 per cent were at diagnosable moderate to severe levels (with 60 per cent registering at the moderately severe to severe level) up from 75 per cent the previous year (D. Wilson, 2014. Response to Freedom of Information request regarding rates of anxiety and depression seen at University of Cumbria. Personal communication).

While diagnostic tools such as these are not yet widely used in the university sector, there is no reason to expect that these rates are unrepresentative of the sector as a whole. And though university counsellors are not, generally, in the business of diagnosis, and the profession has historically tended to resist medicalisation of human distress, we do not need to diagnose all our clients with mood or anxiety disorders in order to recognise the pragmatic relevance of Mair's statement. Stress, low mood, anxiety and depression are constructs that together illustrate a large part of the continuum of distress that unique individual circumstances and distresses map onto, the "common factors" that are present in some form for almost all of the students we see. Homesickness, self-esteem or developmental identity issues, the impact of abuse or other childhood difficulty, parental break up or other losses, relationship or other social difficulties, academic stress and performance anxiety, perfectionism, eating distress and more complex or chronic mental health difficulties all might manifest at least partly in current symptoms of anxiety and/or depression.

Indeed, anxiety and depression are present for everyone as part of the human condition – we cannot escape the fundamental anxiety of being human and the existential given that we are all moving towards death, and associated low mood or anxiety are not conditions to be "cured" but rather lived with. While anxiety and depression are often diagnosed as separate conditions, we know that they very often go hand in hand, two sides to the same coin. It is perhaps helpful, for the purposes of this chapter, to plot a continuum of intensity and complexity along which presentations of anxiety and/or depression can be mapped, in order to better identify what aspects of these issues might be amenable to intervention within the context of short term counselling in HE:

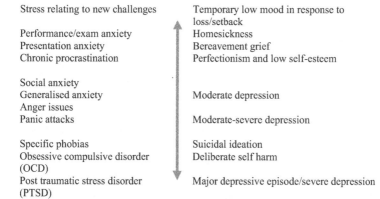

Figure 8.1 Fear (anxiety) and sadness (depression) spectrums

Approaches to working with anxiety and depression

Of course, in a traditional, individual one-to-one approach to counselling there is no need to emphasise anxiety and depression as common factors – counselling in the psychodynamic and humanistic traditions in particular, which have traditionally been the predominant models in the sector, is person-based not issue-based, focusing on forming a therapeutic relationship with a unique individual and their unique life story. However, the revolution in NHS mental health provision, through the IAPT (Increasing Access to Psychological Therapies) roll out with its focus on evidence-based practice as represented in the NICE (National Institute for Health and Care Excellence) guidelines, has brought a more issue-based approach to the fore in recent years. Cognitive-behavioural therapy (CBT), which lends itself to an issue- and protocol-based approach, has been very successful within this paradigm in demonstrating its efficacy and effectiveness for a number of issues, including depression and anxiety (NICE, 2009; NICE, 2011).

This has inevitably affected the university counselling sector to some extent. Many counselling services now offer CBT alongside other counselling approaches, and many more university counsellors have topped up their training in order to be able to integrate CBT techniques into their approach. At the same time, the sector has belatedly started to take more seriously the need for providing rigorous evidence to support the longstanding faith in its efficacy demonstrated by institutional investment in counselling services. The practice-based evidence (using outcome measures) (see McCrea, Chapter 5) and survey data (Wallace, 2012) that has so far been produced gives university counselling a securer basis from which to argue the case for institutions continuing to fund dedicated counselling services in straitened times. In the meantime, international research is beginning to emerge that demonstrates the equivalence of psychodynamic (Monti *et al.*, 2014) and other bona fide therapeutic approaches (Wampold *et al.*, 2002) to CBT for both anxiety and depression. In the UK a randomised controlled trial is underway aiming to prove non-inferiority for a manualised humanistic approach for depression, Counselling for Depression, as compared with standard CBT (Barkham, 2013).

As discussed earlier, however, it is clear that university counselling services are generally no longer in a position to offer a "full course of treatment" of individual sessions, whether CBT or another counselling approach, for students presenting with anxiety, depression or any other issue. Necessity dictates that identifying anxiety and depression as common factors and considering alternative, less resource-intensive means of delivering interventions addressing these issues, might offer a way forward. However, I will argue that the integrated approach emphasising psycho-education explored as follows goes much further than offering a "second-best" way to meet growing demand with fewer resources – like the client-led short-term individual approaches our sector has become skilled in, this model is about making the most of the educational context for the work and focusing on a de-pathologising, skill-building response to student distress.

The starting point for this integrated approach is an aim also to integrate best practice from the range of theoretical models currently informing individual counselling work with students presenting with anxiety and depression. The evidence-based practice debate and its profound effect on the funding landscape has forced a long overdue recognition of the value of CBT among the elitist anti-CBT tribes of my early training. Hopefully the latest research is allowing the pendulum to swing back to a pragmatic middle ground where the value and efficacy of non-CBT approaches are equally evidenced and recognised – and we can all concentrate on using the best aspects of all approaches in order to offer our student clients integrated therapeutic support, which amounts to a whole much greater than the sum of its parts! Single-approach integrations, such as cognitive analytic therapy (CAT), or third-wave CBT models, such as acceptance and commitment therapy (ACT) or schema-focused therapy, are already bridging this divide – but, like all "minority" approaches, they struggle to garner higher-level evidence for their efficacy across the board and they too have protocols depending on considerably more individual sessions than can be delivered routinely in the university setting.

The key to the integrated approach I am proposing for working across a wide range of manifestations of anxieties and depressions is recognition of the flexibility of modern CBT as a framework for delivery of psycho-education and its proven efficacy when delivered in certain self-help formats (NICE, 2009; NICE, 2011). CBT provides an accessible and powerful toolkit of skills, which, once understood and practised in one context, can continue to be used and applied throughout life. I would suggest that an understanding of the basic mechanisms of anxiety and depression, as depicted in the CBT model in terms of unhelpful thinking styles combined with avoidant behaviours, and learning some simple skills for addressing these behaviours and thinking patterns, in itself offers a very useful map for navigating the ordinary ups and downs of life. In addition, third-wave CBT approaches teach active skills, such as mindfulness, to address concepts (implicit in most theoretical approaches) regarding the need to accept life's inherent stress and accompanying anxiety or despondency with learnable skills for resilience and emotional intelligence.

When combined with short-term, focused individual sessions informed by psychodynamic, humanistic or indeed schema-focused CBT or CAT models – which provide a supportive therapeutic relationship engaging in understanding the unique individual narrative within which the anxiety or depression are manifesting – these learnt skills may become further embedded within the transformative *felt* understanding that therapy aims to enable. I believe in this way a powerful and empowering framework can be created for students to learn vital life skills while being appropriately supported in taking charge of their own psychological wellbeing. In this context the aspiration of a university counselling service is not only to keep vulnerable students on their courses, but to make a fundamental contribution to the university's educational mission.

Having identified anxiety and depression as common issues in their own right as well as common factors in many forms of student distress seen at university counselling services, and having recognised the value in students acquiring general skills for tackling these common life problems, we can proceed to consider alternative delivery models that might be able to address these common factors for many of those we see in less resource intensive ways than via individual one-to-one counselling sessions.

Addressing common factors – self-help interventions

The obvious starting point is making targeted use of self-help. Basic self-help materials have long been a staple of university counselling service resources, with advice leaflets on specific issues made available to students in paper form (and more recently online) and self-help books "prescribed" and/or lent to students alongside counselling sessions. More recently, counsellors have also been aware of a range of online resources to refer students to, and counselling service web pages have offered recommendations and links to a range of both online and offline resources. Many counsellors in the sector already see these self-help resources as something to refer students on to when counselling sessions end, in order to try to extend the benefit beyond the limited number of sessions available. Self-help resources might also be signposted when students are on a waiting list. However, it is much less common for self-help resources to be used more proactively and in a structured and supported way.[1]

The evidence for what makes self-help resources most helpful, however, is that *guided* self-help (Gellatly *et al.*, 2007) and, specifically, support in translating learning from self-help resources into constructive action (Varley *et al.*, 2011) is what makes the difference. These principles are incorporated within the "stepped care" approach recommended in the NICE guidelines for both depression and anxiety (NICE, 2009; NICE, 2011) and translated into the IAPT "low intensity" support guidelines (IAPT, 2010). Stepped care gets a bad name when those who clearly need more than this seem to be being "fobbed off" with cursory signposting to self-help materials with which they cannot engage. But the IAPT guidelines (ibid) for use of guided self-help recognise that its effectiveness depends on it being delivered by properly trained practitioners who have the expertise to determine appropriate self-help materials to recommend and who can engage patients with the materials on terms meaningful to them personally (Kahn *et al.*, 2007).

Clearly, counsellors who are skilled in swiftly engaging therapeutically with student clients are very well placed to provide the support and guidance that might allow a student to make full use of appropriate self-help materials in this way. For many students with mild to moderate depression or anxiety one or two individual sessions plus a follow up might be sufficient to support sufficient engagement with a recommended set of self-help resources to set in motion a constructive shift in the student's difficulty. Providing containment and follow up for a client who is being empowered to engage with helpful therapeutic material on their own terms allows the counsellor to offer a significant therapeutic experience within the confines of a very limited number of individual sessions. The benefit to the student of this "light touch" approach is that it is de-pathologising, skill building and also equips the student with resources that can continue to be accessed independently.

Clearly the choice of self-help resources plays an important role in the efficacy of such interventions. The NICE and IAPT guidelines do not endorse specific individual resources, but note that the evidence for effective self-help is for CBT-based resources (ibid). Computerised CBT (CCBT) gains particular recommendation within the depression guidelines, and of course offers the additional benefit of a level of interactivity and reinforcement of learning not available in more static "readable" resources (whether presented on- or off-line). The possibilities for updating and extending the power of such online resources is such that some products may quite quickly become out-dated. For example, the Beating the Blues CCBT software for depression showed early promise in the HE sector (Mitchell & Dunn, 2007), but a follow up paper concluded that despite evidence that it could be an effective treatment for some, low uptake and low user satisfaction indicated that it did not have sufficient appeal in the HE age group (Mitchell, 2009).

Engagement and acceptability to the target audience are therefore important issues for evaluating self-help materials. Two digital resources merit special mention as they were developed specifically for students, with student testers or collaborators participating in the development process to ensure high levels of acceptability to and usability by the target user group – the SAM (Self-help Anxiety Management) smartphone app and the Students Against Depression website are both are also free at the point of use by students and practitioners (see Box 8.1).

Box 8.1 Free digital resources for anxiety and depression

Self-help Anxiety Management (SAM)

The Self-help Anxiety Management (SAM) smartphone app was developed for use by students in a cross-disciplinary collaboration, involving counsellors as well as academics, at the University of the West of England. It offers a personalisable toolkit of anxiety management tools including an anxiety tracker, timed breathing and other relaxation exercises, and meditations, which the user can keep at their fingertips on their mobile phone. The app gains high user ratings and is listed on the NHS Choices Healthy Apps Library.

www.studentsagainstdepression.org

Students Against Depression is an independently clinically-validated website offering information, self-help advice and student peer contributions, which was developed as an action research project with student collaborators (Meyer, 2007) and continues to involve students closely in its delivery. Its printable worksheets and modules (at the time of publication soon to be upgraded to an interactive online support tool) have been carefully designed to help users, or practitioners supporting student users, to formulate the powerful personalised implementation intentions that research has shown to significantly increase the helpfulness of self-help resources (Varley *et al.*, 2011). The site is used by thousands of students (and others) every month.

Other online resources for anxiety and depression

Other well-regarded self-help resources for anxiety, depression and related issues include the excellent modules available from the Australian Centre for Clinical Interventions (CC) – see www.cci.health.wa.gov.au – and the widely-used NHS self-help leaflets developed at Northumberland, Tyne and Wear NHS Foundation Trust – see www.ntw.nhs.uk/pic/selfhelp/.

The advantage of using free online and digital resources is that newer resources can be quickly adopted when they become available, without financial loss. However, well-evidenced commercial CCBT packages, such as Silvercloud (Sharry *et al.*, 2013) – another product developed with students and with emphasis on user engagement – may offer significant advantages in terms of built-in interactivity together with reinforcement via carefully controlled, anonymous use of social media. This, along with some other online CBT packages such as Living Life to the Full (www.llttf.com), offer practical options for online practitioner review and support as clients work through the self-help modules – facilitating the possibility of using these packages as a genuine extension of individual face-to-face sessions. For example, at Teesside University, where the counselling service has been at the forefront of integration of computerised and online packages (Scott-Marshall, 2011), Silvercloud has been successfully integrated into the service in a number of ways, including enrolling students on the waiting list for face-to-face sessions and offering a viable alternative for students on placement or otherwise less able to access counselling.

However, practitioners need to keep themselves updated about developments in the field, as the rate of development and change is high. One useful source for update information in the future is likely to be the MindTech Healthcare Technology Co-operative (www.mindtech.org.uk) – this national centre funded by the National Institute for Healthcare Research was founded in 2013 to co-ordinate research and collaborate in the development and testing of new technologies for mental health and dementia. Another useful source of information about up-to-date resources is the NHS Choices "Health Apps Library" (which only lists apps which have passed its rigorous review process).

Whether high or low tech, the key to successful use of self-help resources is to regard them as ways "for therapists and clients to extend the range and effectiveness of their face-to-face work" – an apt turn of phrase used by one of its developers to describe the SAM app (Topham, 2012). A counsellor orienting a student client to a specifically chosen exercise or module, and then following up the student's application of their learning to their own unique circumstances, will exponentially increase the helpfulness of a referral to these and other resources. The same could equally be said for the next topic we turn our attention to – addressing anxiety and depression via group interventions.

Addressing common factors – group interventions

Given the ubiquity of anxiety and depression, university services are constantly struggling to address these issues on an individual level. Common sense would dictate that group interventions addressing these issues would be an efficient use of resources (Wallace, 2014b). Group interventions also effectively address some of the key factors exacerbating psychological difficulties in general, and low mood in particular – isolation and decreased social contact. Indeed, one of the most consistent pieces of feedback from successful group interventions, in my experience, is the "normalising" effect of meeting others with similar feelings or difficulties.

Unfortunately, a powerful bias towards the idea of individual counselling as preferable or "better" may often be held by both students and many counsellors (whose training will generally have focused on the development of an exclusive one-to-one therapeutic relationship). While workshops on common student issues, such as exam or presentation anxiety (Bradley, 2013), have long been a staple of counselling service offering, and practitioners regularly report a range of useful group interventions developed and offered in their services, with good outcomes for those who attend (Diamond & Proctor, 2011; Mitchell, 2011), successful recruitment to and retention in group interventions remains notoriously difficult by anecdotal report in the sector. This translates into resource inefficiency when a great deal of practitioner/service time is invested in preparing and delivering these interventions.

A key factor seems to be how the group interventions are integrated within the overall offering of the service. As one counsellor offering a successful therapy group puts it: "The support from colleagues is vital to embedding the group in the culture of the counselling team so that groupwork is as much to the forefront as individual counselling" (Porucznik, 2013). I would go further than this to suggest that groups are likely to recruit and run most successfully where they are not presented as part of a "menu" of choices alongside individual sessions, but instead are integrated into pathways through the service as *extensions* of the individual face-to-face work. A "slow, open" therapy group might, for example, be the long-term support option available once a student has used the limited number of individual sessions available (ibid).

A particularly effective way of integrating group interventions is to draw on the context provided by the educational setting and to present them not so much as alternative forms of therapy but instead as *learning opportunities*. Group-based CBT or CBT-based psycho-education interventions are recommended in the NICE guidelines for both depression and anxiety at mild to moderate levels (NICE, 2009; NICE, 2011), and CBT lends itself well to being presented in terms of the learning of skills and strategies. At Portsmouth University we avoid use of the word "group" – all of our group interventions are presented as "courses" or as "workshops" and we have experimented in some courses with using a seminar format with desks rather than the traditional circle of chairs. We find that using upbeat, de-stigmatising language, emphasising the learning aspects and reassuring students that they will not be required to share personal details all help significantly with recruitment, while knowing that students will still benefit from the peer support aspects of the intervention once they arrive.

While the Portsmouth courses and workshops are advertised widely around the university and any student can self-refer, we find that the most effective use of these group interventions is as an extension of, or orientation to, individual counselling sessions. The in-house Mood Boost course (see Meyer, 2014) – a four-week psycho-education course for low mood and mild to moderate depression teaching basic CBT and behavioural activation principles – is run three times within the academic year, making it a practical option for larger numbers as a forerunner or follow-on to a series of individual counselling sessions. We have also been piloting a collaborative venture with the local IAPT service whereby they offer specially-adapted, shorter versions of their CBT-focused anxiety (From Stress to Success) and panic (Keep Calm and Carry On) groups, again presented as "courses" not "groups", open only to students and delivered on campus. By linking the courses with individual counselling sessions we are able to ensure that the skills are learnt or reinforced within a personalised therapeutic context. Akin to the significant benefit of guided self-help, this focused and deliberate integration of distinct psycho-educative experiences has the potential to increase significantly the value of individual short-term counselling.

One of the most popular and widely-spread group interventions being offered in university settings is mindfulness training (e.g. Theaker, 2011). Mindfulness is recommended in the NICE guidelines for relapse prevention in chronic depression (NICE, 2011). There is also solid evidence for its effectiveness in relieving symptoms of a current episode of depression, although not for a current episode of primary anxiety disorder (Strauss *et al.*, 2014). However, mindfulness has been shown to reduce levels of anxiety, depression and stress in the more general sense (Khoury *et al.*, 2013) and to reduce stress in university students (Regehr *et al.*, 2013). Certainly, mindfulness lends itself well to being presented as a positive life skill applicable to students in general, rather than as a therapeutic "treatment". It has been adapted for use with performing arts students to help them cope with competitive pressures and performance anxiety (Faris, 2012) and for "Coping with University Life" (Lynch *et al.*, 2011). Again, such group interventions can offer a very useful extension of therapeutic engagement, empowering student clients with further life skills known to be helpful in managing the stress that might make students susceptible to depression or anxiety. Individual preparatory sessions or follow ups can ensure that students have support in applying the skills effectively to address their particular issues with stress, anxiety or low mood. The Mindfulness for Students website (www.mindfulnessforstudents.co.uk) is a useful resource for both practitioners and students.

Group interventions can also be an effective way to support and augment self-help – a Swedish randomised controlled trial found that bibliotherapy supplemented with online group discussion was as effective as individual therapist-facilitated guided self-help for social anxiety, with both offering outcomes in line with traditional face-to-face CBT (Furmark *et al.*, 2009). At Teesside University, where Silvercloud is used to offer online self-help, the service also offers a three-week Silvercloud Plus "taught and discussion based course", which frames the Silvercloud CCBT materials on stress, anxiety, depression and sleep as a way to "help students learn and develop lifelong key personal skills to help manage a range of emotions".[2] These therapeutic interventions are thereby effectively de-stigmatised and framed as the source of useful life skills for all students.

Another option to consider would include making use of well-integrated student-led peer support groups to deliver guided self-help or other group interventions. The national Student Minds charity (www.studentminds.org.uk) offers peer support training and on-going supervision for campus-based student volunteers running carefully designed peer support programmes. They have collaborated with us at Students Against Depression to develop a six-week Positive Minds peer support course offering a carefully structured, guided self-help programme working through the basic behavioural activation elements of the Students Against Depression website. The course teaches students about the power of implementation intentions, equipping them to continue making constructive use of the Students Against Depression modules or other self-help materials.[3] The course focuses on helping students build their social connections, so may be particularly suitable for students who are isolated or lacking in social support.

A few counselling services have experimented with offering online peer support groups to extend face-to-face services, such as the University of Birmingham's QChat service for anonymous discussion of issues of sexual orientation and gender.[4] Concerns about the risks associated with negative use of such 24/7 spaces, and the corresponding need for resource-intensive monitoring, probably contribute to a lack of such services being widely available. However, some universities are starting to make use of the award-winning Big White Wall service, which offers an anonymous online peer support environment facilitated by trained moderators and reinforced with guided self-help for common issues like anxiety and depression, and one-to-one online therapeutic support options. Students can be referred to this service as individuals if they are willing and able to pay the monthly subscription rate, however the service can also be contracted on an institutional basis including an optional extra making it possible for online support to be offered by the institution's own clinicians via the secure Skype-style BWW platform.

At the time of publication, some universities were offering the Big White Wall service via their students' unions, rather than through the counselling services. However, I would suggest that an integrated approach allowing active referral and monitoring by counsellors or other institutional support staff is likely to ensure that an investment in this service has most benefit for students. Recognising that services such as these are of most benefit when properly integrated and personalised for local conditions also goes some way to addressing concerns that university funders might mistakenly see such services as cheaper straightforward alternatives to in-house counselling support.

Addressing crisis, risk and complex mental health disorders

The 24/7 nature of online resources – particularly those with peer support elements such as Big White Wall – have a further benefit when considering the dilemmas for service provision posed by students affected by severe depression and/or suicidality. If offered as an integrated part of service provision they can play a role in ensuring that students have clear messages about crisis support options and a viable "place to go" out of hours. However, crisis, risk and increasing severity and complexity of student mental health conditions perhaps pose most significant challenges to the routine provision of short-term counselling and, although crisis and risk are by no means restricted to those affected by depression or anxiety, a chapter focusing on short-term work with anxiety and depression needs to consider these challenges in more detail.

In my experience of nearly 20 years' counselling in the HE sector, the most common driver for provision of longer-term counselling has been related to perceptions of risk and/or severity of presentation. Questions such as those posed by Hallett (2012), about the ethics of limiting numbers of sessions for those with increased levels of psychological disturbance, reflect a longstanding staple of the underpinning assumptions and raison d'etre for university counselling services – as "containers" of institutional distress and disturbance, counselling services have traditionally been "left to [their] own devices . . . to balance the books ethically, measure urgency, prioritize from waiting lists and manage the collision of need and entitlement" (ibid, p. 257). Traditionally, services were able to strike this balance by short-term working with the majority of students, thereby "buying" time to provide longer-term counselling with those whose needs seem more urgent or severe.

However, the trend of higher levels of disturbance, noted among university students since the policy of "widening access" (Rana *et al.*, 1999), has continued and intensified (Royal College of Psychiatrists, 2003, 2011), while universities have at the same time experienced cuts and changes to funding formulae putting acute pressure on all institutional spending. In this context a difficult double bind arises as counselling services face higher levels of demand, in terms of both numbers and complexity, often without realistic expectation of gaining higher levels of funding – arguing that a significant amount of student need cannot be met with what the service is generally able to offer (i.e. short-term counselling) risks begging the question whether counselling services are the appropriate format in which the institution ought to invest for student mental health support. Many counselling services have indeed seen active cuts or a shifting of funding to other forms of mental health support.

I would argue that some of this shift is, in fact, appropriate and in the best case scenario facilitates greater clarity about the purpose and value of counselling within an HE setting, i.e. placing it as an essential and valuable part of a wider, multidisciplinary approach to support for student mental health. I agree with Hallett's (2012) contention that care should be taken about raising vulnerable students' expectations of psychological support – university counselling services are increasingly being careful not to present themselves as offering full "treatment" for diagnosed mental health disorders, and are rightly making it clear to students that their needs might require referral to longer-term or NHS-based care (whether medical, psychological or both). Many services are now successfully arguing for their institutions to engage actively at a higher level with local NHS providers to ensure that students' mental health needs are being properly considered and accounted for as part of local mental health provision, and many institutions now employ mental health advisers and co-ordinators to facilitate students' access to appropriate NHS treatment. For example, at the more extreme end of the spectrum of difficulties with anxiety and depression – OCD, phobias, PTSD, chronic self harm, moderately-severe to severe depression and active risk of suicide – it is appropriate for students to be accessing diagnosis and medical treatment via the NHS. Those with moderate anxiety and depression that has not responded to lighter touch interventions in the university setting should also be supported in accessing IAPT higher-intensity provision.

However, I believe that university counsellors can still argue strongly for the valuable contribution made in this context by embedded counselling provision. It can offer containment via short-term therapeutic engagement focusing on how the individual student, with their own unique difficulties and background, can *make use of* such NHS treatment and a wide range of additional resources in order to move forward with greater psychological balance and wellbeing – and with greater ability to engage with their studies. Referral to and follow up after outside treatment or provision provided by in-house counsellors, skilled in orienting the student within the educational setting, can ensure the student is supported to make best use of the available treatment options.

Likewise, I think counsellors are better served by greater clarity around responding to and managing risk in the institution, and by clarifying their own role within a wider institutional response. If counselling is not the only option for containing risk, for example, then short-term counselling could offer a very useful intervention to support a student in crisis and facilitate engagement with other appropriate services and support. In this context it makes sense for services to differentiate clearly between "crisis response" provision and counselling provision. In some institutions, "drop ins" and other forms of immediate access are offered by counsellors but in a format that is clearly distinguished from standard counselling appointments. In others, mental health or wellbeing advisers provide initial crisis response services and support on a flexible basis, including going out into the institution to attend to crises (such as episodes of psychosis, for example), where they arise. Having a clear and reasonable crisis response provision in the institution – a way for students to access appropriate practical support in a crisis – should allow counsellors to provide focused therapeutic support with the emphasis on therapy rather than on safeguarding, and to "let go" of students who have completed a short-term therapeutic engagement rather than prolonging counselling provision simply as a risk containment measure.

Of course, counselling still plays a vital role in the containment and management of risk. Counsellors are very well placed to offer the safe, non-judgemental and confidential space in which students might feel able to acknowledge and address taboo thoughts and feelings around self harm and suicide, and to develop connections and insights about the unique individual circumstances within which these issues have arisen, in itself can play a role in reducing the risk (Reeves, 2010). This does not necessarily require a long-term engagement – a systematic review of the evidence regarding counselling and psychotherapy for the prevention of suicide (Winter *et al.*, 2009) found a significant effect for a range of therapeutic approaches even of less than six sessions' duration. The strongest evidence was for therapy in the CBT family, particularly DBT (dialectical behaviour therapy), but with promising results for a range of other, under-researched approaches particularly when including a problem-solving element.

The aim of short-term therapeutic work in this context might be to address risk issues overtly in a de-stigmatising way, to help the student to evaluate their own risk and to mobilise their own choices and options in response to this risk, possibly working actively on identifying measures which might constitute a personalised "safety plan". Such a plan might include identifying and referring on to appropriate sources of diagnosis and treatment for severe depression or other mental health conditions, if applicable, as well as considering a clear avenue for obtaining crisis support and implementing self-help distress management measures. Facilitating a student's use of a safety plan[5] could form an appropriate focus for a very short series of counselling sessions following an initial assessment of risk of suicide, alongside appropriate onward referral where indicated.

With appropriate treatment ideally in place, or at least with clear avenues for obtaining crisis support, a student with severe anxiety or depression or chronic mental health difficulties might well be able to then make further use of one or more series of short-term focused counselling episodes or of relevant psycho-education opportunities to address specific issues. For example, at Portsmouth a number of students with relatively severe depression have attended the Mood Boost course with the support of the mental health co-ordinator and alongside pursuing appropriate medical and crisis team support. Plans are also underway to offer tailored psycho-education in the form of an Emotional Coping Skills group, run by mental health advisers with DBT training, for students at chronic risk of self harm and crisis but who do not meet criteria for treatment in secondary care.

Referring to the possibility of a "series" of counselling episodes introduces the pragmatic recognition that more than one short-term counselling engagement may be appropriate during a student's time at university – and even within the space of an academic year. However, there is a significant difference between a "revolving door" situation where longer-term support is delivered by default, but without overarching intention, and an approach that makes purposeful use of time-focused engagements within a well-considered overarching framework. The final section summarises the overarching framework within which the approach I have been proposing can be understood and applied.

Time-focused therapy revisited

The basic underlying principle of short-term counselling is its constructive and hopeful engagement with time limits, offering a "light touch" approach that trusts in the client's ability to see through the application in their lives of a focused therapeutic shift or piece of learning. Others have already argued cogently elsewhere in this volume for the "fit" of this perspective with counselling taking place in an educational setting (Coren), and for a practical model of delivery (Groves and Cowley, Chapter 6). What I have proposed builds on these principles, exploring the benefit of integrating the further learning opportunities available through psycho-education and guided self-help in order to extend the impact of a short-term individual therapeutic engagement.

While these ideas may be useful for individual counsellors in the sector to consider and apply, the model makes most sense when applied as a consistent service-wide approach along the lines of the Cardiff Model or a variation of it. The theoretical framework I find most helpful in considering this is an adaptation of Elton-Wilson's (1996) "time conscious psychological therapy", which recognises that a client's development or "psychological transformation" will most often take place through a *series* of therapeutic relationships probably using the services "of a variety of professional helpers, as well as drawing on the support of external resources and facing the common existential challenge of [life]" (ibid, p. 1). For me this translates very well into a service model where clients are offered short time- and content-focused engagements always working to an ending (and, ideally, a break) before committing to any further engagement. This builds in the option of a "revolving door", but in a purposeful and constructive way, which requires both client and therapist to work to a clear ending and then pause before any agreement to engage in a further piece of work.

In the model I have been putting forward in this chapter, for adding value when working with anxiety and depression, the option of undertaking guided self-help or referral to a psycho-educational group might be seen as part of a focused piece of "holding" work with a client for whom this might be enough, or it might be considered as a referral and extension option after a time-focused piece of counselling. A follow-up review session after completion of the guided self-help or psycho-education group, or of a course of treatment within the NHS, would generally be recommended, as a way to ensure that the learning was personalised and embedded within the focus of the individual piece of work, but this could be agreed with the client depending on what felt most appropriate for them. The guiding principle would always be to work with the "lightest touch" possible, creating therapeutic opportunities framed within a context of learning and skill-building to complement the educational experience in which the client is already engaged.

The key framework to keep in view is the mission of a university counselling service to supplement and support *learning* and to frame all therapeutic endeavour in this context. Indeed, I would argue that the emphasis in defining our work has needed to change in recent years away from the confidential, closeted and mysterious receiver and processor of the institution's distress and disturbance and towards an active role in educating both institutions and individual students about mental health and about the imperative for both education and employability of an applied understanding of emotional resilience and psychological wellbeing.

Notes

1 For example, in a workshop at a recent BACP-UC conference most participants said they had referred students to the Students Against Depression website, but very few had used one of the site's worksheets with a client.
2 See www.tees.ac.uk/sections/studentsupport/student_health_counselling2.cfm.
3 See www.studentminds.org.uk/positive-minds-course.html
4 See birmingham.ac.uk/as/studentservices/counselling/services/qchat/index.aspx
5 For example, see 'Desperate right now?' at www.studentsagainstdepression.org for a safety plan worksheet for formulating clear implementation intentions (Varley *et al.*, 2011) for suicide and elsewhere on the site for self harm.

References

Barkham M. (2013) Counselling for Depression vs CBT. *Therapy Today*, 24 (5), 18–20.
Bell, E. (1996) *Counselling in Further and Higher Education*, Maidenhead, Open University Press.
Bradley, A. (2013) At ease with presentations. *University & College Counselling*, May, 6–9.
Coren, A. (1999) Brief Psychodynamic Counselling in Educational Settings, in Lees, J. and Vaspe, A. (Eds) *Clinical Counselling in Further and Higher Education* (pp. 58–74), London, Routledge.
Diamond, L. & Proctor, A. (2011) Making a difference: The roles of groups in developing self-efficacy. *AUCC Journal*, March 2011, 10–13.
Elton-Wilson, J. (1996) *Time Conscious Psychological Therapy: A Life-Stage to Go Through*, Abingdon, Routledge.
Faris, A. (2012), Mindfulness for Students. *Therapy Today*, September 2012, 19–21. Available from:http://mindfulnessforstudents.co.uk/wp-content/uploads/2012/10/Mindfulness-TT Sept12-3.pdf (accessed 30th June 2015).

Furmark, T., Carlbring, P., Hedman, E., Sonnenstein, A., Clevberger, P., Bohman, B., Eriksson, A., Hallen, A., Frykman, M., Holmstrom, A., Sparthan, E., Tillfors, M., Nilsson Ihrfelt, E., Spak, M., Eriksson, A., Ekselius, L. & Andersson, G. (2009) Guided and unguided self-help for social anxiety disorder: randomised controlled trial. *British Journal of Psychiatry*, 195, 440–447.

Gellatly, J., Bower, P., Hennessy, S., Richards, D., Gilbody, S. & Lovell, K. (2007) What makes self-help interventions effective in the management of depressive symptoms? Meta-analysis and meta-regression. *Psychological Medicine*, 37, 1217–1228.

Hallett, C. (2012) Is there time enough? Ethical dilemmas inherent in offering time-limited work in the university. *British Journal of Psychotherapy*, 28 (2), 249–263.

IAPT (2010) *Good Practice Guidance on the Use of Self-Help Materials Within IAPT Services*, NHS Improving Access to Psychological Therapies.

Kahn, N., Bower, P. & Rogers, A. (2007). Guided self-help in primary care mental health: Metasynthesis of qualitative studies of patient experience. *British Journal of Psychiatry*, 191, 206–211.

Khoury, B., Lecomte, T., Fortin, G., Masse, M., Therien, P., Bouchard, V., Chapleau, M. A., Paquin, K. & Hofmann, S. G. (2013) Mindfulness-based therapy: A comprehensive meta-analysis. *Clinical Psychology Review*, 33 (6), 763–771.

Lynch, S., Gander, M-L., Kohls, N., Kudielka, B. & Walach, H. (2011). Mindfulness-based coping with university life: A non-randomized wait-list-controlled pilot evaluation. *Stress and Health*, 27 (5), 365–375.

Meyer, D. (2007) Online self-help: Developing a student-focused website for depression. *Counselling & Psychotherapy Research*, 7 (3), 151–156.

Meyer, D. (2014) Course work. *University and College Counselling*, September 2014, 16–19.

Mitchell, N. (2009) Computerised CBT self-help for depression in higher education: Reflections on a pilot. *Counselling & Psychotherapy Research*, 9 (4), 1–7.

Mitchell, N. (2011) Finding your worth – with group CBT. *AUCC Journal*, March 2011, 6–9.

Mitchell, N. & Dunn, K. (2007) Pragmatic evaluation of the viability of CCBT self-help for depression in higher education. *Counselling & Psychotherapy Research*, 7 (3), 144–150.

Monti, F., Tonetti, L. & Ricci Bitti, P. E. (2014) Comparison of cognitive-behavioural therapy and psychodynamic therapy in the treatment of anxiety among university students: An effectiveness study. *British Journal of Guidance & Counselling*, 42 (3), 233–244.

NICE Guidelines CG90 (2009) *Depression in Adults: The Treatment and Management of Depression in Adults*, National Institute for Care and Health Excellence.

NICE Guidelines CG113 (2011) *Generalised Anxiety Disorder and Panic Disorder (With or Without Agoraphobia) in Adults: Management in Primary, Secondary and Community Care*, National Institute for Care and Health Excellence.

Porucznik, H. (2013) The place where I touch base. *University & College Counselling*. May 2013, 17–19.

Rana, R., Smith, E. & Walkling, J. (1999) *Degrees of Disturbance: The New Agenda. The Impact of Increasing Levels of Psychological Disturbance amongst Students in Higher Education. Heads of University Counselling Services*. Rugby, British Association of Counselling.

Reeves, A. (2010) *Counselling Suicidal Clients*, London, Sage.

Regehr, C., Glancy, D. & Pitts, A. (2013) Interventions to reduce stress in university students: A review and meta-analysis. *Journal of Affective Disorders*, May 2013, 148 (1), 1–11.

Royal College of Psychiatrists (2003) *The Mental Health of Students in Higher Education. Council Report CR112*, London, Royal College of Psychiatrists.

Royal College of Psychiatrists (2011) *The Mental Health of Students in Higher Education. College Report CR166*, London, Royal College of Psychiatrists.

Scott-Marshall, S. (2011) Moving Forward: The Teesside University counselling model. *AUCC Journal*, November 2011.

Sharry, J., Davidson, R., McLoughlin, O. & Doherty, G. (2013) A service-based evaluation of a therapist-supported cognitive behavioural programme for depression. *Journal of Medical Internet Research*, 15 (6), e121.

Strauss, C., Cavanagh, K., Oliver, A. & Pettman, D. (2014) Mindfulness-based interventions for people diagnosed with a current episode of an anxiety or depressive disorder: a meta-analysis of randomised controlled trials. *PLOS ONE*, 9 (4), e96110.

Theaker, C. (2011). Running a mindfulness group. *AUCC Journal*, March 2011, 14–19.

Topham, P. (2012) Making people appy :) *AUCC Journal*, Spring 2012, 10–14.

Varley, R., Webb, T. L. & Sheeran, P. (2011) Making self-help more helpful: A randomized controlled trial of the impact of augmenting self-help materials with implementation intentions on promoting the effective self-management of anxiety symptoms. *Journal of Consulting and Clinical Psychology*, 79 (1), 123–128.

Wallace, P. (2012) The impact of counselling on academic outcomes: A student perspective. *AUCC Journal*, November 2012, 6–11.

Wallace, P. (2014a) *Counselling in universities and colleges*. Available from: www.minded. org.uk (accessed 18th December 2014).

Wallace, P. (2014b) The positive wider impact of counselling provision in colleges and universities. *BACP-UC Journal*, September 2014, 22–25.

Wampold, B. E., Minami, T., Baskin, T. W. & Tierney, S. W. (2002) A meta (re)analysis of the effects of cognitive therapy versus "other therapies" for depression. *Journal of Affective Disorders*, 68 (2–3), 159–165.

Winter, D., Bradshaw, S., Bunn, F. & Wellsted, D. (2009) *Counselling and psychotherapy for the prevention of suicide: A systematic review of the evidence*, British Association for Counselling & Psychotherapy.

Chapter 9

Somatised distress in university students

Sue Anderson and Dorothy Louden

"I feel sick. My throat is tight. I feel jumpy. It's like a physical thing . . ." Words straddle the mind/body divide but what *is* somatised distress? Is it real or imagined, serious or minor, physical or psychological, or both? Are mind and body even separate?

The word "distress" originates from the Latin *districtus* meaning "division of mind". Somatised distress lies at another dividing point, the junction of mental and physical health, with an implied assumption of mind–body partition. Somatisation emerges when mental factors such as stress cause physical symptoms, with somatoform disorders (such as Body Dysmorphic, Conversion and Pain Disorders) being more severe and long-term. But as Kuo and Kavanagh (1994) remind us, many cultures from where our increasingly international student body originate, do not distinguish mind from body, nor illness from other problems of living. Definition is not easy.

In this chapter we take a holistic and pragmatic approach to the phenomenon of somatised distress with its physical *and* psychological manifestations. We explore challenges of working in HE counselling settings, illustrated through two psychotherapeutic models. We debate what services in HE can realistically be expected to offer and what can be achieved by therapists working in a brief way when there is complex need.

Understanding somatised distress – perspectives from medicine, neuroscience and psychological therapy

Somatised distress is an emotive phenomenon, often misunderstood. By its very nature the cause is not immediately apparent. Words and phrases such as "hypochondria", "hysteria", "exaggerated" and "in your head" can be used, by lay and professional people, and the link between physical sensations, biological cause, past and present disturbance can be unclear. In the UK, physical symptoms are usually treated initially within primary care. The medical model aims to diagnose and treat, and may regard a physical symptom as psychosomatic if unexplained, possibly indicative of a psychiatric disorder requiring treatment and symptom alleviation. But might physical manifestations be understood in other ways, as an expression or communication, a disturbance held in the body in a physical form, with meaning, function and potential for resolution?

Physical manifestations can exist both with and without biological cause, so assessment is key. Clearly, not all physical symptoms are somatised distress but it has been pointed out "people who have suffered chronic trauma are much more likely than the average person to suffer from serious medical problems" (Boon, Steele & Van der Hart, 2011, p. 45). A student counselling service will need to liaise closely with professional colleagues in order to clarify physical symptoms and respond appropriately. In this chapter we highlight the importance of inter-agency liaison.

When distress can be verbalised, being held in narrative memory (Rothschild, 2011), it is available for cortical processing (recognition, reflection, understanding) and more helpful perspectives can be developed. We are delighted to work with clients who are able to "work through" issues in counselling, reach a resolution and respond to our talking therapy. But embodied distress cannot so easily be put into words. "Talking just doesn't seem to help", is a familiar response when, as short-term therapists, we can feel stuck, unable to help and aware that the clock of our time-conscious model is ticking.

Distress is expressed in many ways. Commonly recognised symptoms such as tension in our shoulders, headaches, butterflies in the stomach, irritated skin, diarrhoea, feeling sick, cold or numb with fright are forms of somatisation often resulting from stress, fear and anxiety. Therapists are also familiar with manifestations such as digestive problems, panic attacks, pain and physical components of trauma memories as seen in hyper-arousal, hyper-vigilance and sensory memories that feature in flashbacks and nightmares. Clients can become disconnected from their emotions and may engage in physical activities such as addictions, self-harm, problematic eating and excessive exercise due to avoidance or dissociation. There might be an unconscious over-focus on body sensations, as in hypochondria. When distress is expressed non-verbally, through behaviour, body sensations or appears in a dissociated form, such as amnesia, depersonalisation or derealisation, it is not so accessible to cortical process or insight (Boon, Steele & Van der Hart, 2011).

Within psychological therapies, there are various ways of understanding somatised distress. Psychoanalysis refers to defence mechanisms, where the ego can repress emotion, holding it outside awareness as a physical symptom, thereby protecting itself from pain (Errington & Murdin, 2006). Humanistic therapies (Feltham & Horton, 2006) regard physical manifestations as meaningful, requiring acceptance of the relevance to the individual as she grows towards autonomy and self-actualisation. A cognitive-behaviourist might regard somatised distress behaviour such as self-harm as resulting from a "phobia of inner experience" (Boon, Steele & Van der Hart, 2011, p. 315), a coping behaviour linked with, or avoidant of, dysfunctional thoughts and maladaptive core beliefs. The Adaptive Information Processing (AIP) model, which underpins Eye Movement

Desensitisation and Reprocessing Therapy (EMDR) (Shapiro, 2001), states that body sensations (such as jumpiness, tension, breathlessness or pain) may be unprocessed trauma, components of a memory of a previous disturbing experience, which has not been fully processed or integrated into the brain's neural pathways leading to maladaptive functioning and distress. Unprocessed sensory memory is stored in the nervous system, as if frozen in time, and can easily be retriggered if the fight/flight/freeze alarm system is re-activated. Parnell (1999) explains that the "body remembers . . . but the body memory . . . (may not be) . . . consciously linked with a visual memory" (p. 98) of a previous trauma so may be experienced as somatic.

Whatever the approach, distress that has become somatised is tenacious and challenging, particularly for counsellors using brief therapy. Past disturbance for clients may lead to an undervaluing of the body, poor physical care and an inability to enjoy the body's pleasures so that it becomes a target for fear, hatred, shame, attack or avoidance. Entrenched habits such as physical neglect, self-harm, disordered eating can form; myths can become embedded such as body image perfectionism, an increasingly worldwide phenomenon (Orbach, 2009).

Implications for practice

It would be easy to lose hope as therapists when faced with such complex presentations. But we have found two short-term models helpful for working with somatised distress: first, group work combining psycho-education and therapeutic support for students with difficulties around eating and body image; and second, working individually using EMDR with students suffering somatised traumatic stress. Both aim to foster enhanced affect management, modification of body responses to stress, increased understanding through psycho-education about physical and emotional needs, and to promote self-care and informed choice: in short, a more helpful relationship with self, other and the world via the body.

Three challenges pertain to this work. First, the time available at university where students come and go seasonally and rapidly, often presenting with acute, transitional issues but sometimes chronic psychological and/or attachment difficulties. The second challenge is the need to work with the somatisation itself as well as what it might represent or originate from, and the third is the need for clear parameters, careful risk assessment and a preparedness to refer on where appropriate.

Working with students with eating issues

Orbach (2009) speaks about the culture of embodiment in which "the body is both a statement and a site of empowerment" (p. 136) for the individual whose expression of self, identity and belonging often comes "via exhibiting the right kind of body" (p. 137). Students in higher education are typically young adults in transition from adolescence to adulthood, a phase prone to vulnerability and anxiety about identity, differentiation and acceptance of self.

As Orbach suggests, an increasingly global body industry is developing around body transformation, diet and surgical reconstruction. With young adults the world over immersed in instant and globalised visual and cultural references to this industry, it is not surprising therefore that physical manifestations of struggles with identity, belonging and relationships are a common and frequent presentation at a university counselling service. At the University of Birmingham counselling service the percentage of presentations with eating and body-related issues is around 5 per cent. The actual incidence will be higher due to non-disclosure at registration, especially in men, and also due to data collection difficulties. The counselling service works increasingly with international students. Cultural variations affect disclosure, help-seeking and attitudes to difficulties around eating and body image. International students bring their own personal, family and cultural history, which may dovetail or clash but certainly interact with the visual cultural references they find in the UK.

Orbach believes the "binary of good body and bad body" needs addressing as a body anxiety or source of disturbance in the body in and of itself, not just for what it might represent or be expressing, emotionally or psychologically. My (Sue Anderson) approach to working with students with difficulties of eating and body image is informed by the two-fold approach to which Orbach alludes, the physical *and* the emotional/psychological. The implication that eating disorders are somatised distress might suggest that to resolve the distress will eliminate the behaviour. But just as Orbach insists that body anxiety needs its own response, so others (Garner, 1997; Schmidt & Treasure, 1993) have long pointed out that problems of eating and body image need a binary response in both physical and psychological domains. The Minnesota study (Keys, Brozek, Henschel & Mickelsen, 1950) showed the clear physical and psychological effects of prolonged semi-starvation on psychologically healthy individuals akin to the profile of eating disorders. The study was early evidence of the need for a physical as well as psychological intervention.

Liaison with other agencies

In HE, inquiry at assessment about medical history and contact with services is vital. Due to issues of shame, secrecy, attachment to the behaviours and control it is possible that a client with an eating difficulty has not consulted their GP or may have masked symptoms and behaviours. It is therefore possible that risks (electrolyte imbalance, arrhythmia, sudden heart failure) associated with binge and purging behaviours have not been explored. I routinely recommend a GP assessment for all students with eating issues. Due to the severity and high risks associated with eating disorders (Arcelus, Mitchell, Wales & Nielsen, 2011), referral into medical services may be necessary as the sole service providing comprehensive care and in some instances the student may need to take a leave of absence or apply to the Mental Health Advisory Service for reasonable adjustments to continue studying.

University counselling services are nevertheless well placed to provide a pre-ventive service, and brief interventions may be entirely appropriate either with early-onset or with students who have previously had professional input but wish to revisit the issue or prevent further relapse. However, it is important to be clear about the parameters for the service including informed consent for liaison with the GP, for safety of both client and therapy. Supervision and peer support is crucial for this work, which can evoke anxiety and a sense of helplessness in therapists as their competence is challenged by students' apparent reluctance to change and their apparent attachment to damaging eating behaviours and attitudes to food.

One-to-one or group?

There are pros and cons. Individual work can provide more in-depth exploration and is free of peer competitiveness, comparisons and collusions, but lacks the opportunity for peer support and normalisation of experience, e.g. being subject to body and diet industry marketing and gender stereotyping from a young age. Group work gives the opportunity for harnessing the positive side of peer influ-ence and perhaps coverage of a greater range of issues that can ignite personal, private change. But group work can be susceptible to and distracted by difficult dynamics, perhaps particularly with students with eating issues who are especially concerned with identity, body comparisons and anxious differentiation from oth-ers. Careful facilitation is therefore required, as in any group work.

The group may be less attractive to men who are likely to be in a minority, suggesting perhaps a tailored provision focusing on exercise, body image, use of supplements and body enhancements as somatisation in men may manifest as extremes in exercise and body-shaping. Recognising difficulties in men can be problematic due to established diagnostic criteria leading to later presentation at services perhaps with increased shame for what is perceived to be a female issue.

Each therapist will have their own preferred style and each client their own receptivity to varying modalities. I have found the group method of delivery to be well suited to young adults with eating issues and a great opportunity to generate a shared atmosphere of curiosity, openness, fun and possibility not always available in the more intense, individual relationship. Some students choose one-to-one some group. The making of a choice is therapeutic although it may be necessary to provide reassurance about group work so that students do not deprive them-selves of its potential benefits.

The eating issues group

Working with a shared difficulty gives the group an identity, but that is where the commonality ends, and the importance of individual experience is emphasised from the start. The main purpose of the group is to convey the two-fold task recov-ery demands: tackling the physical aspects of eating behaviours as well as emo-tional and life difficulties. The overall aim is to increase awareness of disturbed relationship to the body, enhance motivation to harness more helpful choices and behaviours and develop less self-destructive ways of dealing with distress and experience, whatever form that takes for each group member.

The group is short-term: six weeks, with linking topics. I introduce prospective members to the programme at a pre-group individual assessment at which I assess the suitability of the group for them, establishing whether there is a level of risk that may mean group work is unsuitable, and at which they decide whether to join. Criteria for group membership are engagement in food restriction and/or binge–purge behaviours, and an ability to cope with the rigours of a group experience. On occasions I decline a place if the student's level of functioning is seriously impaired, where urgent medical referral is indicated or where the student is phobic towards food or vomiting but does not have a distorted body image, a fear of becoming fat or an avoidance of weight gain. Individual counselling can be offered. There are 10 places available in the group, which is closed after week one.

Content

The sessions initially cover perpetuating factors (for restrictors, semi-starvation; for binge–purgers, the binge–purge-starve cycle). The remaining sessions cover predisposing factors (socio-cultural attitudes to weight, shape, gender, health and success, the influence of family and the body industry) and precipitating factors (triggers, events, diets, perfectionism, the mindset of good/bad body/self). The sessions are largely topic-led with a small group format familiar to students, using quizzes, pair-work and whole group discussions, letter writing and physical movement to deliver psycho-educational materials and therapeutic support.

The group is based on the principle that change comes about from what we tell ourselves and what we know, not what we are told (Rollnick, Miller & Butler, 2008). However, there is an initial psycho-educational input that aims to expose commonly-held myths about food and eating in order to undermine unhelpful beliefs about weight loss and gain. A key message conveyed is that our bodies are biological entities, programmed for survival, that do their best to adapt to adverse conditions such as starvation and dysfunctional eating. As neither a biologist nor a dietician, my materials have relied on consultation with our local specialist eating disorder service, training materials and resources. The group took over a year to research and plan and I am careful not to overstretch my competence.

The myths explored are:

* diets work
* low fat is best
* it is good to reduce carbohydrates
* BMI is accurate and reliable
* purging works.

Feedback usually rates this input as very useful.

Process

The therapeutic aims of the group are to foster a sense of relationship via shared experience, to enhance safety and support, to increase confidence and self-accep-tance and to reduce shame through opening up to others about this hitherto often secret part of life. In support of the therapeutic function, careful attention is given to agreeing ground rules such as confidentiality and non-competitiveness, check-ing-in at the beginning and end of each session, commitment to attend all six sessions and to communicate about unplanned absences. Establishing my role as a non-participating facilitator encourages a peer-focused experience and enables me to be mindful of group dynamics and any transference. I aim to model an adult way of relating and provide an experience based on attachment theory (Diamond & Marrone, 2003), which is containing, transparent, accepting and empathic. This therapeutic element of the group promotes an alternative to eating behaviours for dealing with feelings, thoughts, confusions, vulnerabilities and distress.

The weekly sessions and their themes

People with eating disorders are often well-versed in information about food, such as calorific values and fat content. Finding motivation for change is crucial and I address this at the start of the group to engage the student as agent in their change process, rather than as a voyeur, and refer back to this in each session. The first session is important for setting the tone, making introductions, expressing hopes and fears but crucially addressing ambivalence. Members address mixed feelings about and attachment to their eating difficulty and begin to question how much choices are influenced by ambivalence and beliefs. The concept of a "mindset" that underpins an eating difficulty is introduced, linking the mind with the body.

The second session focuses on physical aspects – how the body adapts to prob-lematic eating, myths surrounding beliefs about dieting and purging behaviours, how to deal with urges to restrict and binge. Week three looks at socio-cultural influ-ences on body-image and the impact on self-confidence. An important aim of this session is identification of cognitions that provide an internal commentary about appearance, attractiveness, sexuality, success and character, the articulation of the eating disorder "mindset" or "inner bully". Week four explores students' experience

Table 9.1 Weekly group themes

1	Welcome, introductions, hopes and fears, motivation for change
2	Causes, effects and strategies to help
3	Whose body is it anyway?
4	Food and families
5	Thinking traps and your eating difficulty
6	Journey so far, the road ahead and goodbyes

of mealtimes and emotional associations from earlier family life. At this point the group has usually entered its "norming" phase (Tuckman, 1965) where members are opening up, taking a few risks with each other and beginning to acknowledge differences. I notice most years that this session can create a level of protectiveness towards family as a possible root cause for their difficulties. A drawback of short-term work is the need to side-line some issues. I retain this session, however, as it enables the planting of a seed about context and history. Realising without blame that our present lives can be affected by our past can make for fruitful links.

The next two sessions work in more depth with the theme of the eating disorder "mindset" (as distinct from an unchangeable trait) and use training materials developed by Virdi (2010) from research by Serpell *et al.* (1999) into motivational change in eating disorders. Students read two excerpts from "pro-ana" sites (websites that actively encourage living with eating disorders as a life-style choice). Students identify contradictions in the messages promoted by the eating disorder mindset, such as "I will make you perfect" vs. "You will never be perfect" or "I will make others admire you" vs. "You will never cope socially". By identifying an inner bully and an inner friend students help each other to externalise and distance themselves from an unhelpful mindset and create more balance in their inner dialogue. While this is a personal exercise about individual thought process, completing it in a group gives an additional dimension. Students are able to refer to each other, compare experiences, undermine shame and secrecy, exchange support and instil hope (Yalom, 1995).

The final session handles dynamics around endings and returns to focus on ambivalence in an exercise in which students write two letters, one to their eating problem as their friend and the other as their foe or inner bully. The letter to "friend" gives insight; the letter to "foe" gives pointers to change. As cited in Serpell *et al.* (1999) an example from letters to the eating disorder as friend is:

> You make me feel special by making me different. You give me something that none of my friends or family have. I really need you to provide direction in everything I do. You have taught me so many habits and tricks which I have become good at.
>
> (p. 180)

and from letters as foe:

> I'm sick and tired of you ruling my life. You make me devious, unfriendly and unhappy, and very lonely. There are times when I think you've engulfed me and when people look at my body, they don't see me anymore, only you.
>
> (p. 181)

This exercise draws on principles from motivational interviewing (Rollnick & Miller, 1995), highlighting a natural resistance to being told what to do, especially when we are ambivalent about something.

Overall feedback on the group indicates it is relevant and useful. "Feeling less alone" is a frequent remark and "Speaking out loud about what has been wrong in life" has been described as a motivator for change. "I feel less like something bad could happen if I eat, and more like eating will actually help me feel better", is another common comment. Behaviour change is reported but also sometimes that feelings remain similar, suggesting that this is still work in progress, hardly surprising in a short-term intervention. Such comments go some way to countering therapists' frequent sense of incompetence when working with eating issues.

Summary

A brief piece of group work is just that, one piece. Nevertheless it can be important and valuable in itself (Anderson, 2013). An intervention such as the one described is a stepping stone on the path to a healthier and less harmful relationship to body and self. I aim to enable students to see themselves as part of a solution, not just the problem, acknowledging the somatisation and responding with direct action to their body's physical needs. I encourage participants to identify their own feelings, thoughts and behaviours that drive the somatisation and to address their personal motivation for change. This might mean looking at painful aspects of their lives: past experiences, family life or current relationships impacting on self-esteem. Aside from the content of sessions, the students take away an experience of tackling a difficulty of shame and self-harm jointly with others, at their own pace. That in itself is a powerful and therapeutic step.

Working with a student using EMDR

Finding ways to creatively and effectively help students within a time-conscious model is challenging. Alongside group work, some counsellors with additional specialist training use EMDR – an evidence-based psychological treatment for Post-Traumatic Stress Disorder (PTSD) (NICE, 2005). EMDR has also been used in a variety of other psychological presentations including somatised distress and various forms of severe anxiety (Shapiro, 2001), while Shapiro (ibid. p. 234ff) has devised a specific protocol, scripted by Luber (2009) for using EMDR with somatic disorders. The following case study is an example of how EMDR can be utilised in an HE context.

Trauma is thought to cause an imbalance in the nervous system blocking information processing. This unprocessed information is then stored in a raw state, in separate, unconnected neural networks. EMDR is underpinned by the Adaptive Information Processing Model: it is believed that during REM (rapid eye movement) sleep, the eyes dart back and forth while the brain processes stored information. In EMDR, bilateral stimulation (BLS) is used to emulate the movement of the eyes in REM sleep by using various tools and techniques, such as a light bar with a light that moves from end to end; buzzers, which buzz alternately in clients' hand; headphones, where a buzzing alternates in their ears; hand tapping, with the therapist gently tapping the client's hands alternately; therapist hand movements from one point to another in which the client follows the therapists hand. EMDR aims to process somatised trauma in order to make it more adaptive.

EMDR focuses on all aspects of memory: images, thoughts, emotions and bodily sensations, which is essential when working with somatised distress. It seeks to access the distress that is held in the past episodic memory, desensitising and then reprocessing the memory to become more adaptive and held as narrative memory. It is not a reliving of the trauma, rather a re-processing of the memory while remaining in the present. It also helps clients to contemplate the future, thus using a three-pronged approach; past, present and future.

EMDR has the potential for a rapid uncovering of previously unconscious material, and earlier memories may surface during therapy, some of which may be extremely distressing (Shapiro, 2001). A thorough risk assessment needs to be completed with particular attention to the client's ability to handle strong emotions. Royle and Kerr (2010) provide a suggested pre-EMDR questionnaire to use during the first phase of the EMDR protocol in order to accurately assess any possible risk factors.

Working with a student with trauma and PTSD

Steve[1] was a third-year student who had generally coped well with his studies, but one of his lecturers had recently noticed a change in his behaviour during lectures and requested he come to his office for a chat. Steve did not give the lecturer any details, except to say that something had happened while on work experience during the summer vacation; he told the lecturer he did not want to report the event. Concerned about Steve, and that something had happened while working within an organisation frequently used by the university, the lecturer strongly advised steve to attend the university counselling Service.

When I (Dorothy Louden) met Steve there was no eye contact and he kept his distance from me. En route to my counselling room, Steve displayed several startled responses suggesting re-experiencing of trauma-related symptoms. Several weeks later, when Steve was able to verbalise his feelings, he revealed that the narrow corridor to my counselling room reminded him of where he had been assaulted. Each time Steve came to see me he was reliving his traumatic memory before even entering the room, confirming Roschild's theory: "Stimuli from the environment can inadvertently set off a traumatic reaction in a client" (Rothschild, 2000, p. 116).

Once seated, Steve continued to be hyper vigilant, jumping at every noise outside the room. He told me that his lecturer had advised him to come to counselling due to lowered coping abilities as a result of an assault. I asked him how he felt about being here and he replied, "I need to come": he had no previous experience of counselling. At the end of our first session I suggested that Steve visit his GP due to the extent of his symptoms; he agreed but was adamant that he would not take any medication.

Steve told me that he had difficulty concentrating and that placements were also difficult. When asked what he thought would be the most helpful area to focus on, and what changes he would like to make, Steve replied, "Dealing with the memories of what happened so that they are less disruptive to everyday life".

He told me that he had been assaulted, alluding to a sexual nature, while on work experience. He also said that he had often felt trapped and powerless and that he wanted to feel in control again. He could not expand further on his experience. He had come back to university in September having tried to forget the experience. However, as Rothschild (2000) states, "the body of the traumatized individual refuses to be ignored" (cover).

As a matter of course, we also ask our students to complete a CORE 34 questionnaire (see McCrea, Chapter 5). Steve's CORE score was 13 with no disclosed risk factors: a score above 10 is classed as "clinical". We discussed further how he felt he was coping on a day to day basis. Steve described being very jumpy and anxious, not wanting to be around people and said he was not sleeping or eating. He was able to go to lectures, but he was not able to concentrate while there, sitting near the door where he could clearly see who entered. Although during his first two years he had been a model student, on course to achieve a first class honours degree, he now found himself unable to concentrate on his dissertation or study for exams.

I felt drawn to suggest EMDR over other counselling models as it would address Steve's somatised symptoms. However, I pondered if this was the right time for Steve to engage in EMDR as he was due to sit his finals in a few weeks, still had a final work experience placement and dissertation to complete and needed to be able to manage emotionally in order to pass his course and graduate. I asked myself whether Steve was stable enough; could he handle high levels of emotional disturbance, could he self-regulate affect? Would his current levels of disturbance deteriorate further? In essence, what if I made him worse?

Steve was experiencing somatised distress by storing physical memories in his body and as a result was living as if the threat of assault was still current. Although he was attending lectures, he was not engaging in his studies and appeared mentally and emotionally distant. After some thinking, discussion with an EMDR supervisor and with Steve, we agreed to proceed with an EMDR assessment with a view to engage in EMDR if there were no pre-existing risk factors.

The EMDR process is an eight-stage protocol, which begins with history taking. This includes checking if the client has experienced any previous traumas. Steve declared that he had not. He had never taken drugs, or suffered from depression, suicidal ideation or suicide attempts. He had a good support network with supportive parents and a large group of peers, two of whom were aware of the assault.

Although I was anxious about the time constraints and the fact that I had not used EMDR in a short-term setting with a client experiencing such intense somatised symptoms, I reminded myself of one of the core beliefs of EMDR: "trust the process".

Steve's symptoms included: hypervigilance, lack of concentration, intrusive and distressing memories, sleeplessness, flashbacks, intrusive thoughts, an inability to sleep in bed (choosing to sleep on a sofa in the living room) and nightmares when he finally managed to sleep. All these symptoms are described in DSM 4 (APA, 1994) as possible indicators for PTSD. I also used a psychometric tool, the Impact of Event Scale questionnaire revised (IES-R) to assess Steve for these DSM 4 symptoms. His first IES-R score was 49: a score of above 33 suggests possible PTSD (Weiss & Marmar, 1995).

Steve had a clear goal for counselling: to complete his degree with the rest of his cohort. Steve's tutor was concerned about his current wellbeing and his ability to complete the outstanding elements of his course within the time frame. We discussed some of the practicalities that could be implemented, including requesting sitting his exams in a different setting due to his hypervigilance. At first he was against this, believing that he would be able to manage. I reminded him how his hypervigilance could bring up his anxiety at any time, including examples of times that occurred while with me that had caused him to lose focus. After some thought he decided to err on the side of caution and agreed. We wrote a letter to his lecturer requesting sheltered exam conditions.

The second phase of the protocol is preparation, a crucial component of EMDR. This includes explaining the process of EMDR and the various methods used in bilateral stimulation. As well as a verbal explanation, I gave him a written explanation to take away. I let Steve try the different methods of BLS so that he was already familiar with them should we need to use them. I had already checked if he had any medical issues that could interfere with using the lightbar, including any serious eye difficulties. We tested Steve's tolerance of eye movements using the lightbar and there were no negative effects. I told Steve that he would be in control at all times and we agreed a stop signal should he feel overwhelmed. One of the key elements about EMDR is that the client will always be in control even though they may not feel in control at times. I also explained that he might remember things between sessions and gave him a notebook to record anything new that came up. We also discussed any questions Steve had about the process. He understood that this was not a quick fix and that there were no guaranteed outcomes.

Before carrying out the desensitisation phase of EMDR the student needs to have an adequate level of resilience and sufficient resources (Leeds, 2009). To test Steve's ability to self-manage his overwhelming emotions, at the end of the first session we completed an exercise often called "the safe place", or "quiet place", "secure place", "happy place". Here the client chooses a place known to them, or a place that they have seen in a film or picture, which depicts them experiencing a very strong positive emotion. I asked him to remember it during the week when feeling anxious, but also when not so anxious. I then checked his ability to self-regulate and self-soothe using this exercise during the past week. He had found it very effective, saying that he had felt better than he had in ages, and that he had been able to relax a bit and sleep slightly better. This was a positive indication of ability to self-regulate emotions, which, alongside his connection with me and his current support network, gave me confidence to go ahead with EMDR processing.

Despite being keen to engage with EMDR, he was unable to talk about the actual incident. Shapiro describes how some clients are unwilling to talk about specific memories due to shame or guilt but claims that the therapist does not need to know details (Shapiro, 2001). Blore and Holmshaw (2009) devised a "Blind to Therapist" (B2T) EMDR protocol, which enables the therapist and client to process the information without the therapist knowing the details of the memory. Having to reveal a shameful memory can often be why clients avoid seeking help, and not having to share these details can in itself bring some relief. Blore, Holmshaw, Swift, Standart and Fish (2012) have illustrated several different versions of the use of the B2T protocol according to clinical presentations.

Phase three is the assessment; choosing a memory to work on. In this instance Steve's memory was the assault. As we had agreed to use the B2T protocol I checked that he had an image without disclosing any details. I then asked him to choose a word that represented that image. At this point the normal protocol asks the client to think of a negative cognition (NC) to go along with the image, and then a positive cognition (PC) for how they would rather see themselves. The B2T protocol omits these elements as the client may feel too uncomfortable to acknowledge these at this stage (Blore & Holmshaw, 2009).

As Steve had already identified his NC, and his PC, I chose to follow the main protocol for the remainder of the assessment. EMDR measures the validity of the positive cognition (VOC), in other words, how much they believe their positive self-belief on a scale of 1–7. EMDR also rates the client's subjective unit of disturbance (SUD's) on a scale of 0–10, which quantifies how distressing the incident feels to the client here and now. A summary of Steve's assessment is given in Table 9.2.

We were then ready to begin to process the incident in the fourth phase, desensitisation. Processing is the technique of using bilateral stimulation to help both sides of the brain process the traumatic memories. I reassured Steve that although he may experience what seemed to be intolerable emotions, the experience was

Table 9.2 EMDR assessment summary

Target memory:	Assault
IMAGE:	Not disclosed but cued by client's key word, 'Fire'
NC:	I'm powerless, I'm not in control
PC:	I can be in control
VOC:	4
EMOTIONS:	Scared and vulnerable
SUD's:	7
BODY:	Legs and arms

in the past and he was in a safe place now. I told him to notice whatever came to his awareness during processing: thoughts, images, memories, emotions, smells and physical sensations, no matter how strange or irrelevant they seemed to him. I reminded Steve that whatever came up was old material, not current. I also reassured him that he did not have to tell me details of any change he may experience during processing, just if there was change in what he noticed. Steve's physical symptoms continued: he seemed present while simultaneously absent and his breathing sped up. During the beginning stages of processing I never knew specific changes that occurred: he would just say "yes" or "no" to any changes. After a couple of sessions processing, he began to say what some of the changes were. Steve never interrupted or stopped the process even though he knew that he could.

The ending of an EMDR session is classed in one of two ways: "complete" or "incomplete". Complete implies that the client has processed the disturbance and that the SUDs have reduced to 0 and the process then moves to the next phase, installation, the fifth phase of the protocol. This aims to install the client's positive cognition. When the client's SUDS remain above 0–1, this is termed an incomplete session, which ends with the client's safe place. All but one of Steve's sessions ended in an incomplete way.

While engaged in EMDR, Steve undertook some further work experience and his primary lecturer expressed concern to him about his ability to manage emotionally during this time. Steve managed very well until the seventh week when he went to a club with some friends. A man who reminded him of the person who had assaulted him came into the club, causing him to have intrusive memories. This had a powerful impact on Steve's emotional wellbeing and he was unable to move. He also began to have difficulties on his work experience again, requiring him to temporarily withdraw. Although this was a very difficult time for Steve, he understood what was happening. Together we were able to see the positive, i.e. going seven weeks before facing any difficulties. He knew how the desensitisation had helped him so far and was keen to continue. He had to complete his last placement from the beginning again several weeks later and this time he completed it without any further major setbacks.

Steve had used the lightbar for BLS for the first session, but at the second session he asked to try the buzzers and then hand tapping. We found that physical contact from the buzzers or my hand on his hand intensified his somatised body memories and physical re-enactment, probably due to the original trauma being physical. He told me afterwards he wanted to pull his hand away and scream, but managed to resist. After this, he chose hand tapping every session.

Steve came in after the third session of processing and recounted a memory he had forgotten. He had been sexually assaulted at school, and remembered not being able to say "no". This resulted in Steve self-harming by cutting and over exercising; neither of which he had mentioned previously. He had been able to overcome these with support from his parents. He was shocked that he had not remembered this period in his life but pleased he had not defaulted to either of these previous coping strategies as a result of his recent assault. As this was an earlier memory, it became our new target memory to process. It is worth noting that sudden trauma that appears or occurs while at university may not be the original trauma, but may be a trigger to earlier memories.

This was a particularly difficult session; he was very tearful throughout the session and jumped at the touch of my hand and slightest noise. Due to heightened responses and agitation I did not want his safe place to become contaminated and so I chose to end the session in a different way. We did some gentle deep breathing until I noticed that his breathing had slowed down, anxiety had decreased and his body more visibly relaxed. I then used BLS with slow hand tapping on his hands.

After two sessions his SUDs at his new target memory reduced to 0 and we were able to install his PC, "I can be in control". We then moved to the sixth phase: the body scan. This is particularly important when working with body memories as we are looking to check the body has let go of any somatised distress. The seventh phase, closure, is carried out at every session, and as previously mentioned, can be either complete or incomplete.

Phase eight, re-evaluation, checks that the target memory has been resolved and if any other material has surfaced which needs addressing.

The following week we continued with the original assault trauma.

Steve's exams were coming closer but although he was unconcerned about their content, he was anxious about the physical side of attending the exam and the possibility of his somatised distress being triggered. As an additional resource for Steve, we carried out a Resource Development and Installation procedure (RDI) (Leeds, 2009; Leeds & Shapiro, 2000) similar to the safe place exercise. We installed strong positive emotions and physical memories from a previous positive experience to strengthen self-belief and confidence. This proved very effective when he sat his exams as he was able to access those resources.

I saw Steve change from a frightened, almost cowering, young man, ensnared by trauma from his past/present, into someone who walked tall and straight and smiled. This change was evidenced by his CORE score reducing from 13 to 1 in our last session, showing both a clinical and reliable change. His IES-R reduced from 49 to 12.

Steve's SUDs never went to 0. However, in the short term, Steve achieved what he wanted; he attended and passed final exams, attended and passed his final work experience, completed his dissertation, went for interviews and got a new job he wanted, and graduated with a first.

Discussion

While this is perhaps not a text-book use of EMDR, it demonstrates another way of working with somatised distress in a short-term setting. Although there are limitations imposed by the setting, I believe that models such as EMDR can help students get to a position of positive movement. There are potential drawbacks in that an EMDR session is usually planned for 90 minutes, and due to the nature of trauma and PTSD the number of sessions needed is not easily identified at the outset. However, with good history taking and assessment, a planned piece of work can be achieved and I believe that the benefits outweigh the drawbacks. Without a counselling intervention, in this case EMDR, Steve may not have been able to complete his degree with his own peer group. Steve's graduation, alongside improvements in CORE and IES-R, indicate a positive outcome for both Steve and the university. This will probably not be the end of counselling for Steve. Nevertheless, he has had a positive experience, which I hope will encourage him to access further support should he feel the need.

Conclusion

We have looked at two forms of somatised distress in this chapter and at how the body unconsciously stores and expresses distress. We have already said that we can be a stepping stone on the way forward. We cannot take all the student's pain away, but we can help them to take the first, or another step on the journey.

Rothschild (2000) describes "The body as diary: making sense of sensations" (p. 116). We can help our students see themselves as part of the solution, not just the problem and to use those same somatic symptoms to identify triggers, to get in touch with their bodies, to learn to be in the moment and to begin to resolve their difficulties.

Winnicott talks about the "good enough" mother and seeks to also use this analogy for the therapist and client relationship (Abram, 2007). We can be the "good enough therapist"; we *can* make a difference despite the limited time. Focusing on what we can do, rather than what we can't, is key to managing our own, and our clients' expectations, and to offering something of value within a short-term, HE setting.

(With thanks to David Blore for his helpful input and feedback.)

Note

1 All personal details of this case have been changed/anonymised to protect client identity.

References

Abram, J. (2007) *The Language of Winnicott – A dictionary of Winnicott's use of words*, London, Karnac.

American Psychiatric Association (1994) *The Diagnostic and Statistical Manual of Mental Disorders*, Washington DC, London, American Psychiatric Publishing.

Anderson, S. (2013) A group for students with eating issues. *University and College Counselling*, BACP, March 2013, 26–29.

Arcelus, J., Mitchell, A. J., Wales, J. & Nielsen S. (2011) Mortality rates in patients with anorexia nervosa and other eating disorders: A meta-analysis of 36 studies. *Archives of General Psychiatry*, 68, 724–731.

Blore, D. & Holmshaw, M. (2009) EMDR Blind to Therapist Protocol, in Luber, M. (Ed.) *EMDR Scripted Protocols*, New York, Springer Publishing Company.

Blore, D., Holmshaw, E. R., Swift, A., Standart, A. & Fish, D. (2013) The development and uses of the "Blind to Therapist" EMDR protocol. *Journal of EMDR Practice and Research*, 7 (3), 95–105.

Boon, S., Steele, K. & Van der Hart, O. (2011) *Coping with Trauma-Related Dissociation*, New York, W. W. Norton and Company.

Department of Health (2005) Supporting people with long-term medical problems: An NHS and social care model to support local innovation and integration.

Diamond, N. & Marrone, M. (2003) *Attachment and Intersubjectivity*, London, Whurr Publishers.

Errington, M. & Murdin, L. (2006) Psychoanalytic Therapy, in Feltham, C. and Horton, I. *The Sage Handbook of Counselling and Psychotherapy (2nd Edition)*, Sage, London.

Feltham, C. & Horton, I. (2006) *The Sage Handbook of Counselling and Pychotherapy (2nd Edition)*, London, Sage Publications.

Garner, D. M. (1997) Psychoeducational Principles in Treatment, in Garner, D. M. and Garfinkel, P. E. (Eds) *Handbook of Treatment for Eating Disorders (2nd edition)*, New York, The Guilford Press.

Keys, A., Brozek, J., Henschel, A., Mickelsen, O. & Taylor, H. L. (1950) *The Biology of Human Starvation (vols 1 & 2)*, Minneapolis, University of Minnesota Press.

Kuo, C. L. & Kavanagh, K. H. (1994) Chinese perspectives on culture and mental health. *Issues Mental Health Nursing*, Nov–Dec, 15 (6), 551–567.

Leeds, A. M. (2009) Resources in EMDR and other trauma focused psychotherapy: A review. *Journal of EMDR Practice and Research*, 3 (3), 152–160.

Leeds, A. M. & Shapiro, F. (2000) EMDR and Resource Installation: Principles and Procedures for Enhancing Current Functioning and Resolving Traumatic experiences, in Carlson, J. and Sperry, L. (Eds) *Brief Therapy with Individuals and Couples*, Phoenix, Zeig, Tucker and Theisen.

NICE (2005) *Post-traumatic stress disorder (PTSD): The management of PTSD in adults and children*. Available from www.nice.org.uk/guidance/cg26. (accessed 15th December 2014).

Orbach, S. (2009) *Bodies*, London, Profile Books.

Parnell, L. (1999) *EMDR in the Treatment of Adults Abused as Children*, New York, Norton.

Rollnick, S. & Miller, W. R. (1995) What is Motivational Interviewing? *Behavioural and Cognitive Psychotherapy*, 23 (4), 325–334.

Rollnick, S., Miller, W. R. & Butler, C. (2008) *Motivational Interviewing in Health Care: Helping Patients Change Behaviour*, New York, The Guilford Press.

Rothschild, B. (2000) *The Body Remembers (1st Edition)*, New York, W. W. Norton & Company.

Rothschild, B. (2011) *Trauma Essentials*, New York, W.W. Norton and Company.

Royle, L. & Kerr, C. (2010) *Integrating EMDR into Your Practice*, New York, Springer Publishing Company.

Schmidt, U. & Treasure, J. (1993) *Getting Better Bit(e) by Bit(e)*, London, Routledge.

Serpell, L., Treasure, J., Teasdale, J. & Sullivan V. (1999) Anorexia nervosa: Friend or foe? *International Journal of Eating Disorders*, 25 (2), 177–186.

Shapiro, F. (2001) *Eye Movement Desensitisation and Reprocessing: Basic Principles, Protocols and Procedures (2nd Edition)*, New York, Guilford Press.

Shapiro, F. (2009) Illness and Somatic Disorders Protocol, in Luber, M. (Ed.) *EMDR Scripted Protocols Basic and Special Situations*, New York, Springer Publishing Company.

Tuckman, B. (1965) Developmental sequences in small groups. *Psychological Bulletin*, 63, 84–399.

Van der Kolk, B. A., McFarlane, A. C. & Weisaeth, L. (Eds) (2007) *Traumatic Stress*, New York, Guilford Press.

Virdi, P. (2010) Handouts at course training sessions, *From Diet to Disorder*, led by Pam Virdi, Specialist Eating Disorder Psychotherapist. November 2010–May 2011. Birmingham and Solihull Eating Disorders Service, Birmingham.

Weiss, D. S. & Marmar, C. R. (1995) The Impact of Event Scale-Revised, in Wilson, J. P. and Kean, T. M. (Eds) *Assessing Psychological Trauma and PTSD: A Practitioner's Handbook*, New York, Guilford Press.

Yalom, I. D. (1995) *The Theory and Practice of Group Psychotherapy (4th Edition)*, New York, Basic Books.

Chapter 10

Counselling online in HE

Opportunities and challenges

Jo Ames

Chapter overview

The digital age is firmly embedded in our culture and enmeshed within the lives of students in the way they learn and relate. Today's young adults barely even think of things such as computers and smart phones as "technology": they are taken for granted as the means by which communication and learning are conducted. As the reach of technology expands ever wider, counselling services are – whether willingly or reluctantly – also learning that online communication has an important part to play in reaching their clients, especially when those clients are "digital natives" (Prensky, 2001). Technology is currently used in a number of ways in providing a counselling service e.g. online registration, emails about appointments, online feedback forms etc., but this chapter concentrates on the actual delivery of counselling rather than activities associated with it. Addressing the needs of distance learners, students on years abroad or placement, is driving the need to more innovative ways of working and this chapter focuses on how such services can be implemented within a short-term framework. The history and practical application of online counselling will also be discussed, along with legal and ethical considerations pertinent to this approach to therapy provision.

Definition of online counselling for the purpose of this chapter

Online counselling within this chapter addresses the three main modes of delivery of counselling using technology as the medium of delivery: email, internet relay chat – where both parties type messages to each other in real time and web conferencing, an online audio and visual meeting where counsellor and client can see and hear one another. All three approaches to online counselling leave transcripts, recordings or traces of the encounter and these create issues around confidentiality and data protection, which are explored later in this chapter.

History of online counselling and support

It was Chad Varah of the Samaritans, back in 1953, who first introduced the use of the telephone to provide support to people in crisis. Since then the telephone has become a mainstay of our work, with some counsellors specialising in telephone counselling. In 1986, in Cornell University, in the United States, Jerry Feist, the Dean of Students and former director of the Counselling Centre and Steve Worona of Computer Services, collaborated on providing support to students using an online notice board. Their idea was that students could pose any question and "Uncle Ezra" would respond, with the questions and responses available to all students across campus. In essence, this combination of counselling knowledge and computing represents the birth of online counselling as we know it today. Although "Uncle Ezra" was taken offline in 2012, there are a number of student counselling services across the globe using similar methods to support their students.

In 1994 the Samaritans again took the initiative, this time setting up an email service – significant because it was the first of its kind in the UK. It was commonly referred to as "Dear Jo" because all responses were anonymised under the pseudonym "Jo" to protect individual workers.

John Grohol launched Psych Central, an online mental health social network, in 1995. This was the year that saw the first fee-based internet therapy, using email, instant messenger and video conferencing. It was also during this period that the International Society for Mental Health Online was founded, shortly followed by computerised cognitive behaviour therapy (cCBT). More recently avatar therapy, including its use in Second Life (an online virtual world where people create images or avatars of themselves and interact with each other and the environment) has become more commonplace, as have websites dedicated to issue based support. Students Against Depression, established in 2005, is one such website, widely used and recommended by both students and professionals (see Meyer, Chapter 8).

The student context

"Vague, but exciting" was the comment made by Tim Berners-Lee's supervisor in 1989, the year he received approval to go ahead with his concept of the World Wide Web (CERN). That was 26 years ago, which, coincidently, is the same year, or shortly thereafter, that almost 62 per cent of our students (Universities UK, 2013, p. 13) were born. Perhaps it is no coincidence that 62 per cent of 18–24 year olds access their social networking profiles from smartphones and tablets (Sweeney, 2012) and that these are their preferred methods for receiving news updates.

It is difficult for older adults to imagine growing up in a world where technology is so entrenched in everyday life. Young people have moved through their formative years with constant access to friends, navigating through the minefields of "friending" and the angst of being "unfriended" on social networks; evading cyberbullying, cyber trauma or online predators; trying to stay savvy enough not to fall foul of innocent games that encourage "buying more lives" (with real money) and not knowing what it is like to receive a wage packet but instead being familiar with the concept of online purchases and "Bitcoin" (virtual money not related to banks). This is without the added complexities of sexting – sending sexually explicit messages – and easy access or early exposure to online pornography, which opens the virtual door to online pornography addiction.

The way young people relate and attach has expanded dramatically, from gaming and communicating with players across the world, to extending networks using social media. These have implications not only for further developing their interests but also making new connections. The ability to stay connected – for example by texting – with friends or partners can enhance the experience of being in a close and committed relationship, using text to express things that may seem difficult to say "in person", providing an opportunity to engage meaningfully and experience more secure attachment styles.

The nature of some traditional presenting problems are also undergoing change. For example, closer exploration of sleep disturbance may uncover the use of mobile or other screen devices at bedtime or in bed. This artificial light (sometimes known as "blue light") can affect the body's natural functions and sleep patterns and risks being misdiagnosed or treated as insomnia. Another more recent phenomenon is that of digital data hoarding, whereby a student amasses uncontrollable amounts of online data (research papers, course notes, past exam papers etc.). They add too many "favourites" to their internet homepage, finding that their increasing numbers of documents added to their systems means it becomes so full they need to start utilising USB sticks or to invest in external hard drives or cloud storage (where data is stored on remote servers rather than on the device that is being used). After a while the student begins to realise that the thought of trying to organise the information into folders feels overwhelming and they experience anxiety at the idea of deleting any material, "in case they need it". This hidden hoarding would be easier to identify had it appeared in the tangible form of toppling stacks of books or countless bundles of papers impeding a student's ability to navigate through their physical study space. Their (online) learning environment is so full that they struggle to engage with the actual study without being faced by the weight of the data before them, which can then become an emotional battleground (similar to the experience of physical hoarding).

Running alongside all of this is the transitional nature of being a student, a temporary stage in life, where many relationships being forged will not withstand the passage of time; an environment where housing and housemates can change from year to year, where courses are split into modules and study includes regular vacations, reading weeks, placements, and years abroad. Everything seems to be divided into fleeting chunks of time and place. Short-term counselling within this context mirrors the student experience and runs parallel to the pace and shape of their life and studies. Given that counselling itself is moving to a new online platform it is doubtful that even Tim Berners-Lee could have imagined quite the global extent and impact his invention would have on life in general and student life in particular.

Student counselling services within the HE context

Counselling for students has been available for many years and has traditionally been delivered face-to-face (f2f). However, with advances of technology increasingly affecting our lives and the ways we communicate and learn, it is perhaps unsurprising that technology has been exploited to provide counselling. Even within HE there is plenty of evidence that social media is a popular method of engaging students and providing information. The common use of Twitter, Facebook, LinkedIn and ResearchGate are clear examples of this. Another technological development within higher education is online distance learning courses, which have given rise to Massive Open Online Courses (MOOCs). These have been gaining momentum in recent years and have sparked the MOOC debate (Clark, 2014; Holford *et al.*, 2014; Knox, 2014) about whether traditional in-person teaching methods are being diminished or threatened.

In considering the opportunities for "global universities" and the current approach to accessing traditional methods of learning and teaching, Donald Clark (2014) highlights "Ten reasons we should ditch universities lectures". One of these was:

> Students have just one chance to hear a lecture – and mostly it's just someone reading their notes aloud. So, why retain the face-to-face lecture when its value as a pedagogical tool is so limited? There seems to be no other reason than the old justification: We've always done it this way.

There is something here that may ring true for many counsellors and counselling services: why change traditional f2f approaches to counselling when it has been evidenced as an effective way of working? Apart from current and future students being part of the digital age, there has been an emphasis on universities "going global" and increasing the amount of distance learning. In 2010 the Higher Education Funding Council for England (HEFCE) commissioned a report into online distance learning (ODL) and found that there were plans to increase this approach to learning over the next five years. At the time of writing there are 29 (20 per cent) UK universities offering MOOCs through FutureLearn, one of the leading MOOC providers. MOOCs are at the forefront of enticing prospective students to UK institutions, by offering short, free, taster courses. This is significant because the very context in which we work is being transformed by technology. The student body is changing and the way we provide services must reflect these changes; simply because f2f approaches have hitherto dominated our practice does not mean that this is the only way to work effectively. Seeking to embrace more of our student body, using technology to mirror the learning and teaching experience, is a logical direction to take. There is evidence of online counselling and supporting activities (e.g. the use of online self-help resources) occurring in HEIs across the UK suggesting that this response to change is already happening.

Working online: feeding "instant gratification" culture?

According to the UK Universities report of 2013 the majority of students are under 25 years old. This means that they have grown up with an array of technology to a degree unimaginable to previous generations. This phenomenon might beg the question: are counselling services merely pandering to the needs of "digital natives" (Prensky, 2001) and their supposed desire for immediacy in accessing information and services? The answer is possibly yes – to some degree. However, when considering the increasing numbers of students away from campuses on placement, other students who may be considered as time poor (e.g. medical students) and students with known psychological barriers in accessing face-to-face counselling etc. (Vogel *et al.*, 2007), this is clearly not the only factor driving services to extend their reach into cyber space. Indeed, a great deal of thought, planning, training and resources go into the ethical and legally-sound provision of distance counselling using technology (Goss & Hooley, 2015) so it is unlikely to be the main determining factor.

It is possible that a higher element of resistance to online counselling emanates from counsellors, who are less likely to have spent formative years engaging with technology and have had to "grow into" its use as an aspect of current life and working practices. As "digital immigrants" (Prensky, 2001) counsellors are less likely to be familiar and comfortable using written text as the foundation of the counselling process and may require additional training to use this medium. There may be issues with online counselling not being seen as "real", reflecting concerns about losing out on the significance of body language and facial expressions as taught during basic counsellor training along with the fear that something of real importance will be lost when providing text-based counselling. Equally, there may be concern that some individuals have retreated into a "virtual" world to the detriment of "real", "in person" social interaction and an accompanying anxiety that providing online counselling merely compounds social isolation. To the untrained, it can be difficult to imagine providing something close to "real counselling" when direct human contact seems absent. In addition, concerns have been raised by counsellors in HE (Ames, 2014) about how to contain clients when working with technology as the counselling medium and how a particular counselling orientation can be translated into online work. These concerns are evidenced in the desire for reliable guidance in the provision of online counselling. During a specialist online counselling conference (OCTIA, 2013), one of the presenters, Dr Stephen Goss, led Delphi research with the 114 participants, including HE counsellors. The participants attended both in the room and online via a live feed. The purpose of this research exercise was to identify the top priorities for areas of research over the coming years. Three of these priority issues were risk management, confidentiality and contracting (Goss, 2013; Goss & Hooley, 2015).

Understandably there are practitioner fears about the security of communication and the possible public release of written work such as emails with clients. All of these valid concerns underlie the importance of undertaking specific online counselling training and, as endorsed by the British Association for Counselling and Psychotherapy (BACP) Good Practice Guidelines for Online Counselling and Supervision (Anthony & Goss, 2009) engaging in supervision with a practitioner who has knowledge of this way of working and its characteristics, as well as developing robust systems with related policies and procedures.

Helping services under pressure?

It may be tempting to imagine that online work creates only benefits for services under pressure, and while it is true that these are clear benefits, they are not without potential drawbacks, which need careful consideration. Online counselling fits seamlessly into existing service provision with the added benefit of being able to provide ongoing counselling throughout the academic year, which is normally subject to breaks when using the traditional f2f approach. While these breaks can in themselves be part of the therapeutic process, services with trained online counsellors who are employed year round can not only complete existing contracts with clients but also take clients off waiting lists during vacation periods. This allows them to be seen more quickly, thus reducing overall service waiting times. On the other hand, there is a natural reduction of client numbers during university breaks as they return home. The urgency of academic needs may pass or their situation may change, and providing distance counselling could counteract the benefits of clients problem-solving for themselves, or discovering the truth that environment often has a significant impact on levels of distress.

Another benefit of online work in services where space is an issue is that there is always the potential for online counsellors to work from home (complying with in-house policies and procedures) or to utilise a space that may not be suitable for f2f counselling e.g. a room without a panic alarm. Nevertheless, in terms of the time taken to provide either a real time session or email response there is little difference between online and f2f counselling. The administrative tasks are at least the same if not a little more than in f2f counselling.

Avoiding the pitfalls in providing online counselling

Given that there are potential downsides to providing online counselling, I now outline some of the areas to avoid, and others to explore further, when considering such provision. Before moving into the actual development of services, it may be helpful to consider some of the background thinking and learning gleaned from HE counselling services that have initiated online counselling.

- Being both confident and competent in counselling online is important, so undertaking specific online counselling training prior to offering a service (Anthony, 2014) enables the counsellor to practise being in cyberspace, working out how their theoretical orientation translates into online practice and generally becoming more familiar with the platform that will be used as the therapeutic meeting space. Jones and Stokes (2008) and Evans (2008) have written accessible books that are recommended reading resources for counsellors thinking about and currently working online. Evans is an author with specific counselling knowledge and experience in the HEI context and wrote the original *Pullout guide for online counsellors in universities and colleges* in 2007.

The latest good practice guidelines for Online Counselling Guidelines (third edition) are available to members on the BACP website; these cover the aspects of the work that require consideration and provide a comprehensive approach to offering a legal and ethical service.

- Check that service institutional insurance policies covers online counselling; it is important to verify that this is the case before proceeding to offer services online.
- In terms of policies and procedures it is possible to rework existing documents rather than "reinventing the wheel". Standing back and looking at these documents through an online counselling lens, especially with regards to confidentiality, can save a considerable amount of time and any gaps that appear due to the nature of working online can be easily rectified. For example, changes to the storage and access to transcripts or recordings of the online counselling agreement and subsequent sessions.
- Plan for crises and emergencies in advance; not only for clients with presenting or emerging risk, but in determining how the service will respond to counsellor absence or technology breakdown for either the client or the counsellor.
- Have clear criteria about how onward referral will be managed and how this will be conveyed to the client.
- Aim for *informed* consent during the contracting process.
- Use transparency and clarity when providing information on web pages and when contracting with clients remember to be explicit about the extent and limitations of the service e.g. short term work, when online counselling is not suitable and that the counsellor will not accept friend requests on social media, etc.
- Build working relationships with institutional IT and/or Elearning, Legal and Disability Departments as these are important partners in providing online services. Remember to inform the legal department of any databases kept containing the processing of sensitive and personal data for online clients. Security online is a two-way process and clients need to be informed about

ways to manage their online security as part of the contract and on supporting web pages.

- Whether using email as a general means of correspondence in providing the service e.g. sending out appointments or as the actual counselling approach i.e. email counselling, use only secure encrypted email. Store all emails, transcripts, contracts etc. securely offline, ensuring that they are deleted on any platform where they will not be stored.
- When working with audio/visual (web conferencing) avoid "talking heads" by setting your camera further back and encouraging your client to do likewise. This allows for observation of clients' physical responses during sessions.
- Practise with the online counselling medium e.g. instant messenger, before going "live" as clients will feel more comfortable about using technology if the counsellor demonstrates confidence.

Legal and ethical issues

There are a number of legal and ethical issues to consider when setting up and delivering online counselling services. These are outlined as follows and include eliciting informed consent, complying with the Data Protection Act 1998 (DPA 98) in handling sensitive personal data and meeting the requirements of the Disability Discrimination Act 2005 in the provision of services, which means promoting and encouraging wider but equally accessible participation, by students who present with a range of abilities (DDA 2005, Part 5A, 49A, (1)(a & c)). One of the significant benefits of working online is that psychological as well as physical barriers to counselling can be overcome more easily (King *et al.*, 2006; Oravec, 2000; Vogel *et al.*, 2007).

Informed consent

We know from our f2f counselling practice that informed consent is a process that is undertaken between the counsellor and client, whereby the counsellor provides all necessary information about the service/treatment that is being offered, such as the duration, extent and limitations of confidentiality. The client, having considered this information, then conveys to the counsellor that they understand the boundaries and implications of undertaking counselling and consents to participate in it. A clear distinction needs to be drawn between "obtaining consent" – a legal, often formulaic process – and "obtaining *informed* consent". Informed consent can be more difficult to achieve when there may be no f2f contact with the client to gauge physical and facial responses and, depending on the online medium used, verbal responses to the contracting process. Readers will no doubt have experienced being asked to agree to an impossibly long online contract or terms and conditions, full of jargon, clauses and sub-clauses. Most will have simply taken on trust that the contract is sound and scrolled to the end, without reading, before clicking in a box to "confirm that I have read and understood these terms and conditions".

While this practice is unlikely to be eradicated, hopefully this casual response can be mitigated to some degree when faced with an online agreement presented in a way that requires that the client input personal information at key points within the text, by dividing the agreement into distinct elements. The requested information can include a contact number in the event of a technology failure, student identification number, GP contact details, full name and date or whatever information the counselling service deems is necessary to both verify the identity of the student and elicit informed (which here means *considered*) consent.

An example of a lay-out that makes informed consent more likely would be:

Section 1: brief points about what the service is offering to the client in terms of assessment, number of appointments, how confidentiality will be managed, what will be done in the event of counsellor absence, technology failure or the emergence of risk.

Section 2: what is expected of the client with regards to respect for the counselling process and content (protection of intellectual property), information about how the client can protect their privacy in accessing the counselling and the safekeeping of passwords; also that the client will agree to alert the counselling service of any breaches of security or changes to their circumstances where online counselling may no longer be appropriate within this context e.g. risk of harm to self or another.

Section 3: statements of confirmation acknowledged by the client for their suitability for online counselling, which includes having read supplementary information regarding the online counselling service. Within HE counselling services there may be specific presenting problems or difficulties the client experiences that may be deemed unsuitable for online work (such as self harm or suicidal ideation). Being explicit with clients at the outset is an important aspect of gaining informed consent and working within the parameters of a service.

Section 4: client to select from list of options available for their online counselling e.g. email, IRC or web conferencing.

Within the agreement, it is advisable to incorporate information regarding legal jurisdiction and, in the event that the student is studying or living abroad at the time that the agreement is undertaken, that the agreement is governed by English or Scottish law and subject to the exclusive jurisdiction of the English or Scottish courts.

The intent behind breaking contracts into sections is to slow the process of giving consent and by doing so, to encourage the client to read the expectations, extent and limitations of the service before agreeing to proceed with online counselling. This agreement can be checked with the client for accuracy during the initial counselling assessment session.

In addition, it is useful to have dedicated web pages for students with full information about the online counselling provided. These pages can explicitly cover issues such as the extent and limits of the service, ways to increase online privacy and safety, links to other sources of help, what clients can do in an emergency etc. Directing prospective online clients to these web pages will promote a greater understanding about what to expect from the counselling and what is outside of the remit of their counsellor, e.g. "friending" on social media (e.g. Facebook) or professional networking sites (e.g. LinkedIn).

After receiving a copy of the contract from a client, it is important to carefully read through the document, checking that the information has been completed in full as requested.

Data protection, confidentiality and security

Clients are covered by Data Protection Act (DPA 1998) and the storage and handling of their sensitive and personal data is of paramount importance. This is addressed in a number of ways in online counselling.

For email counselling, or indeed any correspondence with the client regarding their use of the counselling service, encryption is a minimum standard. As previously mentioned, providing clients with information on web pages and, as part of the online agreement, about safer storage of emails by copying them onto a password protected Word document before deleting them from their email inbox, offers greater protection of their privacy and email content. This privacy often extends to include a clause regarding respect for the counselling process by not posting or sharing any part of the counselling as a way of protecting the intellectual property rights of the counsellor.

In thinking about the ways that the counsellor manages the clients sensitive personal data, which includes emails and any transcripts, the Data Protection Act 1998 (Principle 5) states that "Information that does not need to be accessed regularly, but which still needs to be retained, should be safely archived or put offline".

The simplest way to implement this principle, is to copy and paste the email or transcript into a password protected Word document and store it on a limited access area/drive on the university network or onto whichever note storage facility is provided by the counselling service. CoreNet, when enabled for confidential note storage, is one example of an appropriate secured alternative to storage on the university server.

There are currently few counselling services providing one-to-one web conferencing in HE and those that do need to be mindful of access to and ownership of content of sessions as these are routinely recorded by web conferencing providers. Using the in-house iVLE will have high levels of security and access limitations with polices regarding its use already agreed by students, who are likely to be familiar with its functions. In instances where using the in-house iVLE is not an option, there are an increasing number of platforms available specifically designed for the purpose of providing confidential counselling.

Providing equitable services

There are guidelines available through www.abilitynet.org.uk regarding ways to make web pages and text-based services more accessible to clients with disabilities and these guidelines address issues such as layout, use of colour, headings and font sizes.

Some research (e.g. Dunn, 2012) suggests that online counselling acts as a bridge to f2f counselling. This is where the client may experience psychological barriers to speaking with a counsellor in person and initially may use online counselling as a means to building trust and using the therapeutic alliance as a path or bridge to accessing counselling by the more traditional means. Although online counselling in a range of approaches has been researched (Richards, 2009; Richards & Viganó, 2013; Rochlen et al., 2004; Simpson, 2009) and found to be more than adequate as a standalone approach the profession currently lacks a significant body of empirical evidence (Richards & Viganó, 2013) to support which presenting problems are suitable or contra-indicated for online work. One study (Wagner et al., 2014) used one-to-one short-term (eight weeks) cognitive behaviour therapy with clients alongside f2f provision, directly comparing the interventions. While both approaches were found to have equal benefit, the online clients continued to experience symptom reduction following the therapy. Paxton (2007) discovered that for eating disorders the f2f clients fared better than their online counterparts post-treatment; again this was over a short-term, eight-session contract. The inflow of more evidence becoming available to the counselling profession will mean that services are better able to respond to client need within a short-term time frame.

With the increasing emphasis occurring within HE on widening participation and also with the growth of distance learning, counselling services need to engage with the challenges such students bring including the provision of distance counselling. All students, irrespective of geographical distance from campus might reasonably have an expectation of such provision. In addition this requirement may be documented within individual institutional legislation or as part of the organisational strategic vision in supporting all students.

Time frames for online counselling

In providing equitable services to all students, online counselling must, of course, reflect the number of sessions offered to f2f clients. The initial assessment serves the same purposes in online as face-to-face counselling (see Dufour, Chapter 4) – to clarify psychological mindedness, to clarify the extent and limitations of the service, to outline process, e.g. counsellor theoretical orientation, confidentiality, to assess for risk and to agree to the counselling contract. The contracting process can incorporate desired outcomes for the client and having a clear sense of direction, even if that is purely a space to explore a client's experience of distress, helps keep the focus of counselling within a short-term time frame. Counsellors who set "homework" with clients can share this using password protected Word documents and, if forwarded in advance by the client, afford the counsellor more time to contemplate client progress or identify stumbling blocks.

Using email as a medium allows the counsellor time to read through and consider what the client is expressing before a response is sent. The counsellor also has the flexibility to change the time slot for this response depending on other commitments, providing it remains within the contracted response time. Some counsellors prefer to work using email as they value the opportunity to reflect on the client's needs. Counsellors' email responses can be contracted to be delivered within five working days and so keep within the time frame for f2f counselling, thus maintaining the same rhythm over the period of counselling.

There is no evidence to suggest that clients cannot benefit from time-limited or shorter-term online counselling. In fact as little as a single session has been shown to benefit certain client groups, including problem gamblers, alcohol users and those who present as socially isolated (Chester & Glass, 2006; Rochlen *et al.*, 2004) although it could be argued that single session contact is not "therapy" in the more traditional sense.

Referring on and monitoring risk

Clients who are actively engaging in risky behaviours or have suicidal ideation can access a number of professional online counselling services. There are independent practitioners and counsellors working within organisations who have been trained in services that have been developed to incorporate working with risk. In most cases this is provided professionally and ethically within BACP and legal frameworks.

Institutions such as universities tend to approach their online practice and care for clients (students) differently from these online counselling providers, especially where risk is present at the outset or emerges during the counselling. This is reflected in the agreement with the client that online counselling may cease in the event that the client discloses emerging risk to self or others and that onward referral or face-to-face counselling will be offered instead. The use of outcome measures is widely recognised as being helpful to the counselling process and this is especially true for online counselling, particularly when the mode of communication is text based. Counsellors' ability to monitor and regularly discuss clients' responses aids their understanding of what is going on for the client outside of the sessions.

Protocols that are in place for face-to-face counselling for such an eventuality can then be actioned with the full knowledge of the client. This is where an online trained and experienced supervisor is key to the online counselling process. Their knowledge and understanding of the context and limitations of the service alongside the actual online counselling process can reduce levels of concern and anxiety for the client, the counsellor and the service.

Using supervision to discuss concerns and explore ways forward in supporting the client through this transition is important. "Risk" and "harm" may be defined within individual institutions to not only include physical self harm, risk of harm to others and suicidal ideation, but also eating disorders, or excessive risky drug and alcohol use. Sometimes it is beneficial for the counsellor to actually have sight of the client in order to better ascertain the extent and nature of the presenting risk. It is worth noting that when the online counselling is text based, subtle clues can be missed regarding any deterioration in the client's health, which may manifest for example in reduced self care or hygiene. This is one of the reasons that specific online training and clear contracting with the client can help to counter inadvertently working outside of the limits of the service.

Differences between online and face-to-face work

Apart from the more obvious aspects of working at distance with text or with a web camera and microphone, one of the most striking aspects of working online is the difference in the shift of power. Although as counsellors we often consider the imbalance of power in the favour of the counsellor within the relationship, this is somewhat diminished as clients often have a greater ability to engage equally when working in cyberspace. Although it remains the counsellor's responsibility to care for the client in the way services are set up and provided and that clients continue to be treated with respect, there can be a greater sense of client expertise within this environment.

Understandably, the quality of the online relationship is often questioned but research has found it to be equal to that found in face-to-face therapy (Barak *et al.*, 2008; Cook & Doyle, 2002). In 2002 Fenichel *et al.* wrote of the "Myths and Realities of Online Clinical Work". The differences and quirks of online working were described in some depth by Suler (1996) in his exploration into online therapy and this is where the phenomenon of potential early disclosure by clients was identified and where the phrase "online disinhibition effect" originated. This is a powerful dynamic counsellors need to be fully aware of as they begin online work – both as it affects their client, but also, potentially, themselves. There can be a temptation to say more, to reveal more, because the other person is not physically present, and the risks involved in doing so need careful consideration.

Using text and its therapeutic benefits has long been established and carries the added bonus for the client of being able to look back at transcripts and review their progress and even "take the counselling with them", reflecting back in a way that is lost in traditional face-to-face work.

There are a number of disadvantages to working online with text based counselling and these include the need for clients to possess a certain level of literacy and computing skills along with a place of privacy. Some clients, for example students with dyslexia or those using assistive technology, may find text-based counselling inaccessible.

There is also a risk of misunderstanding between parties as the written word can be ambiguous and there is a lack of visual clues that may leave these words without context and explicit meaning, which can affect how the text is interpreted. This could lead to the client disengaging (Hunt, 2008) and the counsellor being left unsure why this has occurred.

Spontaneity and immediacy are lost with email and the client's situation may have changed by the time they receive the counsellor's response, rendering it irrelevant.

With real time chat, difficulties may arise from computer processing or typing speed and the counsellor or client may feel pressure to respond quickly rather than spend a few moments thinking through their response. This can be overcome by typing [thinking] or [pft, k?] – pause for thought, ok? – a concept shared by Anthony and Nagel (2010, p. 28).

So while there are many advantages of moving online to encounter our digital-native clients, we must also bear in mind that some of the unique qualities of f2f counselling relationships can seem even more valuable in the digital age. At what other times during the week might young people actually put their phones aside, or even turn them off and not take sneaky peeks at incoming messages? The communication generation who take their smartphones to bed and are assaulted by the "need to know now" culture that brings forth news feeds, blogs and messages with tempting opportunities for constant live streaming of information. No wonder then, that f2f "in person" intimacy might feel like a welcome relief, a place where the request for phone silence is agreed as two people sit opposite one another and communicate about inner and outer worlds. Online counselling provision is not a panacea for service delivery; but it does form an essential role in delivering therapy to a new generation.

The online counselling experience

Working online can be a daunting experience especially when new to the work and/or recently familiarised with a new platform. For the counsellor, there is often a level of uncertainty about what to expect from the client, how they present, how they will express themselves, their own experience of being online and how to guide a student through the contracting process during initial assessment session. Often, hovering in the back of the counsellor's mind is the knowledge that at some point the technology may fail and that they need to be prepared to calmly manage this with the client. This can be particularly tricky if it occurs during a sensitive part of the process and especially when this occurs during an IM session. One of the benefits of working in HE is that students have ready access to IT support so any incompatibility issues can be easily resolved as they are fully supported by the IT department.

When working online the playing field, so to speak, is suddenly more level, as the environment while "controlled" to some extent by the counsellor, is often more readily familiar to the client. For those counsellors who prefer to work with immediacy, the use of instant messaging or one-to-one web conferencing really comes into its own and the experience of being "in the moment with the client" can be as real as when working f2f.

Conclusion

As research into this emerging field continues, so will the evidence base for the impact, approaches, models and outcomes of counselling using technology. As this literature emerges, there may be evidence to inform services where distance counselling is less efficacious or unhelpful to clients that can be applied to working (short term) within the higher education environment.

As this way of working is no less resource-intense than face-to-face counselling, there is unlikely to be any organisational financial gain from adopting this approach. However, as the student body reaches across the globe to access our institutional teaching and learning, student counselling services need to respond in kind by incorporating distance therapy while remembering that online counselling may not suit everybody and that it is not, essentially, intended to replace f2f therapy.

Although the initial set up requires careful thought, planning and training with support from legal, technical and disability departments, the actual provision can comfortably sit alongside other short-term therapy approaches within a service and can, indeed, inform good practice with regards to the handling and storage of data.

At the time of writing, the BACP Ethical Framework for Good Practice in Counselling and Psychotherapy is undergoing consultation and revision, so it remains to be seen how online counselling (training, supervision and practice) will be reflected in the revised document. In the meantime, the existing good practice guidelines provide a sound framework with additional resources available from authors mentioned within this chapter and organisations such as the Association for Counselling and Therapy Online (ACTO) the Online Therapy Institute (OTI) and the International Society for Mental Health Online (ISMHO).

In 2001, Coren wrote: "In education, short term therapy captures the developmental fluidity of the process of being a student and parallels the student's experience of learning" (p. 195). He identifies the essentially transitory nature of much of student life – relationships, self-concept, knowledge. Sometimes when clients return to a service for further help after an initial episode of counselling, they are unable to recall the name of the counsellor with whom they worked. They may – just – remember their gender. For counsellors, this can be a salutary reminder that our relationship with students is not necessarily as important as we might like to imagine, and that some of the changes that are reflected in outcome measures can be attributed to factors beyond therapy. It may signal that online help, when offered compassionately and with full presence, can be as useful and effective as f2f work. Students are not, primarily, seeking a *relationship* with a counsellor but rather a *presence* with whom they can grapple with issues and who can act as witness to that struggle. As we are beginning to learn, and as I have shown in this chapter, online presence and witness offers much that is of real benefit, when we have developed the confidence and the skills to provide such a service to our student populations.

Glossary

Avatars: a visual portrayal of self using an image which is not a true likeness e.g. cartoon type image
HEI: Higher Education Institution
DDA: Disability Discrimination Act 2005 is the law governing the equitable provision of services for disabled persons
DPA: Data Protection Act 1998 is the law governing the handing and storage of personal and sensitive personal data
Equality Act 2010: Available at www.legislation.gov.uk/ukpga/2010/15/section/149
Platform: technology medium used to provide the services e.g. in house iVLE or email provider
Web con: web conferencing with audio and visual
IM: instant messaging or internet relay chat IRC
IRC: internet relay chat or instant messaging (IM)
iVLE: integrated Virtual Learning Environment

References

Ames, J. M. (2014) Get the message. *British Association for Counselling & Psychotherapy University & College Journal*, September 2014, 10–13.
Ames, J. M. (2014) *Being Present – Exploring Practice and Process in Our Counselling Services. Being Present Online*, Exeter, BACP Universities and Colleges Conference.
Anthony, K. E. & Goss, S. P. (2009). *Guidelines for Online Counselling and Psychotherapy, including Guidelines for Online Supervision. (3rd Edition)*, Lutterworth, BACP. Available to BACP members at: www.bacp.co.uk/online/index.php (accessed 3rd February 2015).
Anthony, K. (2014) *Training Therapists to Work Effectively Online and Offline within Digital Culture*, London, Routledge.
Anthony, K. & Nagel, D. M. (2010) *Therapy Online. A Practical Guide*, London, Sage.
Barak, A., Hen, L., Boniel-Nissim, M. & Shapira, N. (2008) A comprehensive review and a meta-analysis of the effectiveness of internet-based psychotherapeutic interventions. *Journal of Technology in Human Services*, 26 (2–4), 109–160.
CERN website. European Council for Nuclear Research. Available from: http://timeline.web.cern.ch/timelines/The-birth-of-the-World-Wide-Web (accessed 2nd February 2015).
Chester, A. & Glass, C. A. (2006) Online counselling: A descriptive analysis of therapy services on the Internet. *British Journal of Guidance & Counselling*, 34 (2), 145–160.
Clark, D. (2014) *10 reasons we should ditch university lectures*. Guardian Professional. Available from: www.theguardian.com/higher-education-network/blog/2014/may/15/ten-reasons-we-should-ditch-university-lectures (accessed 17th January 2014).
Cook, J. E. & Doyle, C. (2002) Working alliance in online therapy as compared to face-to-face therapy: Preliminary results. *CyberPsychology & Behavior*, 5 (2), 95–105.

Coren, A. (2001) *Short Term Therapy. A Psychodynamic Approach*, London, Palgrave.

Data Protection Act (1988) Available from: www.legislation.gov.uk/ukpga/1998/29/contents (accessed 6th January 2015).

Disability Discrimination Act (2005) Available from: www.legislation.gov.uk/ukpga/2005/13/crossheading/public-authorities (accessed 6th January 2015).

Dunn, K. (2012) A qualitative investigation into the online counselling relationship: To meet or not to meet, that is the question. *Counselling and Psychotherapy Research: Linking research with practice*, 12 (4), 316–327.

Evans, J. (2007) A pullout guide for online counselling in universities and colleges. *AUCC Journal*. Available through the British Association for Counselling & Psychotherapy. BACP, Lutterworth.

Evans, J. (2008) *Online Counselling & Guidance Skills: A Practical resource for Trainees & Practitioners*, London, Sage.

Fenichel, M., Suler, J., Barak, A., Zelvin, E., Jones, G., Munro, K., Meunier, V. & Walker-Schmucker, S. (2002) Myths and realities of online clinical work. *CyberPsychology & Behavior*, 5 (5), 481–497.

Goss, S. P. (2013) *Attending to the Sad, the Mad, the Bad and the Glad in Shaping the Future of Online Counselling and Psychotherapy*. Bristol, Online Counselling and Therapy in Action Conference.

Goss, S. P. & Hooley, T. (2015) Symposium on online practice in counselling and guidance. *British Journal of Guidance & Counselling*, 43 (1), 1–7.

Holford, J. Jarvis, P. Milana, M. Waller, R. & Webb, S. (2014) The MOOC phenomenon: Toward lifelong education for all? International Journal of Lifelong Education, 33 (5), 569–572.

Hunt, S. (2008). In favour of online counselling? *Australian Social Work*, 55 (4), 260–267.

Jones, G. & Stokes, A. (2008) *Online Counselling: A Handbook for Practitioners*, London, Palgrave Macmillan.

King, R., Bambling, M., Lloyd, C., Gomurra, R., Smith, S., Reid, W. & Wegner, K. (2006) Online counselling: The motives and experiences of young people who choose the Internet instead of face to face or telephone counselling. *Counselling & Psychotherapy Research Journal*, 6 (3), 169–174.

Knox, J. (2014) Digital culture clash: "Massive" education in the E-learning and Digital Cultures MOOC. *Distance Education*, 35 (2), 164–177.

Oravec, J. (2000) Online counselling and the Internet: Perspectives for mental health care supervision and education. *Journal of Mental Health.* 9 (2), 121–135.

Paxton, S. J., McLean, S. A, Gollings, E. K., Faulkner, C. & Wertheim, E. H. (2007) Comparison of face-to-face and internet interventions for body image and eating problems in adult women: An RCT. *International Journal of Eating Disorders*, 40 (8), 692–704.

Prensky, M. (2001) Digital natives, digital immigrants, *From On the Horizon* (NCB University Press, 9 (5), October 2001). Available from: http://www.nnstoy.org/download/technology/Digital%20Natives%20-%20Digital%20Immigrants.pdf (accessed 30th June 2015).

Richards, D. (2009) Features and benefits of online counselling: Trinity College online mental health community. *British Journal of Guidance & Counselling.* 37 (3), 231–242.

Richards, D. & Viganó, N. (2013) Online counseling: A narrative and critical review of the literature. *Journal of Clinical Psychology.* 69 (9), 994–1011.

Rochlen, A. B., Zack, J. S. & Speyer, C. (2004) Online therapy: Review of relevant definitions, debates, and current empirical support. *Journal of Clinical Psychology.* 60 (3), 269–283.

Simpson, S. (2009) Psychotherapy via videoconferencing: A review. *British Journal of Guidance & Counselling*, 37 (3), 271–286.

Suler, J. (1996) Psychology of cyberspace. Available from: http://truecenterpublishing. com/psycyber/psycyber.html (accessed 3rd January 2015).

Sweeney, M. (2012). UK leads world in mobile web use thanks to Facebook . . . and Gangnam. *Guardian Online*. Available from: www.theguardian.com/technology/2012/dec/13/ mobile-web-facebook-gangnam (accessed 2nd February 2015).

Universities UK (in collaboration with the Higher Education Statistics Agency) (2013) *Higher education: A diverse and changing sector.* Available from: www.universitiesuk. ac.uk/.../PatternsAndTrendsinUKHigherEducation2013 (accessed 26th January 2015).

Vogel, D. L., Wester, S. R. & Larson, L. M. (2007) Avoidance of counseling: Psychological factors that inhibit seeking help. *Journal of Counseling & Development*, 85, 410–422.

Wagner, B., Horn, A., & Maercker, A. (2014) Internet-based versus face-to-face cognitive-behavioral intervention for depression: A randomized controlled non-inferiority trial. *Journal of Affective Disorders*, 133–141, 152–154.

Chapter 11

Managing demand and surviving the work

Samantha Tarren

Monday morning, 9 a.m. Emily arrives at work and checks her diary. Full. Six clients. Her heart sinks. This is week eight of a really busy term – looking down the list of names she realises that she can't even remember who some of them are. A feeling of shame takes over. "I bet other counsellors never forget their clients" a voice whispers in her ear. Also, a feeling of real fatigue. She recognises one of the names, and she knows that this client is very vulnerable, and tends to push the boundaries of sessions a lot. Today Emily really needs time to get her credit card bill paid – it's the last date before she'll incur late payment charges. But when will she find time to phone the bank? Her phone rings: it's reception. "Your client is here."

Jane manages a small team of counsellors – a mixture of full and part-time staff, with a few trainees coming in several days a week. She was promoted to this position a year ago and still finds it quite hard to realise that this has changed the relationship she had with colleagues who she has become accustomed to thinking of as friends. Now she finds that she is viewed differently and expectations of her have shifted fundamentally. Staff who used to talk to her about their concerns and problems, now seem more interested in "getting" from her – time off, funding for training, advice about difficult clients. This week she's been asked to make a presentation to senior management outlining the cost-benefits of keeping the counselling service in-house. This is both exciting and terrifying, and she's not sure who she can really talk to about how she's feeling.

Introduction

Working as a therapist in University Counselling Services is particularly challenging: demand for counselling continues to increase yet resources are often limited. As the profile of students changes, so counselling services are continually tasked with creatively meeting their needs. Institutions may appreciate that comprehensive support services are an essential aspect of their overall provision, but may not always be willing to provide the resources staff feel are necessary in order to fulfil their professional roles. This gap between demand and resource means that working as a counsellor in HE is no easy task, and is something that requires resilience and imagination as well as good management in order to not only survive, but thrive.

The challenges of the work

Defining "survival" in the context of short-term work in Higher Education counselling services is a challenge in itself. It could be said that counselling is an inherently dangerous occupation, not dissimilar to rock climbing, metaphorically. Like the rock climber, we learn the (counselling) ropes, build up experience, continually check our "kit" is safe and fit for purpose. Yet there is always the inherent danger of a fall off the rock face, or the rock structure may give way beneath us. Hopefully robust equipment and thorough preparation will ensure any stumble is not fatal and so the process of the climb is continually exciting, perhaps because of, rather than in spite of, its precarious nature. So it is with counselling. However, challenges in HE counselling have shifted over the years. The key challenge used to be to ensure the concept of student support was accepted and recognised as important. Now there is a need for wide-ranging sophisticated student support services in universities. However, acknowledgement of this need has generally not been met with sufficient resources to keep pace with demand, so pressure has increased on services to continue to do more with less. This generates a raft of issues for service managers to contend with, attempting simultaneously to balance serving the needs of the institution and paying attention to the professional and personal needs of the counselling team. If service managers only respond to the demands of the institution, the fundamental tenets of counselling may be jeopardised; if only the needs of the counselling team are considered, institutional requirements may suffer. To survive the contemporary challenges of counselling in HE in a vigorous and healthy way, service managers need to understand the requirements of all stakeholders and find creative and effective ways of ensuring an excellent counselling service is delivered. How successfully the counselling service is embedded within the university relates to the skill of a manager in championing their service, as well as the level of resources available to support service staff in maintaining their professional integrity, ensuring they can successfully survive the rigours of the job of counselling in an HE institution.

Surviving the challenges

"Surviving the work" may seem a rather dramatic chapter title, as if a service may be in mortal danger if matters are not attended to appropriately. Sadly, some services have indeed been severely under threat in organisations under pressure to cut costs significantly, or where the work of a counselling service has not been adequately valued. Institutions have had to scrutinise their expenditure and some have considered that student support, particularly counselling, is extraneous to their core academic task and have looked at ways to reduce costs by cutting resources. In some cases "the spectre of outsourcing university counselling lurks in the shadows" (Pointon, 2014, p. 16). Most institutions, however, realise that offering a comprehensive package of university-based student support is important, not least from a public relations perspective, as evidence that it provides a supportive space for its students that can assist in the achievement of academic goals as well as adding value to the overall student experience. Nevertheless, as Ruth Clowes, Media and Communication Manager at BACP suggests, "it has never been more important for services to successfully promote the many benefits of in-house counselling" (Clowes, 2014, p. 5). Service managers need to pay close attention to this challenge as well as to protecting their teams in highly stressful work. Institutions have a legal duty of care to staff to ensure good working conditions. Service managers must protect counsellors who are working with dangerous or risky clients and ensure that the ongoing stress of working with disturbing client material is managed and supported appropriately. Otherwise the institution may be in danger of incurring legal proceedings for failing to meet its duty of care to staff (see Jenkins, Chapter 3).

What do institutions expect from their counselling services?

May reminds us that "how we define and publicise our work may be crucial to our survival" (May, 1999, p. 14). Inevitably this challenge tends to fall predominantly to the managers of counselling services as they act as a conduit between the counsellors and the institution. This position can be uncomfortable for all concerned. Institutions may simply want the "distress to go away" (whatever that may mean): stop students taking their own life, stop them disrupting others. The counselling team may be the best placed service within the institution to be able to make some inroads into this challenge if they have sufficient counsellors with adequate time to provide significant therapeutic intervention. And there's the rub: institutions are continually requiring "more for less" from counselling services and significant additional resources are not an option. In 2010, Les McMinn, former director of the Centre of Wellbeing at the University of Surrey, wrote about his experience of attending an AMOSSHE[1] conference entitled "Facing the economic downturn – creative solutions in challenging times", where it became clear that the

> challenge we all face is to demonstrate the value we add to the institution . . . we need to be putting our energies in to what we are contributing to the organisation and our value. What is the actual impact of a counselling centre . . . What is our strategic contribution?
>
> (AUCC, 2010, p. 7)

In order to ensure HE counselling services survive, service managers need to pay attention to facing outwards towards the institution and beyond, keeping abreast of national strategies. They also need to be skilled at presenting a viable business case and seeking out routes in to senior managers who can be ambassadors for the counselling service wherever possible, to ensure survival in the institution.

Managing demand

Student counselling services within higher education are often over-subscribed with demand frequently outstripping capacity. This inevitably creates the potential for waiting times for counselling to increase. Service managers need to carefully consider their model of service delivery so that clients can be seen swiftly and expediently both in terms of wait time and in terms of number of sessions offered, whilst ensuring the core task of therapeutic counselling remains their central activity. It is important that counsellors aim for an optimum balance of securing sufficient time and space to reflect and process their work, whilst still engaging with the therapeutic task with integrity.

Counselling short-term

Counsellors in HE have had to develop their skills in practice to embrace a service delivery model that emphasises offering briefer interventions to more clients. This can lead to counsellors carrying larger caseloads than they used to, but the BACP professional guidelines, originally drawn up in 2004 and revised in 2010, state that "An average of 20 contact hours for a full time counsellor is considered best practice and while this may fluctuate according to local conditions, 25 hours should be the maximum in any one week". However the guidelines also recognise that "some counselling services experience high demand all the year round and a low rate of missed sessions" and "Counsellors working in such situations are unlikely to be able to function effectively if their caseload is consistently at the high end of this range" (BACP, 2010, p. 13). It is essential when working to brief therapeutic contracts that caseload management is carefully monitored throughout the academic timeframe to ensure counsellors are not exceeding the guidelines so they can successfully survive the work. It could be argued that working to briefer contracts means counsellors have less chance to be professionally stimulated by a range of longer-term counselling relationships with clients. Fortunately, for traditional 18- to 21-year-old undergraduates, issues may not be significantly entrenched; they may be able to make significant personal changes quite swiftly. Also, the nature of the context of the HE institution is continually requiring the student to examine, explore and critically evaluate – often essential tools for successful therapy. As Coren (1999) notes, brief work

> is appropriate for the context in which educational settings work, but also because it speaks to the adolescent/young adult's developmental drive. Many young adults, having just left home and their families, do not necessarily want, or need, to be pulled back into what can be experienced as a regressively frightening (or comforting – which can be equally problematic at this age) relationship.

(pp. 65–66)

However, it is important for both clients and counsellors, where possible, to offer the capacity to engage in some longer-term therapeutic contracts. From the client perspective, this may be important to meet specific therapeutic needs on occasion when the situation requires it. Several experienced service managers anecdotally report the importance of offering variety in work to their counsellors to sustain them professionally, and to continue to thrive as ethical professionals in the predominantly short-term environment. As service managers, it is essential to respond to the institution's requirements to meet demand with limited resources, but not at the expense of the core counselling tenets of offering sufficient time and space to explore and think.

Working with increasingly severe and complex cases

One of the key challenges for university counselling services that has arisen over recent years is the increased severity and complexity of clients' presentations. As Caleb (2014) notes,

> university support services are trying to cope with a huge wave of students with serious and complex mental health problems that need medical intervention. . . . specialist mental health services, such as eating disorders clinics, are being cut or even closed, and waiting lists for psychiatric assessments and psychological therapy are growing.
>
> (p. 2)

Support for students from GPs and specialist NHS mental health services has often been problematic as the academic timeframe may mean that students are in different areas of the country at different times of the year, which makes continuity of care difficult. However, counselling services, and even the growing number of mental health services within universities, cannot take the place of specialist NHS treatment provision. The best case scenario for students would be

> a caring and responsive NHS that understands the stresses and nature of university life. Where this is offered, students with mental health issues will be able to reach their academic potential which will serve them for the rest of their lives.
>
> (Caleb, 2014)

In practice, counselling services are being challenged to contain and manage some severely disturbed students. Institutions may be pushing for support staff to provide intervention for disruptive students with serious mental health difficulties. It is the service manager's job to ensure that the counselling service is seen as robust and responsive by the university while ensuring the counselling team is practicing safely. Drawing up clear protocols about who can benefit and who should not be referred to counselling is an ongoing challenge. It is imperative that counselling service managers establish good links with local GP practices or health centres and support challenges to local trusts and commissioning bodies to meet their duty of care and lobby for the resources to do so. This may go some way to help ensure counsellors are not being required to work beyond their competency with clients who are too disturbed and chaotic to benefit from counselling as this working practice is a threat to counsellor's healthy survival in the workplace.

Summary of the challenges/pressures on counselling services

* Coping with increasing demand
* Adapting to briefer therapeutic contracts
* Being creative with the range of therapeutic intervention
* Evidencing the worth of an embedded counselling service
* Demonstrating accountability and effectiveness
* Managing with limited resources
* Working with increasingly complex and severe students as clients
* Adding value and impact to the student experience
* Containing the anxiety and distress of the staff of the institution

Surviving as counsellor

At the core of a heathy, functioning counselling service in any HE organisation lie healthy, functioning counsellors. Counsellors are aware through their training of their motivations for becoming therapists and for many there is a "wounded healer" within. This needs attention throughout practice, especially when working with undergraduates as they are passing through developmental psycho-social stages counsellors will have also passed through. There is the potential for our own issues to become re-activated when working with students. It is essential for counsellors to become aware of unconscious drives and desires that continue to resonate in order to avoid getting re-ensnared those issues ourselves. If we fail to pay good attention to these, as Wicks notes:

> [the] . . . potential for developing such psychological problems as emotional blunting at one end of the spectrum or extreme affectivity at the other are quite great. Many of us deny personal emotional needs as a survival mechanism. However, clinicians who follow the implicit advice to protect themselves by not allowing themselves to feel too much emotion, sympathy, or sadness run the risk of shutting down entirely in the process and losing the joy and empathy that are so necessary for being clinicians who can thrive and be a true healing presence to others.
>
> (2008, p. 11)

Working to briefer counselling contracts and seeing more clients may affect thera-peutic stress levels in different ways. Dipping briefly but intensely into many clients' narratives will have an impact because as we listen to and try and make sense of the stories of distress and disturbance "we catch some of the futility, fear, vulnerability and hopelessness rather than experiencing mere frustration or concern" (Wicks, 2008, p. 30). No matter how skilled and how experienced, it is not possible for counsellors to be unaffected by their clients: indeed it is important that we *are* affected in order to fully empathise and understand the frame of refer-ence of the client. But it is the level of impact and its sometimes insidious nature that needs monitoring with a range of self-care strategies to help to manage the chronic effect of secondary stress. Some stress is acute in that there may be a spe-cific and obvious indicator that all is not well. This may be physical – the onset of a migraine or a cold – or mental, where the thought of seeing a client seems over-whelming; most stress builds up cumulatively over time. Moving towards burn out can be identified by the counsellor feeling constantly cynical about the process of therapeutic change for many clients; feeling continually bored or depleted by the work, or isolating from colleagues in an attempt to keep on top of workload. These are all clues that need attention. It is essential that "we face stress con-structively, [so that] not only do we lessen the chances of it turning into extreme distress, but we also are in a position to learn from it in a way that deepens us" (Wicks, 2008, p. 27).

Counsellors' self-care

The BACP Ethical Framework has as one of its core principles self-respect, or "fostering the practitioners' self-knowledge and care for self . . . The principle of self-respect means that the practitioner appropriately applies all the . . . principles as entitlements for self" (BACP, 2013 p. 19). This principle "encourages active engagement in life-enhancing activities and relationships that are independent of relationships in counselling or psychotherapy". Indeed, the guidelines go on to note, "practitioners have a responsibility to themselves to ensure that their work does not become detrimental to their health or wellbeing" (BACP, 2013 p. 19). Individual counsellors must take personal responsibility for adhering to this guid-ance and find what works for them whilst ensuring they deliver the counselling service required by their institution. Commonly-used self-care strategies include paying attention to primary physical basics such as maintaining healthy eating, exercise and sleeping patterns; practising mindfulness or meditative techniques to practice psychological stillness and replenishment to restore mental equilibrium.

Petra works four days a week in a busy university counselling service. It is near-ing the end of the term and today is Thursday, her fourth and final working day of the week, and so far she's had 19 clients booked in to see her this week. This is alongside supervising an associate counsellor, attending a business meeting and a student care session with colleagues across student support services. One client telephoned the service this morning to say he was unwell and would not be able to come in for his appointment today. Petra was aware of a sense of relief at having some breathing space in her day. She has noticed as the term has gone on that she has needed to increase her self-care strategies to keep herself sufficiently alert in order to process the many levels of overt and covert communication with her clients. She commits to going for a brisk walk in the fresh air in her lunch break then does a brief body scan – checking in with where the tension is being held physically and trying to breathe it away with each out-breath. Petra knows that, although she still has a set of case notes to write up, it is more important for her overall wellbeing to step out of her consulting office and connect with colleagues whilst eating a healthy lunch. Petra returns to prepare her notes and herself for her afternoon counselling sessions feeling much more centred and able to concentrate on her clients and their concerns.

Ensuring a healthy work-life balance is in place, with time for play as well as rest and work, and time to connect with others and with the self in a way that is self-supporting is important as is an ability to manage times when our own lives are under stress or when we are coping with our own difficult issues. Atkinson, during her online workshop event, "Self-care – who cares for the carers" (Atkinson, 2014), shared her ideas for therapists to develop their own mental health first aid kits, or "kindness kits", which ranged from being outdoors to creative cooking and beyond. At worst, if counsellors fail to attend sufficiently to their own self-maintenance, there is the possibility, perhaps particularly in the short-term model within the pressured environments of HE with repeated, quick engagement and disengagement, for counsellors to suffer burnout due to vicarious trauma. This is described by one author as

> a state of physical, emotional and mental exhaustion caused by long term involvement in emotionally demanding situations...where the culture of the place is one that colludes with the idea that fatigue is seen as part and parcel of the role.
>
> (Royle, 2006, p. 25)

Staying connected

Service managers in HE counselling services can play a vital role in ensuring the environment, physical and emotional, is as secure and appropriate as possible, to ensure the culture of self-care is embodied throughout the service. For example, at Warwick University, during weekly business meetings there is an ongoing agenda item, "team check-in" time, where all colleagues including the service manager and the administrator as well as the counselling staff comment on how they feel they are managing generally with their case-loads. Each fortnight there is a peer supervision session with counsellors to check in with each other regarding any significant personal or professional issues as appropriate. These sessions are given priority in each counsellor's diary. Each term during a one-to-one line-management session the impact of the work is discussed, as well as a check-in on the physical environment to ensure it continues to be fit for purpose. Over time a culture has developed of encouraging each other to meet for regular breaks around a structured daily calendar as well as an ethos of working to time boundaries and generally not working over scheduled hours in the working week.

The pressures and intensity of the work needs, where possible, to be contained and offset by the support of colleagues and team members, so attention needs to be paid to the ethos of the service as being one that embodies self-care and affirmation to encourage general positivity. It can be important to create opportunities to celebrate achievements and to acknowledge professional success, perhaps using team meetings to note individuals and teams for a job well done, for example, when a particularly challenging term has been successfully worked through. Giving positive strokes where possible can help to boost and sustain morale, which can have the effect of enhancing team optimism as a helpful counterpoint to the struggle of the work.

Encouraging social opportunities to connect with other counsellors can be another way of facilitating positive and supportive morale within a team of hard-working professional counsellors. This may take the form of team socials or encouraging involvement in staff or institutional community events that facilitate team bonding. However, service managers need to tread a careful line to ensure family dynamics are not re-enacted as inevitably the service manager takes on a quasi-parental role, regardless of their age, simply by the authority vested in their job title. Spending time with one member of the team could be interpreted as favouritism.

The importance of structure and time management

Even for those counsellors in HE who may enjoy the benefits of working in a team, counselling can be a lonely occupation. We are generally in the counselling room, on our own with our clients; so, it is important for healthy counselling practice to create frequent points of contact and connection with others. Working to a team schedule each day, which structures breaks at set times in a designated area, can go far to provide a context for counsellors to check in with each other. Although this prescribed working pattern may seem dogmatic, a defined shape throughout a working day can provide clear anchor points, which can help restore emotional balance to enable the counsellors to engage robustly with the random and often disturbing places their clients may take them. This coming together of colleagues, albeit briefly, can be grounding and important. As well as the basic good practice of taking regular breaks throughout an intense working day – the sort of strategy that we encourage our students to adopt for themselves – has added value if the break is taken both out of the consulting room and also with familiar and, to all intents and purposes, sane and safe colleagues. As the service manager, as well as setting up and encouraging the fullest use of this structure, it is of course also important to adhere to it oneself as much as possible. It can be tempting to work through a scheduled break, especially as it is unlikely that you are working to the same 50-minute session rhythms that the core counselling staff work to. But in practice it is not only modelling good self-care but it is also an opportunity to take a break and connect with team members in a less formal setting. It is also an important way of gauging the mood in general and to check in with individuals. This is often where a team of colleagues might notice that someone seems more tired than usual, more stressed, disengaged, or otherwise preoccupied, in a way that may not be evident in a more formal meeting. This can then be attended to in a light-touch way, that might be sufficient to rebalance something, or it might lead to the surfacing of a trend of disturbance that needs discussing in a more formal setting such as a scheduled team meeting. As well as regular breaks within the working day, it is essential to take breaks away from the work entirely:

> all of us need breaks in the sense that being able to *detach* as well as *attach* is a vital aspect of relating. We all need them, not just to relax and unwind, but because they can bring vitality, change, new possibilities into life.
>
> (Rose, 2004, p. 28)

The importance of clinical supervision

A key tenet of the counselling and psychotherapy profession is clinical supervision. There is a requirement from training and throughout practice to ensure adequate supervision. This is an imperative for securing accreditation and re-accreditation. Supervision is generally viewed positively by counsellors as an essential and important aspect of their clinical work. Although there is always an element of monitoring involved in supervision, where the supervisor is ensuring the counsellor is practicing ethically and appropriately, supervision is generally an activity that is welcome and perceived as an extremely useful and supportive space. The service manager has a duty to ensure all counsellors have access to and make full use of supervision, to help all concerned survive the work successfully. In practice this should not simply be borne out of a necessity to adhere to the regulations of BACP accreditation requirements, but should actually be integral to the ethos of the counsellor and the counselling service. Supervision is a space to think, to reflect, to critically examine and to ponder in a way that is invaluable to help the overall therapeutic process for counsellors. It could be said to be even more essential to help contain the amount of material worked with in briefer therapeutic contracts common in HE counselling. It is vital to work with a supervisor who is willing and able to work within the context of shorter-term counselling work in the HE context. Supervision can help to keep the core aims and purpose of counselling clearly at the centre of the work while weaving the needs and idiosyncrasies of the organisation around and through it.

A range of supervision options

There are many different models of supervision in university counselling services: some services may allow counsellors to select their own supervisor with whom they have an ongoing supervisory relationship and perhaps supervises other areas of the clinical work of the individual counsellor. This model may or may not involve the counsellors travelling out to visit their supervisor. The advantage of this model is that it fosters autonomy in the counsellors as they can take responsibility for selecting a supervisor who works well with them personally. Some services opt for one supervisor who supervises all counsellors in-house. A key advantage of this model is that the supervisor has a sense of the team and can be alert to themes that may emerge through the client work or with the team members, but the disadvantage is that the supervisory relationship will not be "pure" and uncontaminated by the input from all team members. The delivery model of supervision also varies throughout HE institutions. Some counselling teams work solely with one-to-one supervision support; some may have peer supervision groups either facilitated by an external or an in-house supervisor; many have a combination of individual and group supervision. The key to supervision helping counsellors to survive the work, in whatever mode of delivery and whichever model, is that it suits the ethos of the service and there is a culture of willingness to engage in the process at all levels. It is important for the institution to acknowledge the importance of supervision by paying for it and ensuring that time for supervision is included in the working hours of counselling staff. However it is essentially the service manager's task to ensure the institution funds the practice of supervision as an essential element of a respectable and creditable university counselling service. This may entail reminding senior managers of their duty of care for staff who are working in a high-stress environment.

Professional development

All counsellors have an ethical duty to update their clinical practice by engaging in continuing professional development. As part of providing a good standard of practice and care, there is a requirement "to keep up to date with the latest knowledge and respond to changing circumstances. They should consider carefully their own need for continuing professional development and engage in appropriate educational activities" (BACP, 2013, p. 5). Counsellors working in HE settings undertaking predominantly short-term counselling work need to pay special attention to make the time to arrange appropriate training to ensure they are working to the principle of beneficence for the client and also to keep themselves sufficiently nourished to undertake the strenuous exigencies of the role. Where possible, and when related to strategic service objectives, service managers should support professional development activity for their team members. BACP:UC organise an annual conference for counsellors working in university or college settings to meet together to discuss and explore the challenges of the role and is an excellent opportunity for counsellors to understand their work from a wider national perspective.

When considering creative ways to support counselling colleagues with professional development it can be resourceful to run cascade CPD sessions where members of staff who have attended a conference or training session share the key learning with other members of the team. Occasionally a university counselling service may arrange with another local service to run joint training days for continuing professional development topics that would benefit the whole team, thus sharing the costs and resources.

Summary of challenges/pressures for counsellors in HE counselling services and possible antidotes

Table 11.1 Challenges for HE counsellors

Challenges/pressures for counsellors in HE counselling services:	Possible antidotes:
• Continuing need to be adaptable and creative and embrace change • Carrying a full and diverse case load • Often working to brief therapeutic contracts • Counselling clients with severe and complex issues • Needing to manage time and tasks smartly • The risks of burn out/vicarious trauma/secondary stress	• Engage with continuing professional development opportunities to keep practice fresh and progressive • Offer a range of therapeutic interventions to add variety to keep revitalised • Engage fully in supervision • Keep connected with colleagues • Develop robust self-care strategies • Maintain high levels of self-awareness • Maintain a work-life balance with interests and relationships outside of work • Be alert to primary and secondary stressors and manage stress appropriately • Develop excellent time management skills

Surviving as a manager

Counselling service managers are often promoted to the role from within a team and are therefore familiar with being a colleague carrying a clinical caseload. One of the challenges of a counselling service manager is to be a leader within our peers – a kind of "first among equals". This has both advantages and disadvantages. The counselling skills of understanding how people and teams behave, especially in groups, is essential, as well as the capacity to listen well and be empathic. However, taking a clear, decisive lead and direction may not come naturally to those who are experienced counsellors, but is nonetheless necessary for an effective service manager. Taking a service forward requires assertiveness and authority, sometimes in the face of adversity and challenge.

It requires the counsellor to learn a new vocabulary of budgets, to cultivate strategic awareness and to develop networking skills along with a boldness and tenacity to manage successfully up the management line as well as downwards. The transition from team member to team leader inevitably changes the relationship between colleagues. Halpern commented heads of service need to "be able to contain the anxiety for the team and be able to bear both their love and their hate" (Halpern, 2008).

Effective leadership is essential to ensuring the healthy survival of the whole counselling team. An experienced service manager recalls realising during a meeting, after a year in post, that the team wanted a leader to influence and shape the service, to take responsibility for setting up operations to successfully respond to the patterns of clients' presentations and to help reduce the anxieties about the work for the team. Holding a vision for the counselling team while also focussing attention on the day-to-day operational mechanisms of the service is a challenge that, if successfully mastered, can help the team survive and thrive. A litmus test for gauging the levels of stress or anxiety could be taken from the administrator perspective, as this is often the initial point of contact for disturbed clients and the reception staff could be said to be responsible for receiving some of the raw distress of clients or members of staff, however it may manifest. The service manager needs to involve administrative staff, where feasible, in workload management discussions and take seriously their sense about what is occurring within the service. Where services are working to briefer therapeutic contracts with clients, there is inevitably an increase in the footfall of clients to the service. Administrative staff are likely to get an overview of the presentation of clients, and their input is invaluable in helping to shape the manager's strategy to manage demand.

Leading a counselling service in HE can be exciting and invigorating, but in order to be effective, the service manager also needs to keep fit and well to survive the rigours of the role. Monitoring levels of physical health and being aware of any changes is important for the whole team, including the service manager, as stress or disturbance can often manifest somatically. For example, if ongoing injury or illness flares up, it is important to consider the holistic implications rather than simply treating the physical symptoms. The recurrence may be caused by tension as a result of increased work pressure. If the cause can be identified, it is sensible to make adjustments at the root of the problem to keep sufficiently physically robust and healthy to undertake the work. Developing a culture of psychological curiosity in the service around the causes of physical issues can help the team to stay as well as possible to survive the work.

It is important for a counselling service manager, where possible, to work with a line manager who understands the complexities of the counselling profession. Where this is not feasible it can be helpful to identify a colleague within the organisation who can be trusted to maintain confidentiality, to talk frankly with about any institutional issues. As one experienced manager commented, "Having someone who you both trust and respect, who understands the service and the organisation, who you can talk to openly, in confidence, without fear of criticism, is enormously helpful to keep safe and well as a Head of Service". Making time to meet with a member of a senior management team who can act as ambassador and champion for the counselling service while also being a trusted confidante can be important, where possible, in surviving the challenges of counselling service management. It is also helpful to secure external organisational consultancy supervision (alongside clinical supervision for counselling work) to talk about service management issues in general and to contain some of the complexities and frustrations of heading up a counselling service. This can ensure any difficulties within a team are considered from an organisational dynamic perspective rather than taken personally. As another experienced service manager observed, simply modelling the importance of a sense of humour where appropriate is often an essential tool in the survival kit of service managers who head up teams of counsellors, helping to keep a balanced perspective on situations.

Seeking out support for the unique role of counselling service manager is essential. Colleagues in the counselling profession working in a similar HE context can be an invaluable support. There is an extremely lively, interactive and well-used mail base for Heads of University Counselling Services (HUCS). This forum was set up via BACP:UC specifically for service heads who can share ideas of good practice among each other and check in for support about any issues. Reading the email threads, even if not directly or currently relevant to each individual service, is interesting and informative, and the archives can be accessed if or when the issue arises in any service in the future. Heads of University Counselling Services also host regular national and regional meetings throughout the year where colleagues can meet and consider relevant topics. These are often well attended and testify to their importance in a busy service manager's schedule. From these sessions, professional connections are developed as a positive networking resource to help keep service managers continuing to think and function clearly to survive the work. Service managers also need to learn to tolerate a certain amount of creative chaos in their work, while remembering to keep a perspective on what can realistically be achieved in the context in which they are working.

Good time-management is an important skill to master, as well as the ability to be responsive and flexible with time, as the service and the institution requires, as no longer are time boundaries prescribed by the therapeutic hours throughout the day. Although service managers need to reduce their clinical caseload to allow sufficient time to attend to management tasks, it is nonetheless important to continue to see clients. This ensures that the service manager stays connected with the therapeutic task and the whole team recognises, in practice, the importance of the clinical work and jointly holds some responsibility for the therapeutic work of the service. This can help avoid unhelpful team splits where the manager is seen as solely understanding the service from a managerial and institutional perspective and the counsellors perceive they alone understand the clinical aspects and perhaps then do not so readily share in institutional and service thinking. Securing a workable balance of clinical work and managerial tasks is important to ensure everyone in the team is thinking both clinically and institutionally where appropriate.

Encouraging and ensuring all team members uphold firm boundaries of time and purpose in all aspects of their work is important to ensure healthy professional survival. Of course modelling this as the service manager is also important – not encouraging a culture of routinely working over contracted hours and ensuring that all staff leave on time, whenever possible, is vital to longer-term stress management, and helps develop healthy, functioning counselling teams.

Summary of challenges and pressures of counselling specific to counselling service managers in Higher Education and possible antidotes

Table 11.2 Challenges for service managers in HE

Challenges and pressures of counselling service managers:	Possible antidotes:
• Continuing to creatively manage the increased demand • Focusing simultaneously on operational and institutional/strategic matters • Ensuring the counselling service is responsive and flexible yet ethical and safe • Being continually creative with the range of therapeutic interventions whilst ensuring the core tenets of counselling are upheld • Offering an excellent counselling service with limited resources • Demonstrating the professional counselling service's added value to and impact on the institution • Managing high expectations of institutions • Creatively championing and promoting the counselling service to the institution • Containing and managing the institution's anxiety • Needing to convey confidence when unsure • Responding to counselling staff requests for resources • Maintaining counsellor skills e.g. of empathy and understanding with both clients and counselling staff while being decisive and directive	• Recruiting a high calibre team of robust counsellors and administrative staff • Developing clear protocols for managing need with appropriate onward referrals • Developing good links with the institution using ambassadors for the service where possible • Frequent managerial/case-work supervision • Supportive networks – e.g. HUCS, other trusted managers within institutions, GPs • Good self-care: ensuring regular time-out for reflection • Developing specific management skills to enhance effectiveness as team leader • Maintaining a sense of perspective and a sense of humour

Surviving together

The whole counselling team needs to be personally and professionally robust to respond to the inevitable times in the academic cycle when services experience increased demand or where it may be necessary to re-prioritise, to perhaps increase capacity to take on more new clients when waiting times begin to build, or possibly, where funding allows, to welcome and support locum or bank counsellors into the team to help manage demand. This extra pressure on an already busy caseload requires staff to be sufficiently intellectually and emotionally robust, as well as agile and flexible in their approach and attitude in order to survive the work. It is important that practitioners in the HE context have let go of any "private counselling practice mentality" and are able to fully commit to the challenges of working in an educational context. This involves not simply understanding the impact of the academic cycle time frame, but also being responsive when necessary to institutional crisis situations. For example, in the unfortunate event of a student (or staff) death, it is not unusual that the institution turns to the University Counselling Service for guidance. It is essential that the counselling service respond with compassion, expedience and care, while at all times modelling professionalism to calm and contain the distress that will inevitably abound in such circumstances. Employing responsive, experienced counselling staff willing to respond in a co-operative and supportive, yet thoughtful and calm way is imperative. Those who are not overly-attached to their theoretical model, and can be flexible to embrace multiple styles and techniques are better able to survive these demands and indeed are better able to employ their flexible approach to effectively work with short-term therapeutic contracts with clients in general. The service manager needs to effectively lead through these fortunately infrequent situations, carefully meeting the ebbs and flows of demand, but also gently but firmly holding the shape of the service to maximise dynamic flow while containing anxiety, which ensures the team is kept safe and well.

There is an interesting relationship between managing demand successfully and surviving the work. Feeling totally overwhelmed is an interesting mix of inner and outer worlds. Some days one can drown in a puddle and yet on others thrive in an ocean. Perhaps the service manager's challenge is to present the illusion of swimming along calmly whilst paddling hard underneath. It could be argued that to be an effective counsellor we need to be bold enough to take risks, to venture into unknown territory where it is sometimes unclear whether we will survive at all. Like the rock climber, we need to be continually alert to the dangers, to update our knowledge, keep ourselves fit and alert, monitor ourselves and seek support to ensure others can help us be vigilant, proceed with mindful care, to scale the challenging terrain with competence and confidence. Service managers must support and challenge counsellors to ensure they remain fit and healthy in a busy counselling service, and can survive the challenges of undertaking short-term work. In the counselling room, we all still need to be prepared to take risks to meet our clients in their many fascinating and intriguing places in order to effectively carry out our therapeutic tasks.

Note

1 AMOSSHE (Association of Managers of Student Services in Higher Education). AMOSSHE is a professional membership association for leaders of student services in UK higher education.

References

Atkinson, J. (2014) *Self care – who cares for the carers*? Online interview through www. onlineevents.co.uk. Broadcast live on 6th October 2014.

BACP (2010) *AUCC Guidelines for University and College Counselling Services (2nd Edition)*, Rugby, BACP.

BACP (2013) *Ethical Framework for Good Practice in Counselling and Psychotherapy (Revised Edition January 2013)*, Lutterworth, BACP.

Caleb, R. (2014) *Uni counselling services challenged by growing demand*. The Guardian, 27th May. Available from: www.theguardian.com/higher-education-network/blog/2014/may/27/students-mental-health-risk-cuts-nhs-services (accessed 28th May 2014).

Clowes, R. (2014) #promote. *University & College Counselling*, September 2014, New Ways of Being and Doing, 4–7.

Coren, A. (1999) Brief Psychodynamic Counselling in Education, in Lees, J. and Vaspe, A. (Eds) *Clinical Counselling in Further and Higher Education* (pp. 58–74), London, Routledge.

Halpern, L. (2008) On Being a Head of Service: Temptations of Power and Certainty, in *Heads of University Counselling Services Conference*, Cambridge, 19th June 2008, p. 3 slide 18.

May, R. (1999) Doing Clinical Work in a College or University: How Does the Context Matter?, in Lees, J. and Vaspe, A. (Eds) *Clinical Counselling in Further and Higher Education* (pp. 13–25), London, Routledge.

McMinn, L. (2010) Higher ambitions. *BACP AUCC,* May 2010, 6–7.

Pointon, C. (2014) The changing role of the university counselling service. *Therapy Today*, 25 (8) 12–17.

Rose, C. (2004) Needing a break. *Counselling and Psychotherapy Journal*, 15 (7), 26–28.

Royle, L. (2006) Are we getting sick of caring? *Therapy Today*, 17 (6), 25–27.

Wallace, P. (2012) The impact of counselling on academic outcomes: The student perspective. *AUCC Journal*, November, 6–11.

Wallace, P. (2014) The positive wider impact of counselling provision in colleges and universities. *BACP University & College Counselling*, September, 22–25.

Wicks, R. J. (2008) *The Resilient Client*, London, Oxford University Press.

Index

Entries in **bold** denote tables; entries in *italics* denote figures.

Taylor & Francis eBooks

Helping you to choose the right eBooks for your Library

Add Routledge titles to your library's digital collection today. Taylor and Francis ebooks contains over 50,000 titles in the Humanities, Social Sciences, Behavioural Sciences, Built Environment and Law.

Choose from a range of subject packages or create your own!

Benefits for you
» Free MARC records
» COUNTER-compliant usage statistics
» Flexible purchase and pricing options
» All titles DRM-free.

Benefits for your user
» Off-site, anytime access via Athens or referring URL
» Print or copy pages or chapters
» Full content search
» Bookmark, highlight and annotate text
» Access to thousands of pages of quality research at the click of a button.

 REQUEST YOUR **FREE** INSTITUTIONAL TRIAL TODAY

Free Trials Available
We offer free trials to qualifying academic, corporate and government customers.

eCollections – Choose from over 30 subject eCollections, including:

Archaeology	Language Learning
Architecture	Law
Asian Studies	Literature
Business & Management	Media & Communication
Classical Studies	Middle East Studies
Construction	Music
Creative & Media Arts	Philosophy
Criminology & Criminal Justice	Planning
Economics	Politics
Education	Psychology & Mental Health
Energy	Religion
Engineering	Security
English Language & Linguistics	Social Work
Environment & Sustainability	Sociology
Geography	Sport
Health Studies	Theatre & Performance
History	Tourism, Hospitality & Events

For more information, pricing enquiries or to order a free trial, please contact your local sales team:
www.tandfebooks.com/page/sales

 Routledge
Taylor & Francis Group

The home of
Routledge books

www.tandfebooks.com